NON SANZ DROICT.

William Shakespeare

The Second Part of [KING] HENRY IV

EDITED BY NORMAN N. HOLLAND

THE SIGNET CLASSIC SHAKESPEARE
GENERAL EDITOR: SYLVAN BARNET

PUBLISHED BY THE NEW AMERICAN LIBRARY,
NEW YORK AND TORONTO
THE NEW ENGLISH LIBRARY LIMITED, LONDON

First Printing, July, 1965

SIGNET CLASSICS are published *in the United States* by
The New American Library Inc.,
1301 Avenue of the Americas, New York, New York 10019,
in Canada by The New American Library of Canada Limited,
156 Front Street West, Toronto 1, Ontario,
in the United Kingdom by The New English Library Limited,
Barnard's Inn, Holborn, London, E.C. 1, England

Contents

Shakespeare: Prefatory Remarks

Between the record of his baptism in Stratford on 26 April 1564 and the record of his burial in Stratford on 25 April 1616, some forty documents name Shakespeare, and many others name his parents, his children, and his grandchildren. More facts are known about William Shakespeare than about any other playwright of the period except Ben Jonson. The facts should, however, be distinguished from the legends. The latter, inevitably more engaging and better known, tell us that the Stratford boy killed a calf in high style, poached deer and rabbits, and was forced to flee to London, where he held horses outside a playhouse. These traditions are only traditions; they may be true, but no evidence supports them, and it is well to stick to the facts.

Mary Arden, the dramatist's mother, was the daughter of a substantial landowner; about 1557 she married John Shakespeare, who was a glove-maker and trader in various farm commodities. In 1557 John Shakespeare was a member of the Council (the governing body of Stratford), in 1558 a constable of the borough, in 1561 one of the two town chamberlains, in 1565 an alderman (entitling him to the appellation "Mr."), in 1568 high bailiff—the town's highest political office, equivalent to mayor. After 1577, for an unknown reason he drops out of local politics. The birthday of William Shakespeare, the eldest son of this locally prominent man, is unrecorded; but the Stratford parish register records that the infant was baptized on 26 April 1564. (It is quite possible that he was born on

23 April, but this date has probably been assigned by tradition because it is the date on which, fifty-two years later, he died.) The attendance records of the Stratford grammar school of the period are not extant, but it is reasonable to assume that the son of a local official attended the school and received substantial training in Latin. The masters of the school from Shakespeare's seventh to fifteenth years held Oxford degrees; the Elizabethan curriculum excluded mathematics and the natural sciences but taught a good deal of Latin rhetoric, logic, and literature. On 27 November 1582 a marriage license was issued to Shakespeare and Anne Hathaway, eight years his senior. The couple had a child in May, 1583. Perhaps the marriage was necessary, but perhaps the couple had earlier engaged in a formal "troth plight" which would render their children legitimate even if no further ceremony were performed. In 1585 Anne Hathaway bore Shakespeare twins.

That Shakespeare was born is excellent; that he married and had children is pleasant; but that we know nothing about his departure from Stratford to London, or about the beginning of his theatrical career, is lamentable and must be admitted. We would gladly sacrifice details about his children's baptism for details about his earliest days on the stage. Perhaps the poaching episode is true (but it is first reported almost a century after Shakespeare's death), or perhaps he first left Stratford to be a schoolteacher, as another tradition holds; perhaps he was moved by

> Such wind as scatters young men through the world,
> To seek their fortunes further than at home
> Where small experience grows.

In 1592, thanks to the cantankerousness of Robert Greene, a rival playwright and a pamphleteer, we have our first reference, a snarling one, to Shakespeare as an actor and playwright. Greene warns those of his own educated friends who wrote for the theater against an actor who has presumed to turn playwright:

> There is an upstart crow, beautified with our feathers,
> that with his *tiger's heart wrapped in a player's hide* sup-
> poses he is as well able to bombast out a blank verse as
> the best of you, and being an absolute Johannes-factotum
> is in his own conceit the only Shake-scene in a country.

The reference to the player, as well as the allusion to
Aesop's crow (who strutted in borrowed plumage, as an
actor struts in fine words not his own), makes it clear
that by this date Shakespeare had both acted and written. That Shakespeare is meant is indicated not only by
"Shake-scene" but by the parody of a line from one of
Shakespeare's plays, *3 Henry VI:* "O, tiger's heart wrapped
in a woman's hide." If Shakespeare in 1592 was prominent enough to be attacked by an envious dramatist, he
probably had served an apprenticeship in the theater for
at least a few years.

In any case, by 1592 Shakespeare had acted and written, and there are a number of subsequent references to
him as an actor: documents indicate that in 1598 he is
a "principal comedian," in 1603 a "principal tragedian,"
in 1608 he is one of the "men players." The profession
of actor was not for a gentleman, and it occasionally drew
the scorn of university men who resented writing speeches
for persons less educated than themselves, but it was
respectable enough: players, if prosperous, were in effect
members of the bourgeoisie, and there is nothing to suggest that Stratford considered William Shakespeare less
than a solid citizen. When, in 1596, the Shakespeares
were granted a coat of arms, the grant was made to Shakespeare's father, but probably William Shakespeare (who
the next year bought the second-largest house in town)
had arranged the matter on his own behalf. In subsequent
transactions he is occasionally styled a gentleman.

Although in 1593 and 1594 Shakespeare published two
narrative poems dedicated to the Earl of Southampton,
Venus and Adonis and *The Rape of Lucrece,* and may
well have written most or all of his sonnets in the middle nineties, Shakespeare's literary activity seems to have
been almost entirely devoted to the theater. (It may be

significant that the two narrative poems were written in years when the plague closed the theaters for several months.) In 1594 he was a charter member of a theatrical company called the Chamberlain's Men (which in 1603 changed its name to the King's Men); until he retired to Stratford (about 1611, apparently), he was with this remarkably stable company. From 1599 the company acted primarily at the Globe Theatre, in which Shakespeare held a one-tenth interest. Other Elizabethan dramatists are known to have acted, but no other is known also to have been entitled to a share in the profits of the playhouse.

Shakespeare's first eight published plays did not have his name on them, but this is not remarkable; the most popular play of the sixteenth century, Thomas Kyd's *The Spanish Tragedy,* went through many editions without naming Kyd, and Kyd's authorship is known only because a book on the profession of acting happens to quote (and attribute to Kyd) some lines on the interest of Roman emperors in the drama. What is remarkable is that after 1598 Shakespeare's name commonly appears on printed plays—some of which are not his. Another indication of his popularity comes from Francis Meres, author of *Palladis Tamia: Wit's Treasury* (1598): in this anthology of snippets accompanied by an essay on literature, many playwrights are mentioned, but Shakespeare's name occurs more often than any other, and Shakespeare is the only playwright whose plays are listed.

From his acting, playwriting, and share in a theater, Shakespeare seems to have made considerable money. He put it to work, making substantial investments in Stratford real estate. When he made his will (less than a month before he died), he sought to leave his property intact to his descendants. Of small bequests to relatives and to friends (including three actors, Richard Burbage, John Heminges, and Henry Condell), that to his wife of the second-best bed has provoked the most comment; perhaps it was the bed the couple had slept in, the best being reserved for visitors. In any case, had Shakespeare not excepted it, the bed would have gone (with the rest of his household possessions) to his daughter and her husband. On 25 April 1616 he was buried within the chancel of the church at Stratford. An unattractive monument to his memory, placed on a wall near the grave, says he died on 23 April. Over the grave itself are the lines, perhaps by Shakespeare, that (more than his literary fame) have kept his bones undisturbed in the crowded burial ground where old bones were often dislodged to make way for new:

> Good friend, for Jesus' sake forbear
> To dig the dust enclosèd here.
> Blessed be the man that spares these stones
> And cursed be he that moves my bones.

Thirty-seven plays, as well as some nondramatic poems, are held to constitute the Shakespeare canon. The dates of composition of most of the works are highly uncertain, but there is often evidence of a *terminus a quo* (starting point) and/or a *terminus ad quem* (terminal point) that provides a framework for intelligent guessing. For example, *Richard II* cannot be earlier than 1595, the publication date of some material to which it is indebted; *The Merchant of Venice* cannot be later than 1598, the year Francis Meres mentioned it. Sometimes arguments for a date hang on an alleged topical allusion, such as the lines about the unseasonable weather in *A Midsummer Night's Dream,* II.i.81–87, but such an allusion (if indeed it is an allusion) can be variously interpreted, and in any case there is always the possibility that a topical allusion was inserted during a revision, years after the composition of a play. Dates are often attributed on the basis of style, and although conjectures about style usually rest on other conjectures, sooner or later one must rely on one's literary sense. There is no real proof, for example, that *Othello* is not as early as *Romeo and Juliet,* but one feels *Othello* is later, and because the first record of its performance is 1604, one is glad enough to set its composition at that date and not push it back into Shakespeare's early years. The following chronology, then, is as much indebted to informed guesswork and sensitivity as it is to fact. The dates, necessarily imprecise, indicate something like a scholarly consensus.

PLAYS

1609–10	*Cymbeline*
1610–11	*The Winter's Tale*
1611	*The Tempest*
1612–13	*Henry VIII*

POEMS

1592	*Venus and Adonis*
1593–94	*The Rape of Lucrece*
1593–1600	*Sonnets*
1600–01	*The Phoenix and Turtle*

Shakespeare's Theater

In Shakespeare's infancy, Elizabethan actors performed wherever they could—in great halls, at court, in the courtyards of inns. The innyards must have made rather unsatisfactory theaters: on some days they were unavailable because carters bringing goods to London used them as depots; when available, they had to be rented from the innkeeper; perhaps most important, London inns were subject to the Common Council of London, which was not well disposed toward theatricals. In 1574 the Common Council required that plays and playing places in London be licensed. It asserted that

> sundry great disorders and inconveniences have been found to ensue to this city by the inordinate haunting of great multitudes of people, specially youth, to plays, interludes, and shows, namely occasion of frays and quarrels, evil practices of incontinency in great inns having chambers and secret places adjoining to their open stages and galleries,

and ordered that innkeepers who wished licenses to hold performances put up a bond and make contributions to the poor.

The requirement that plays and innyard theaters be

licensed, along with the other drawbacks of playing at inns, probably drove James Burbage (a carpenter-turned-actor) to rent in 1576 a plot of land northeast of the city walls and to build here—on property outside the jurisdiction of the city—England's first permanent construction designed for plays. He called it simply the Theatre. About all that is known of its construction is that it was wood. It soon had imitators, the most famous being the Globe (1599), built across the Thames (again outside the city's jurisdiction), out of timbers of the Theatre, which had been dismantled when Burbage's lease ran out.

There are three important sources of information about the structure of Elizabethan playhouses—drawings, a contract, and stage directions in plays. Of drawings, only the so-called De Witt drawing (c. 1596) of the Swan—really a friend's copy of De Witt's drawing—is of much significance. It shows a building of three tiers, with a stage jutting from a wall into the yard or center of the building. The tiers are roofed, and part of the stage is covered by a roof that projects from the rear and is supported at its front on two posts, but the groundlings, who paid a penny to stand in front of the stage, were exposed to the sky. (Performances in such a playhouse were held only in the daytime; artificial illumination was not used.) At the rear of the stage are two doors; above the stage is a gallery. The second major source of information, the contract for the Fortune, specifies that although the Globe is to be the model, the Fortune is to be square, eighty feet outside and fifty-five inside. The stage is to be forty-three feet broad, and is to extend into the middle of the yard (i.e., it is twenty-seven and a half feet deep). For patrons willing to pay more than the general admission charged of the groundlings, there were to be three galleries provided with seats. From the third chief source, stage directions, one learns that entrance to the stage was by doors, presumably spaced widely apart at the rear ("Enter one citizen at one door, and another at the other"), and that in addition to the platform stage there was occasionally some sort of curtained booth or alcove allowing for "discovery" scenes, and some sort of playing space "aloft" or "above" to represent (for example) the top of a city's walls or a room above the street. Doubtless each theater had its own peculiarities, but perhaps we can talk about a "typical" Elizabethan theater if we realize that no theater need exactly have fit the description, just as no father is the typical father with 3.7 children. This hypothetical theater is wooden, round or polygonal (in *Henry V* Shakespeare calls it a "wooden *O*"), capable of holding some eight hundred spectators standing in the yard around the projecting elevated stage and some fifteen hundred additional spectators seated in the three roofed galleries. The stage, protected by a "shadow" or "heavens" or roof, is entered by two doors; behind the doors is the "tiring house" (attiring house, i.e., dressing room), and above the doors is some sort of gallery that may sometimes hold spectators but that can be used (for example) as the bedroom from which Romeo—according to a stage direction in one text—"goeth down." Some evidence suggests that a throne can be lowered onto the platform stage, perhaps from the "shadow"; certainly characters can descend from the stage through a trap or traps into the cellar or "hell." Sometimes this space beneath the platform accommodates a sound-effects man or musician (in *Antony and Cleopatra* "music of the hautboys is under the stage") or an actor (in *Hamlet* the "Ghost cries under the stage"). Most characters simply walk on and off, but because there is no curtain in front of the platform, corpses will have to be carried off (Hamlet must lug Polonius' guts into the neighbor room), or will have to fall at the rear, where the curtain on the alcove or booth can be drawn to conceal them.

Such may have been the so-called "public theater." Another kind of theater, called the "private theater" because its much greater admission charge limited its audience to the wealthy or the prodigal, must be briefly mentioned. The private theater was basically a large room, entirely roofed and therefore artificially illuminated, with a stage at one end. In 1576 one such theater was established in Blackfriars, a Dominican priory in London that had been suppressed in 1538 and confiscated by the Crown and thus was not under the city's jurisdiction. All the actors in the Blackfriars theater were boys about eight to thirteen years old (in the public theaters similar boys played female parts; a boy Lady Macbeth played to a man Macbeth). This private theater had a precarious existence, and ceased operations in 1584. In 1596 James Burbage, who had already made theatrical history by building the Theatre, began to construct a second Blackfriars theater. He died in 1597, and for several years this second Blackfriars theater was used by a troupe of boys, but in 1608 two of Burbage's sons and five other actors (including Shakespeare) became joint operators of the theater, using it in the winter when the open-air Globe was unsuitable. Perhaps such a smaller theater, roofed, artificially illuminated, and with a tradition of a courtly audience, exerted an influence on Shakespeare's late plays.

Performances in the private theaters may well have had intermissions during which music was played, but in the public theaters the action was probably uninterrupted, flowing from scene to scene almost without a break. Actors would enter, speak, exit, and others would immediately enter and establish (if necessary) the new locale by a few properties and by words and gestures. Here are some samples of Shakespeare's scene painting:

> This is Illyria, lady.

> Well, this is the Forest of Arden.

> This castle hath a pleasant seat; the air
> Nimbly and sweetly recommends itself
> Unto our gentle senses.

On the other hand, it is a mistake to conceive of the Elizabethan stage as bare. Although Shakespeare's Chorus in *Henry V* calls the stage an "unworthy scaffold" and urges the spectators to "eke out our performance with your mind," there was considerable spectacle. The last act of *Macbeth,* for example, has five stage directions calling for "drum and colors," and another sort of appeal to the eye is indicated by the stage direction "Enter Macduff, with Macbeth's head." Some scenery and properties may have been substantial; doubtless a throne was used, and in one play of the period we encounter this direction: "Hector takes up a great piece of rock and casts at Ajax, who tears up a young tree by the roots and assails Hector." The matter is of some importance, and will be glanced at again in the next section.

The Texts of Shakespeare

Though eighteen of his plays were published during his lifetime, Shakespeare seems never to have supervised their publication. There is nothing unusual here; when a playwright sold a play to a theatrical company he surrendered his ownership of it. Normally a company would not publish the play, because to publish it meant to allow competitors to acquire the piece. Some plays, however, did get published: apparently treacherous actors sometimes pieced together a play for a publisher, sometimes a company in need of money sold a play, and sometimes a company allowed a play to be published that no longer drew audiences. That Shakespeare did not concern himself with publication, then, is scarcely remarkable; of his contemporaries only Ben Jonson carefully supervised the publication of his own plays. In 1623, seven years after Shakespeare's death, John Heminges and Henry Condell (two senior members of Shakespeare's company, who had performed with him for about twenty years) collected his plays—published and unpublished—into a large volume, commonly called the First Folio. (A folio is a volume consisting of sheets that have been folded once, each sheet thus making two leaves, or four pages. The eighteen plays published during Shakespeare's lifetime had been issued one play per volume in small books called quartos. Each sheet in a quarto has been folded twice, making four leaves, or eight pages.) The First Folio contains thirty-six plays; a thirty-seventh, *Pericles,* though not in the Folio, is regarded as canonical. Heminges and Condell suggest in an address "To the great variety of readers" that the republished plays are presented in better form than in the quartos: "Before you were abused with diverse stolen and surreptitious copies, maimed and deformed by the frauds and stealths of injurious impostors that exposed them; even those, are now offered to your view cured and perfect of their limbs, and all the rest absolute in their numbers, as he [i.e., Shakespeare] conceived them."

Whoever was assigned to prepare the texts for publication in the First Folio seems to have taken his job seriously and yet not to have performed it with uniform care. The sources of the texts seem to have been, in general, good unpublished copies or the best published copies. The first play in the collection, *The Tempest,* is divided into acts and scenes, has unusually full stage directions and descriptions of spectacle, and concludes with a list of the characters, but the editor was not able (or willing) to present all of the succeeding texts so fully dressed. Later texts occasionally show signs of carelessness: in one scene of *Much Ado About Nothing* the names of actors, instead of characters, appear as speech prefixes, as they had in the quarto, which the Folio reprints; proofreading throughout the Folio is spotty and apparently was done without reference to the printer's copy; the pagination of *Hamlet* jumps from 156 to 257.

A modern editor of Shakespeare must first select his copy; no problem if the play exists only in the Folio, but a considerable problem if the relationship between a quarto and the Folio—or an early quarto and a later one—is unclear. When an editor has chosen what seems to him to be the most authoritative text or texts for his copy, he has not done with making decisions. First of all, he must reckon with Elizabethan spelling. If he is not producing a facsimile, he probably modernizes it, but ought he to preserve the old form of words that apparently were pronounced quite unlike their modern forms—"lanthorn," "alablaster"? If he preserves these forms, is he really preserving Shakespeare's forms or perhaps those of a compositor in the printing house? What is one to do when one finds "lanthorn" and "lantern" in adjacent lines? (The editors of this series in general, but not invariably, assume that words should be spelled in their modern form.) Elizabethan punctuation, too, presents problems. For example in the First Folio, the only text for the play, Macbeth rejects his wife's idea that he can wash the blood from his hand:

> no: this my Hand will rather
> The multitudinous Seas incarnadine,
> Making the Greene one, Red.

Obviously an editor will remove the superfluous capitals, and he will probably alter the spelling to "incarnadine," but will he leave the comma before "red," letting Macbeth speak of the sea as "the green one," or will he (like most modern editors) remove the comma and thus have Macbeth say that his hand will make the ocean *uniformly* red?

An editor will sometimes have to change more than spelling or punctuation. Macbeth says to his wife:

> I dare do all that may become a man,
> Who dares no more, is none.

For two centuries editors have agreed that the second line is unsatisfactory, and have emended "no" to "do": "Who dares do more is none." But when in the same play Ross says that fearful persons

> floate vpon a wilde and violent Sea
> Each way, and moue,

need "move" be emended to "none," as it often is, on the hunch that the compositor misread the manuscript? The editors of the Signet Classic Shakespeare have restrained themselves from making abundant emendations. In their minds they hear Dr. Johnson on the dangers of emending: "I have adopted the Roman sentiment, that it is more honorable to save a citizen than to kill an enemy." Some departures (in addition to spelling, punctuation, and lineation) from the copy text have of course been made, but the original readings are listed in a note following the play, so that the reader can evaluate them for himself.

The editors of the Signet Classic Shakespeare, following tradition, have added line numbers and in many cases act and scene divisions as well as indications of locale at the beginning of scenes. The Folio divided most of the plays into acts and some into scenes. Early eighteenth-century editors increased the divisions. These divisions, which provide a convenient way of referring to passages in the plays, have been retained, but when not in the text chosen as the basis for the Signet Classic text they are enclosed in square brackets [ ] to indicate that they are editorial additions. Similarly, although no play of Shakespeare's published during his lifetime was equipped with indications of locale at the heads of scene divisions, locales have here been added in square brackets for the convenience of the reader, who lacks the information afforded to spectators by costumes, properties, and gestures. The spectator can tell at a glance he is in the throne room, but without an editorial indication the reader may be puzzled for a while. It should be mentioned, incidentally, that there are a few authentic stage directions —perhaps Shakespeare's, perhaps a prompter's—that suggest locales: for example, "Enter Brutus in his orchard," and "They go up into the Senate house." It is hoped that the bracketed additions provide the reader with the sort of help provided in these two authentic directions, but it is equally hoped that the reader will remember that the stage was not loaded with scenery.

No editor during the course of his work can fail to recollect some words Heminges and Condell prefixed to the Folio:

It had been a thing, we confess, worthy to have been wished, that the author himself had lived to have set forth and overseen his own writings. But since it hath been ordained otherwise, and he by death departed from that right, we pray you do not envy his friends the office of their care and pain to have collected and published them.

Nor can an editor, after he has done his best, forget Heminges and Condell's final words: "And so we leave you to other of his friends, whom if you need can be your guides. If you need them not, you can lead yourselves, and others. And such readers we wish him."

SYLVAN BARNET
Tufts University

Introduction

Betrayal, someone has said, is the quintessential Shakespearean theme. Certainly, it would seem to be in *Henry IV* [*Part Two*], for this play hinges on two betrayals. Prince John promises the rebels in a battlefield parley their "griefs shall be with speed redressed. Upon my soul, they shall." Then, once the rebels' troops are discharged, he tells them he will indeed redress their grievances "with a most Christian care"—but executes them as rebels. "God, and not we, hath safely fought today." (Some outraged critics have called the line blasphemous.) Then, at the end of the play, after the death of Henry IV, Falstaff expects to be "one of the greatest men in this realm" in something other than size. He cheers his newly crowned Hal only to be answered by one of the most magnificent and brutal lines in all literature: "I know thee not, old man. Fall to thy prayers." Dismissed, banished, he dies in *Henry V* because "The King has killed his heart."

The ethical rightness or wrongness of these actions[1] constitutes one of the two bones of contention this play has cast among critics. The other is the relation of this play to Part One: are Parts One and Two[2] separate plays

[1] Mr. Stanley McKenzie, in an unpublished paper, very skillfully analyzes the ethical problem of the two "betrayals" in terms of the structure and imagery of the play. I am indebted to him for a number of the ideas which follow.

[2] "Part Two" in the title of an Elizabethan history play simply means that the play deals with events later in the reign of the king named in the title than those the Part One play deals with. It does not imply that the play in question is an integral part of a series, like a chapter in a novel.

or one long ten-act play? The answers to both (like all questions we ask of Shakespeare) must come from a recognition of the significant wholeness of the work of art he has created, for these two seeming betrayals, morally ambiguous as they may appear, make only two among a host of other such incidents in the play.

For example, in an episode that Shakespeare carefully retained from his sources, the old king, believing a prophecy he is to die "in Jerusalem," expects to die on a Crusade. Instead, he finds himself dying, not in the city Jerusalem but in a room in Westminster called "Jerusalem." Once Henry IV is dead, the Lord Chief Justice (who had clapped Hal in prison) thinks himself a man doomed, but instead, the new king creates him Chief Justice anew, "a father to my youth," and puts him in charge of Falstaff. Bringing these and many other such reversals to a fullness and completion is, of course, the reformation of Hal himself from the madcap prince to what he will be in *Henry V,* "the mirror of all Christian kings." "Let the end try the man," he had warned earlier; and at the end he acts

> To mock the expectation of the world,
> To frustrate prophecies, and to raze out
> Rotten opinion, who hath writ me down
> After my seeming.

"Expectation mocked" is the key, a theme that pervades and informs the comic scenes as well as the serious ones. To the Lord Chief Justice's amused outrage, Falstaff, who illustrates "all the characters of age," has the gall to set down his name "in the scroll of youth" and —even—call the Justice old. He manages to elude the legal powers of the Lord Chief Justice (roughly equivalent to the Chief Justice of the U. S. Supreme Court), and then he has the effrontery to try to borrow a thousand pounds from him. Mistress Quickly believes Falstaff will marry her (perhaps the silliest of all expectations in a play of silly expectations), and thus Falstaff manages to turn her lawsuit into a cozy dinner party. Old Justice

Shallow, in one of the most exquisite moments of the play, turns away from that death that hovers over all the characters to a startling image of vitality and (in Elizabethan English) virility:

> *Shallow.* Jesu, Jesu, the mad days that I have spent! And to see how many of my old acquaintance are dead!
> *Silence.* We shall all follow, cousin.
> *Shallow.* Certain, 'tis certain, very sure, very sure. Death, as the Psalmist saith, is certain to all, all shall die. How [much for] a good yoke of bullocks at Stamford Fair?

Shallow, the classic portrait of the old grad, makes much of "the wildness of his youth," but we find that his talk is all an old man's lying. Young Shallow was thin, puny, "ever in the rearward of the fashion," and yet, notes Falstaff ruefully, "Now has he lands and beeves." Everywhere expectation is overturned. Falstaff picks (from Shallow's point of view) precisely the wrong men for his recruits. Yet even so, Francis Feeble of valorous name turns out to have that stoical acceptance of destiny that constitutes (as we shall see) the essential ethic the play puts forward.

The same sense of expectation mocked permeates the language and imagery of the play. What should give hope or security does not. Armor "worn in heat of day . . . scald'st with safety," while, conversely, "In poison there is physic." Hopes, like ships, "touch ground and dash themselves to pieces," while even houses are "giddy and unsure." The very buds,

> which to prove fruit,
> Hope gives not so much warrant as despair
> That frost will bite them.

Fathers who care for their sons, like bees that gather honey, "are murdered for [their] pains." Sleep, in the King's lovely apostrophe, comes to the least likely, the shipboy suffering a storm in the crows' nest:

> Canst thou, O partial sleep, give thy repose
> To the wet sea-son in an hour so rude,
> And in the calmest and most stillest night,
> With all appliances and means to boot,
> Deny it to a king? Then happy low, lie down!
> Uneasy lies the head that wears a crown.

The least fortunate are most fortunate—one cannot predict, for premonitions themselves run by opposites:

> Against ill chances men are ever merry,
> But heaviness foreruns the good event.

Even the mere dramaturgic context of *2 Henry IV* mocks expectation. The madcap prince of Part Two reverses the reformation we have already seen in Part One (see pp. 219–23). The odd epilogue treats the plays as the unsuccessful payment of a debt—an expectation—and goes on to contract a further debt: "Our humble author will continue the story, with Sir John in it." But Falstaff does not appear in *Henry V,* and further, he is not to be confused with the character you expected him to be; "Oldcastle died martyr, and this is not the man" (see p. 169n.).

Even odder than the epilogue is the induction with Rumor as the presenter. Shakespeare, as always, sets up the internal logic of his work from the very opening lines: Rumor, whatever else he may be, is the creator and defeater of expectations par excellence, bringer of "smooth comforts false, worse than true wrongs." Here, he announces falsely a rebel victory at Shrewsbury and the death of Prince Hal under the sword of Northumberland's son Hotspur. Then, almost the entire first scene of the play deals with expectations created and defeated (even down to the opening lines in which a porter says that Northumberland will be found in the orchard, but then the Earl himself unexpectedly appears). And, of course, no one expected the madcap prince to overcome "the never-daunted Percy." Learning of his son's death, Northumberland says,

> these news,
> Having been well, that would have made me sick,
> Being sick, have in some measure made me well.

Much later in the play, another old man, King Henry IV, will echo his paradox: "Wherefore should these good news make me sick?" In either case, news—words—seem to have an effect opposite to what one would expect.

The first scene shifts to the second, from one diseased old man to another:

> *Falstaff.* Sirrah . . . what says the doctor to my water [i.e., urine]?
> *Page.* He said, sir, the water itself was a good healthy water; but, for the party that [owned] it, he might have [more] diseases than he knew. . . .

The Page's response, itself a mockery of what we might expect from a doctor, continues from the previous scene the tension between words and body.

As we might expect from Falstaff's "throng of words" or, indeed, the figure of Rumor, "painted full of tongues," words—"prophecies," "seeming," "rotten opinion," "news"—all play a key role in *2 Henry IV* in creating expectations that deeds and persons then defeat in fact, as

> chances, mocks,
> And changes fill the cup of alteration
> With divers liquors.

Most notably, Prince John tricks the rebels with his "princely word": "I give it you, and will maintain my word"—though the letter, not the spirit. But there are others whose words create false expectations: Mistress Quickly's malapropisms and Pistol's ranting in garbled quotations make us expect to hear one thing; then, when we hear their blunder, our expectation is mocked. And the rebels, too, create false hopes with words:

> We fortify in paper and in figures,
> Using the names of men instead of men,

> Like one that draws the model of an house
> Beyond his power to build.

As Lord Bardolph's words hint, this play uses (unusually often for Shakespeare) names that tag their bearers in a manner almost Dickensian: Pistol, Shallow, Shadow, and Moldy; Doll Tearsheet and Jane Nightwork of amorous name; the sheriff's men, Fang and Snare; Mistress Quickly, whose name, in Elizabethan pronunciation, conceals a ribald pun; Goodman Puff, fat as Falstaff, and hungry Francis Pickbone; Traverse, who, in the opening scene, denies ("traverses") Lord Bardolph's report. Yet, as one would expect in a play of expectations mocked, the actual, physical characters often belie their tags; Sampson Stockfish is a fruiterer, Bullcalf a coward, and Feeble brave.

We would be wrong, though, to conclude that words always build up false expectations, that *2 Henry IV* envisions no larger plan that one can trust—such a skepticism would be utterly foreign to Shakespeare and the Elizabethans' sense of cosmic order. There is, as the King says, a plan, though a bitter one, "the book of fate" that lists the defeats of our expectations:

> O, if this were seen,
> The happiest youth, viewing his progress through,
> What perils past, what crosses to ensue,
> Would shut the book, and sit him down and die.

And Warwick goes on to make an important statement of the Elizabethans' anecdotal or symbolistic view of history:

> There is a history in all men's lives,
> Figuring the nature of the times deceased,
> The which observed, a man may prophesy,
> With a near aim, of the main chance of things
> As yet not come to life.

There is, then, a larger order, and some of the characters find their place in it. Others, notably Falstaff and the rebels who are "betrayed," do not. What is the essential difference between those who find a place and those who are "betrayed"?

As so often in Shakespeare, a peripheral episode tells us, a scene superfluous to the main plot but one which Shakespeare spent some pains to improve from his sources (see pp. 183–89). Hal, thinking his father dead, takes his crown into another room. His father revives and accuses him of wishing parricide. It is, of course, one more episode of expectations mocked, but the King's words tell us more: he accuses Hal of being "hasty," unable to "stay," of wishing his father's death: "What! Canst thou not forbear me half an hour?" Slowly, Hal answers. He did not "affect," that is, crave, desire, the crown. Rather, he took it as an enemy: it "hath fed upon the body of my father." Its gold is no medicine, but rather "hast eat thy bearer up." The King is pleased with his son's "pleading so wisely." Wherein does the wisdom lie?

The King explains in his next speech, "the very latest counsel that ever I shall breathe," presumably, therefore, the most important. He recalls the way he took the crown from Richard in *Richard II,*

> How troublesome it sat upon my head.
> To thee it shall descend with better quiet.

> It seemed in me
> But as an honor snatched with boisterous hand.

> And now my death
> Changes the mood, for what in me was purchased
> Falls upon thee in a more fairer sort,
> So thou the garland wear'st successively.

The word "purchased" is important: a legal term, it refers to the acquiring of land other than by inherited succession ("successively"). The word reflects, as the whole play does, the feudal and Renaissance prejudice against those who violate the natural order of things by taking for themselves against the ordained patterns of birth and inheritance. Henry sinned when he "snatched" the crown, but Hal will wear it free of such sin, for he inherits it. The King's accusations tell us Hal's wrong in taking the crown from his sleeping father lay in his inability to "forbear," to "stay," in his "wish," his being "hasty."

> Thou hast stolen that which after some few hours
> Were thine without offense.

Hal's answer is wise in that he says he did not crave the crown, but rather recognized that the crown is an enemy that feeds on its bearer, eats its bearer up.

Appetite is both the sin and the danger, that appetite which, as the Prince had jokingly confessed earlier, "was not princely got." To be truly a prince, one must not crave and try to take, but rather forbear, wait, trust, put oneself in that larger order: God's, nature's, his father's. Appetite governs the common man, not the prince, and, indeed, it was the common people's appetite that let Henry take the crown from Richard, though, says the Archbishop,

> The commonwealth is sick of their own choice;
> Their overgreedy love hath surfeited.
>
> Thou, beastly feeder, art so full of [Henry]
> That thou provok'st thyself to cast him up.
> So, so, thou common dog, didst thou disgorge
> Thy glutton bosom of the royal Richard;
> And now thou wouldst eat thy dead vomit up,
> And howl'st to find it. What trust is in these times?

The wise monarch provides for his people's appetites. Henry's last counsel—for his expectation was again foiled, his statement of Hal's rightful title was not his "latest counsel"—Henry's last advice is to "busy giddy minds with foreign quarrels," to turn appetite elsewhere, for Henry knows all too well the rebel and vain spirit is one that seeks to take for itself rather than accept the natural order of monarchy.

That larger order is not wholly beneficent, for it includes, as Shallow reminds us, death. "Death, as the

Psalmist saith, is certain to all, all shall die," all: Northumberland, the King, Shallow, Silence, Falstaff, the Lord
Chief Justice—all the old men in this play of old men
are dying. Some try to put it aside, like Falstaff: "Peace,
good Doll! Do not speak like a death's head. Do not bid
me remember my end." But death cannot be put aside.
In Sir Thomas Browne's beautiful sentence, "This world
is not an inn but an hospital," not a place to feed but a
place to die in. One may consult the doctor as Falstaff
does; or, as the Archbishop's rebellion tries to do,

> diet rank minds sick of happiness
> And purge the obstructions which begin to stop
> Our very veins of life.

But purges and potions, be they the medicinable gold
that the crown so distinctly is not or the sherris-sack
whose virtues Falstaff so eloquently proclaims, are of no
real use, for death is certain. Though it may be unexpected, in a chamber named Jerusalem instead of the city,
death itself is certain.

The play's images of medicines represent one kind of
defense against the acceptance of a larger, cosmic order
that includes disease and death; words represent another.
Thus, the rebels project and plan, emitting words, "publish[ing] the occasion of our arms." They "fortify with
the names of men." The Archbishop, so "deep within the
books of God," turns himself into "an iron man talking."
In general, the rebels emit words and then take them for
things, as their predecessor Hotspur did,

> who lined himself with hope
> Eating the air and promise of supply.

They forget their physical selves and ask only for their
"articles," "this schedule," their "conditions" in a "true
substantial form." And verbal form is all John gives them.

Falstaff, too, emits a "throng of words" that wrench
the "true cause the false way." Contrasted with them,
taking language in,

The Prince but studies his companions
Like a strange tongue, wherein, to gain the language,
'Tis needful that the most immodest word
Be looked upon and learned,

but once learned, he will no longer speak, emit, such words, but rather take them "as a pattern or a measure" with which to judge the lives of others.

In other words, the Prince will not thrust up a merely verbal reality against the larger order. Rather, he will make himself and his language a part of that larger order, as Prince John does: "God, and not we, hath safely fought today." Pathetically, the rebels themselves try to become part of some larger order: "We are time's subjects."

✓ We see which way the stream of time doth run,
And are enforced from our most quiet there
By the rough torrent of occasion.

But "occasion" is a transitory thing, a creature of time, and time itself is a great betrayer. The King's party fits into a firmer order: "Construe the times to their necessities." When Warwick states the Elizabethan view of history, he speaks of it as a "necessary form." When King Henry disclaims any intent on his part of seizing Richard's crown, he says,

Necessity so bowed the state
That I and greatness were compelled to kiss.

And he accepts the rebel threat—

Are these things then necessities?
Then let us meet them like necessities.

The rebels, however, are responding, not to "necessities," but their "most just and right desires," the "demands" they seek to "enjoy." Appetite is their failure, and John's strategy simply traps them as animals are baited and trapped by their appetites. They drink as token of their wishes granted, but the drink also symbolizes their failure and defeat through appetite. (Indeed, the Archbishop after drinking finds himself "passing light in spirit.")

The real drinker, though, the very essence of appetite, is, of course, Falstaff. "He hath eaten me out of house and home," Mistress Quickly complains. "The old boar" (earlier he had been a sow) doth "feed in the old frank," monetarily, emotionally, and gastrically. At Shallow's, "We shall do nothing but eat, and make good cheer." Falstaff feeds on Shallow, too, taking a thousand pounds from him, promising to turn him into verbal jokes just as he himself ("the cause that wit is in other men") turns himself to words. Hal's succession provokes him into a riot of appetite: "Let us take any man's horses; the laws of England are at my commandment."

Thus, it is supremely appropriate that Hal reject him ("the feeder of my riots") in terms of food, as, earlier, he had taken leave of a Falstaff richly symbolized as a withered apple. In the coronation scene, Falstaff calls out, "My King! My Jove!" (thus identifying himself with Saturn, the titan who devoured his own children). Hal replies:

> I know thee not, old man. Fall to thy prayers.
> How ill white hairs becomes a fool and jester!
> I have long dreamt of such a kind of man,
> So surfeit-swelled, so old, and so profane,
> But, being awaked, I do despise my dream.
> Make less thy body hence, and more thy grace.
> Leave gormandizing. Know the grave doth gape
> For thee thrice wider than for other men.
> Reply not to me with a fool-born jest.

Not only does Hal put aside appetite—he fends off Falstaff's wordmongering (even as he himself lapses into two jokes—though he immediately counters, "Presume not that I am the thing I was"). Saddest of all, most brutal but most necessary, he reminds Falstaff of his role as an old man and of the grave's mouth that gapes so widely for him.

The mouth, food and medicine going into it, words

coming out, these images dominating a play of appetites and expectations mocked—Shakespeare here harks back to a truth of infancy, to a time when life was a life of the mouth. Psychologists such as Erik Erikson have been stressing in recent years the crucial importance of that time when we must discover our own identities; when we learn, taught by our own appetites, that we must await, trust, expect another to feed us. It is this ability to trust in another that enables the infant to experience that other as an existence separate from his own desires, to experience, therefore, his own separateness, his identity. The paradox continues into later life: it is the ability to give up one's own desires, to trust, even to merge and identify with the "necessity" represented by others, even, in a sense, to tolerate being engulfed by or devoured by it (as King Henry's crown, emblem of the larger order, has eaten its bearer up), that enables us to reemerge, as we did in earliest infancy, into a new sense of identity, a new role. In a paradox almost Biblical, we must lose ourselves to find ourselves.

So with Falstaff: to grow into the new role he should assume now that Hal is king, he must curb his appetites ("Leave gormandizing") and learn to depend on another (the "competence of life" his new king allows him). He must live with the certainty that the grave gapes for him, that he will himself be devoured. As for the rebels, they do not let themselves be merged into the larger necessity represented by the monarch; instead, they try to create roles for themselves out of their own words (or mouths). Necessarily, they fail.

Prince Hal, too, must give up an identity based on his own appetites, that of the madcap prince, and accept an identity set out for him, that of the hero-king. As Ernst Kris points out in a psychoanalytic study of this play,[3] Hal, until his father's death, refuses to fall back into the role his father has planned for him. Rather, he puts aside his father, stained and imperfect as a curber of appetites

---

[3] The critics referred to in this Introduction are either reprinted in the Commentaries section of this edition, pp. 190–233, or listed in the Suggested References, pp. 239–40.

because he himself "snatched" the crown "with boisterous hand," and he takes an identity from Falstaff, a father-substitute. Once his real father is dead, however, he can put aside Falstaff (ultimately rendering him as dead as his true father) and be taken into the role his father wished for him. Indeed, he can even accept a proper father-substitute in the person of the Lord Chief Justice.

Food is our earliest experience of trust; justice is a later one. Again, we must learn to wait rather than try to grab—we must trust in the larger necessity of law. *2 Henry IV* gives us a pair of justices: a true one in the Lord Chief Justice, a false one in Shallow, who succumbs to his servant's entreaty to "bear out a knave against an honest man." Shallow lets himself merge into a larger order, but one of his servants' making, so that, as Falstaff points out, they become like foolish justices, he a justice-like servingman. The Lord Chief Justice, however, speaks to Hal with "the person of your father"; "the image of his power lay then in me." He justifies his earlier action of imprisoning the Prince by reminding the new young king that he, now, has a new identity—"As you are a king, speak in your state." And Hal responds by assuming his kingly role, merging himself in his father's identity so that "I live to speak my father's words." To the Lord Chief Justice,

> You shall be as a father to my youth.
> My voice shall sound as you do prompt mine ear.
> And I will stoop and humble my intents
> To your well-practiced wise directions.
>
> My father is gone wild into his grave,
> For in his tomb lie my [appetites]
> And with his spirits sadly I survive
> To mock the expectation of the world. . . .

Thus, Hal merges into his father and contrasts with the Archbishop, who rebelled though he was "the imagined voice of God himself"; he did

> misuse the reverence of [his] place,

> Employ the countenance and grace of heaven,
> As a false favorite does his prince's name,
> In deeds dishonorable.

The right people of the play merge into a larger order;
the wrong people resist or misuse that larger order. Shallow's very name tells us something about their failure:
as Prince John says to the rebels,

> You are too shallow, Hastings, much too shallow,
> To sound the bottom of the after-times.

The image is of a river, and the Archbishop had earlier
compared himself and the other rebels to a river in flood,
saying that, if their demands are granted, "We come
within our awful banks again." Henry IV, too, is linked
to a flooding river: in a detail Shakespeare retained from
his sources, Henry (who was himself a rebel) dies as the
Thames thrice floods without ebb. As for Hal,

> The tide of blood in me
> Hath proudly flowed in vanity till now.
> Now doth it turn and ebb back to the sea,
> Where it shall mingle with the state of floods
> And flow henceforth in formal majesty.

He has put aside flooding and merged himself into the
identity ordained for him by that larger order, vast as the
sea. The play can end now, as it began, with a rumor.
But now a true rumor, for a bird sings the music of true
expectation, the King's will merged into the nation's
destiny.

In short, the theme of betrayal permeates and informs
the language, incidents, and characters of *2 Henry IV*,
but it is betrayal in a special sense: "expectations
mocked." That is, the play begins with a sense of hunger
or appetite:

> Open your ears, for which of you will stop
> The vent of hearing when loud Rumor speaks?

Then, against selfish or foolish appetite, the play poises a larger, parental plan of justice or monarchy or necessity that threatens to swallow up the characters by danger, disease, or death. And yet this larger necessity offers the paradoxical and unexpected possibility of a new identity, a kind of rebirth into a new self for those who can merge themselves into it. True princeliness calls for this ability to trust in the larger order, to achieve identity by the very act of curbing the self and its appetites and being merged into the greater plan. True rebellion means—in its most primitive sense—feeding oneself, resisting trust in that larger order by substituting one's own medicines, words, appetite, food, plans: "eating the air." And thus, the play itself answers the critics who have been troubled by Prince John's trick on the political rebels and Prince Hal's rejection of the appetitive rebel, Falstaff. These two "betrayals" become necessary and inevitable if we take the play on its own emotional and intellectual terms: the original failure of trust was the rebels' own inability to merge (without wordy conditions) into the larger order of nature.

Again, if we take the play on its own terms, we can see the answer to the second critical issue: the relation of Part Two to Part One. The external evidence from Elizabethan stage-practice that the two plays must have been separate and self-sufficient entities is clear enough. The internal evidence is clear, too. Part One and Part Two are quite different in their essential dramatic ideas, but they make a matched pair.

We can see the difference in the Falstaffs of the two parts. Twinned in avoirdupois, soldiering, and appetites, they nevertheless differ in some important ways. In both parts, Falstaff is a creature who defeats expectation, not only in the action, but also in our response (as Freud notes). From the point of view of the literary historian, as Bernard Spivack has shown, this mocking of our expectations places him in the tradition of the deceptive Vice of the morality plays or the tricky Ambidexter of a *Cambises*. But in Part One, Falstaff seems more triumphant: the Chaplinesque clown who, by his ability to play many parts, triumphs even over death, as (in the final battle) he feigns a death-and-rebirth. In Part Two, Falstaff resists, but succumbs to, the preordained role pointed out by Philip Williams and C. L. Barber. He becomes the slain god, the Lord of Misrule who must be banished to restore health to the land. Hal is absorbed into the role of the hero-king, while Falstaff is engulfed by a mythic significance that demands his rejection and death.

Miss Caroline Spurgeon noted some years ago that the Falstaff of Part One uses many images from books and the Bible, while the Falstaff of Part Two speaks in grotesque, rough, coarse similes drawn from body functions and appetites. We can add that Falstaff One uses a very distinctive figure of speech, the enthymeme: "If I travel but four foot by the squire further afoot, I shall break my wind." "If the rascal have not given me medicines to make me love him, I'll be hanged." "And 'twere not as good a deed as drink to turn true man and to leave these rogues, I am the veriest varlet that ever chewed with a tooth." (These all occur within ten lines in Part One, suggesting the frequency of the figure.) Falstaff Two almost entirely lacks this figure of speech; instead, he has become something of a monologist. He takes in a character, then turns him into a satirical portrait: we see Falstaff Two do this with himself, his page, his tailor, Pistol, Prince Hal, Poins, Bardolph, Shallow, Prince John, and, of course, sherris-sack, in monologues quite different in style from his catechism of honor in Part One (which tests a role). Falstaff Two may be responding to the same taste that led Jonson to put such incidental character sketches into *Every Man Out of his Humor* and *Cynthia's Revels* or that accounts for the popularity of the character-books of Hall, Overbury, and others in the early seventeenth century, but, in any case, he has shifted from acting out different roles (often taken from books and the Bible) to a more passive taking in of what he sees, then spewing it out in words (the image of vomit occurs several times in *2 Henry IV*). Falstaff One's big comic scene is the play-within-the-play in the tavern, when he tries on the roles of King

Henry and Prince Hal. Falstaff Two's big comic scene is
the recruiting, when he looks at the prospective draftees
and coins them into a mint of witty remarks. In short,
he becomes the walking embodiment of everything the
play rejects: appetite, wordmongering, resistance to one's
proper role. He becomes, like Iago in the tragedies, or
Autolycus and Caliban in the last plays, Shakespeare's
homo repudiandus, the character who focuses in himself
everything to be rejected. This, then, is the essential difference between the Falstaffs of Part One and Part Two:
the earlier Falstaff actively tries on different roles; the
later and more passive Falstaff finds himself forced into a
pattern laid down for him by his context.

And so does Hal. In Part One, he actively chooses the
role of hero; in Part Two, he lapses into kingship. The
rest of the characters show the same passivity. Part One
gave us an active, scrappy group of rebels; Part Two rep-
resents rebellion by talkers and bargainers. Part One
sharply opposed characters as good son—bad son; good
father—bad father; hot spur and false staff; and Hal
forged a role for himself between such extremes. Part Two
makes only one such sharp pairing: the good justice, who
merges into his master's voice, as against the bad justice,
who merges into his servant's. Mostly, Part Two bunches
fairly nondescript characters into the roles they must assume—and so the Folio text lists them, in bracketed
groups as "Opposites against King Henrie the Fourth,"
"Of the Kings Partie," "Country Soldiers," "Irregular Humorists," and the women. In the same way, Part Two
abounds in references to parts of the body, parts of a
house, parts of a kingdom—the later play constantly
stresses a sense of role within a larger plan.

These different ways of dealing with role are what make
Parts One and Two quite separate but nevertheless a
matched pair. In both, the problem is to bring Hal to the
role laid down for him by his father, his King, his God.
Part One offers the active solution; Part Two, the passive.
In the first play, Hal takes from the takers, robs Hotspur
and Falstaff of the honors or money they had robbed
from others. In the second, Hal is the taker taken: he

learns to put down his cravings and appetites and be taken up into the larger plan. Part One is the sunnier version—my pun is intentional—for it looks at the problem of Hal's achieving at-oneness with his father from the point of view of the son who actively battles the rebel within and without. Part Two sees the theme with the eyes of a dying father, in terms of passive expectation, trust, and acceptance of necessity. It is this atmosphere of passivity that keeps the magnificent fighter-Hal of Part One out of the action—what action there is—in Part Two. Finally, in *Henry V*, these active and passive solutions fuse. Hal's active battling fulfills the role he must passively accept. He brings the drives and appetites of others and their roles as Scot, Irishman, Welshman, or French princess into the service of his kingly function:

> Upon the King! Let us our lives, our souls,
> Our debts, our careful wives,
> Our children, and our sins, lay on the King!

The King must bear all—all but a few traitors and "irregular humorists" who insist on keeping separate. They must die.

Betrayal is the quintessential Shakespearean theme—provided we recognize the special tone that Shakespeare gives it. All his works deal with the taming of shrewishness: the masking over or mastery of hate by love. Betrayal, for Shakespeare, seems to mean a situation in which one can expect love, but in which love falls away and reveals an unsuspected or unmastered hate beneath. Iago is the obvious example, but we can look at all the tragedies as situations in which the love between a man and a woman, love either new or preexisting or expectable, fails to master hate. When love succeeds, the issue is comic, as in *Measure for Measure* and *The Merchant of Venice*, which temper hard justice with feminine mercy. All's well that ends well—that ends in love as Henry V's wars in France will.

So understood, *2 Henry IV*, written near the end of

1597 or early in 1598, occupies a pivotal point in the Shakespearean canon. In the early comedies, romantic love overcomes feuds and hatreds, while in the early histories and tragedies, family or romantic love fails to control political and social aggressions. In the plays of 1598–1601, Shakespeare seems to play with the thought that passivity best counters aggression or romantic assertiveness. Claudio in *Much Ado* lets his Prince do his wooing for him. In *Twelfth Night,* the woman takes the role of wooer, as she does in *As You Like It. 2 Henry IV* also looks forward to the tragedies, the uncurbed and parricidal drives of Brutus and Cassius, and even more, to that character who, more than any other in Shakespeare, resists the role his father had set up for him, putting up instead his own smokescreen of words—Hamlet. In many ways, but notably in the special, paternal way love controls rebellion and aggression, *2 Henry IV* seems closer to the tragedies and "problem plays" than to the earlier histories.

The passivity of *2 Henry IV* may also explain why it has become less popular than the other histories. It was apparently as popular as Part One in the eighteenth century, but, then, eighteenth-century audiences were still committed to a larger, hierarchical plan in society. The nineteenth and twentieth centuries prize precisely the acquisitive, assertive behavior that resists inherited patterns and plans, and this particular history play, which so sharply rejects such social individualism, has fallen in popularity. But *2 Henry IV* can look for better days with newer approaches to Shakespeare. Nineteenth-century audiences concentrated on the events represented by the plays rather than on the plays as themselves events and, therefore, they wanted to see in the histories one long epic glorifying England's history—to them, *2 Henry IV* marked a sordid low. Today, however, we recognize that Shakespeare's histories embody Elizabethan political views, not nineteenth-century Whiggery, and we are better at accepting Shakespeare's plays on their own terms, as things-in-themselves. When we do so accept *2 Henry IV,* we find it offers moments as fine as any in the Shakespearean canon: the brilliant and pathetic portrait of Shallow; the grotesquery of Pistol; the Prince's reconciliation with his father; the King's apostrophe to sleep; the rejection of Falstaff. More important, when we accept the play itself as an event, our experience of the play becomes our own act of trust.

NORMAN N. HOLLAND
Massachusetts Institute of Technology

The Second Part of [King] Henry IV

The Actors' Names

Rumor, the Presenter
King Henry the Fourth
Prince Henry, afterwards crowned King Henry the Fifth
Prince John of Lancaster ⎫
Humphrey of Gloucester ⎬ sons to Henry IV and
Thomas of Clarence   ⎭ brethren to Henry V

[Earl of] Northumberland ⎫
[Richard Scroop] the Arch- ⎪
  bishop of York ⎪
[Lord] Mowbray ⎪
[Lord] Hastings ⎬ opposites against
Lord Bardolph ⎪ King Henry IV
Travers ⎪
Morton ⎪
[Sir John] Coleville ⎭

[Earl of] Warwick ⎫   Poins ⎫
[Earl of] Westmoreland ⎪   [Sir John] ⎪
[Earl of] Surrey ⎪   Falstaff ⎪
[Sir John Blunt] ⎬ of the   Bardolph ⎬ irregular
Gower ⎪ King's   Pistol ⎪ humorists
Harcourt ⎪ party   Peto ⎪
Lord Chief Justice ⎭   [Falstaff's] ⎪
                               Page ⎭

[Robert] Shallow ⎫ both coun-
Silence ⎬ try justices   Northumberland's
Davy, servant to Shallow   Wife
Fang and Snare, two sergeants   Percy's Widow
[Ralph] Moldy ⎫   [Lady Percy]
[Simon] Shadow ⎪   Drawers   Hostess Quickly
[Thomas] Wart ⎬ country Beadles   Doll Tearsheet
[Francis] Feeble ⎪ soldiers Grooms [A Dancer as]
[Peter] Bullcalf ⎭   Epilogue

[Porter, Messenger, Soldiers, Lords, Attendants

Scene: England]

The Second Part of
[King] Henry IV

[INDUCTION]

Enter Rumor, painted full of tongues.

[*Rumor.*] Open your ears, for which of you will stop
  The vent of hearing when loud Rumor speaks?
  I, from the orient to the drooping west,
  Making the wind my post-horse, still unfold
  The acts commencèd on this ball of earth.   5
  Upon my tongues continual slanders ride,
  The which in every language I pronounce,
  Stuffing the ears of men with false reports.
  I speak of peace while covert enmity
  Under the smile of safety wounds the world.   10
  And who but Rumor, who but only I,
  Make fearful musters and prepared defense
  Whiles the big year, swoln with some other grief,
  Is thought with child by the stern tyrant, war,
  And no such matter? Rumor is a pipe°1   15
  Blown by surmises, jealousies, conjectures,
  And of so easy and so plain a stop
  That the blunt° monster with uncounted heads,
  The still-discordant wav'ring multitude,
  Can play upon it. But what need I thus   20
  My well-known body to anatomize
  Among my household?° Why is Rumor here?

---

1 The degree sign (°) indicates a footnote, which is keyed to the text by line number. Text references are printed in **boldface** type; the annotation follows in roman type.
Ind.15 **pipe** wind instrument   18 **blunt** dull   22 **my household** i.e., the audience

I run before King Harry's victory,
Who in a bloody field by Shrewsbury
25 Hath beaten down young Hotspur° and his troops,
Quenching the flame of bold rebellion
Even with the rebels' blood. But what mean I
To speak so true at first? My office is
To noise abroad that Harry Monmouth° fell
30 Under the wrath of noble Hotspur's sword,
And that the King before the Douglas' rage
Stooped his anointed head as low as death.
This have I rumored through the peasant towns
Between that royal field of Shrewsbury
35 And this worm-eaten hole of ragged° stone,
Where Hotspur's father, old Northumberland,
Lies crafty-sick.° The posts come tiring° on,
And not a man of them brings other news
Than they have learned of me. From Rumor's
      tongues
They bring smooth comforts false, worse than true
40   wrongs.   *Exit Rumor.*

---

25 **Hotspur** Harry Percy, the Earl of Northumberland's son, a rebel
against King Henry IV, killed by the Prince of Wales   29 **Harry
Monmouth** the Prince of Wales, Prince Hal   35 **ragged** rough-edged
37 **crafty-sick** feigning sickness   37 **tiring** exhausting themselves

Scene I. *Northumberland's castle.*]

Enter the Lord Bardolph at one door.

Lord Bardolph. Who keeps the gate here, ho? Where
  is the Earl?

Porter. [*Within*] What shall I say you are?

Lord Bardolph.   Tell thou the Earl
  That the Lord Bardolph doth attend him here.

Porter. His lordship is walked forth into the orchard.
  Please it your honor, knock but at the gate,   5
  And he himself will answer.

        Enter the Earl [of] Northumberland.

Lord Bardolph.   Here comes the Earl.

Northumberland. What news, Lord Bardolph? Every
  minute now
  Should be the father of some stratagem.
  The times are wild. Contention, like a horse
  Full of high feeding, madly hath broke loose   10
  And bears down all before him.

Lord Bardolph.   Noble Earl,
I bring you certain news from Shrewsbury.

Northumberland. Good, and° God will!

Lord Bardolph.   As good as heart can wish.
The King is almost wounded to the death;
15 And, in the fortune of my lord your son,
Prince Harry slain outright; and both the Blunts
Killed by the hand of Douglas; young Prince John
And Westmoreland and Stafford fled the field;
And Harry Monmouth's brawn,° the hulk Sir John,
20 Is prisoner to your son. O, such a day,
So fought, so followed, and so fairly won,
Came not till now to dignify the times
Since Caesar's fortunes!

Northumberland.   How is this derived?
Saw you the field? Came you from Shrewsbury?

Lord Bardolph. I spake with one, my lord, that came
25   from thence,

Enter Travers.

A gentleman well bred and of good name,
That freely rend'red me these news for true.

Northumberland. Here comes my servant Travers,°
    who I sent
On Tuesday last to listen after news.

Lord Bardolph. My lord, I overrode° him on the
30   way,
And he is furnished with no certainties
More than he haply° may retail from me.

Northumberland. Now, Travers, what good tidings
    comes with you?

Travers. My lord, Sir John Umfrevile turned me back
35   With joyful tidings, and, being better horsed,
Outrode me. After him came spurring hard

I.i.13 **and** if   19 **brawn** fattened boar   28 **Travers** (to "traverse" is
to deny)   30 **overrode** outrode   32 **haply** perhaps

A gentleman, almost forspent° with speed,
That stopped by me to breathe his bloodied horse.
He asked the way to Chester, and of him
I did demand what news from Shrewsbury.   40
He told me that rebellion had bad luck,
And that young Harry Percy's spur was cold.
With that, he gave his able horse the head,
And bending forward struck his armèd heels
Against the panting sides of his poor jade°   45
Up to the rowel-head, and starting so
He seemed in running to devour the way,
Staying no longer question.

Northumberland.   Ha? Again.
Said he young Harry Percy's spur was cold?
Of Hotspur Coldspur? That rebellion   50
Had met ill luck?

Lord Bardolph.   My lord, I'll tell you what.
If my young lord your son have not the day,
Upon mine honor, for a silken point°
I'll give my barony. Never talk of it.

Northumberland. Why should that gentleman that
     rode by Travers   55
Give then such instances of loss?

Lord Bardolph.   Who, he?
He was some hilding° fellow that had stol'n
The horse he rode on, and, upon my life,
Spoke at a venture. Look, here comes more news.

Enter Morton.

Northumberland. Yea, this man's brow, like to a title-
     leaf,   60
Foretells the nature of a tragic volume.
So looks the strond° whereon the imperious flood
Hath left a witnessed° usurpation.
Say, Morton, didst thou come from Shrewsbury?

---

37 **forspent** totally used up   45 **jade** nag   53 **point** lace (used to tie
breeches up)   57 **hilding** base   62 **strond** shore   63 **witnessed** evidence of

65 *Morton.* I ran from Shrewsbury, my noble lord,
      Where hateful death put on his ugliest mask
      To fright our party.

   Northumberland.   How doth my son and brother?
      Thou tremblest, and the whiteness in thy cheek
      Is apter than thy tongue to tell thy errand.
70   Even such a man, so faint, so spiritless,
      So dull, so dead in look, so woebegone,
      Drew Priam's curtain in the dead of night,
      And would have told him half his Troy was burnt.
      But Priam found the fire ere he his tongue
75   And I my Percy's death ere thou report'st it.
      This thou wouldst say, "Your son did thus and
         thus;
      Your brother thus. So fought the noble Douglas,"
      Stopping my greedy ear with their bold deeds.
      But in the end, to stop my ear indeed,
80   Thou hast a sigh to blow away this praise,
      Ending with "Brother, son, and all are dead."

   Morton. Douglas is living, and your brother—yet;
      But, for my lord your son—

   Northumberland.   Why, he is dead!
      See what a ready tongue suspicion hath!
85   He that but fears the thing he would not know
      Hath by instinct knowledge from others' eyes
      That what he feared is chanced. Yet speak, Morton.
      Tell thou an earl his divination lies,
      And I will take it as a sweet disgrace
90   And make thee rich for doing me such wrong.

   Morton. You are too great to be by me gainsaid.
      Your spirit is too true, your fears too certain.

   Northumberland. Yet, for all this, say not that Percy's
         dead.
      I see a strange confession in thine eye.
95   Thou shak'st thy head and hold'st it fear, or sin,
      To speak a truth. If he be slain, say so.
      The tongue offends not that reports his death;

And he doth sin that doth belie the dead,
Not he which says the dead is not alive.
Yet the first bringer of unwelcome news   *100*
Hath but a losing office, and his tongue
Sounds ever after as a sullen bell,
Remem'bred tolling a departing friend.

Lord Bardolph. I cannot think, my lord, your son is
    dead.

Morton. I am sorry I should force you to believe   *105*
That which I would to God I had not seen.
But these mine eyes saw him in bloody state,
Rend'ring faint quittance,° wearied and out-
    breathed,
To Harry Monmouth, whose swift wrath beat down
The never-daunted Percy to the earth,   *110*
From whence with life he never more sprung up.
In few,° his death, whose spirit lent a fire
Even to the dullest peasant in his camp,
Being bruited° once, took fire and heat away
From the best-tempered courage in his troops.   *115*
For from his mettle was his party steeled,
Which once in him abated, all the rest
Turned on themselves, like dull and heavy lead.
And as the thing that's heavy in itself,
Upon enforcement flies with greatest speed,   *120*
So did our men, heavy in Hotspur's loss,
Lend to this weight such lightness with their fear
That arrows fled not swifter toward their aim
Than did our soldiers, aiming at their safety,
Fly from the field. Then was that noble Worcester   *125*
So soon ta'en prisoner. And that furious Scot,
The bloody Douglas, whose well-laboring sword
Had three times slain th' appearance of the King,°
'Gan vail his stomach° and did grace° the shame
Of those that turned their backs, and in his flight,   *130*

---

108 **quittance** repaying (of blows)   112 **few** i.e., few words   114
bruited noised about   128 **th' appearance of the King** noblemen disguised as the King   129 **'Gan vail his stomach** began to abate his
courage   129 **grace** favor

Stumbling in fear, was took. The sum of all
Is that the King hath won, and hath sent out
A speedy power to encounter you, my lord,
Under the conduct of young Lancaster
135   And Westmoreland. This is the news at full.

Northumberland. For this I shall have time enough to
    mourn.
In poison there is physic;° and these news,
Having been well, that° would have made me sick,
Being sick, have in some measure made me well.
140   And, as the wretch whose fever-weak'ned joints,
Like strengthless hinges, buckle under life,
Impatient of his fit, breaks like a fire
Out of his keeper's arms, even so my limbs,
Weak'ned with grief, being now enraged with
    grief,°
Are thrice themselves. Hence, therefore, thou nice°
145   crutch!
A scaly gauntlet now with joints of steel
Must glove this hand. And hence, thou sickly
    quoif!°
Thou art a guard too wanton° for the head
Which princes, fleshed with° conquest, aim to hit.
150   Now bind my brows with iron, and approach
The ragged'st° hour that time and spite dare bring
To frown upon th' enraged Northumberland!
Let heaven kiss earth! Now let not Nature's hand
Keep the wild flood confined! Let order die!
155   And let this world no longer be a stage
To feed contention in a ling'ring act!°
But let one spirit of the firstborn Cain
Reign in all bosoms, that, each heart being set
On bloody courses, the rude scene may end,
160   And darkness be the burier of the dead!

137 **physic** medicine   138 **Having been well, that** that, had they been
well   144 **grief . . . grief** sickness . . . sorrow   145 **nice** delicate
147 **quoif** nightcap   148 **wanton** light   149 **fleshed with** having sa-
vored   151 **ragged'st** roughest   156 **act** (1) deed (2) section of a
play

Lord Bardolph. This strainèd passion doth you wrong,
   my lord.

Morton. Sweet Earl, divorce not wisdom from your
   honor.
   The lives of all your loving complices
   Lean on your health, the which, if you give o'er
   To stormy passion, must perforce decay.   *165*
   You cast th' event° of war, my noble lord,
   And summed the account of chance, before you
      said,
   "Let us make head."° It was your presurmise
   That, in the dole° of blows, your son might drop.
   You knew he walked o'er perils, on an edge,   *170*
   More likely to fall in than to get o'er.
   You were advised his flesh was capable
   Of wounds and scars and that his forward spirit
   Would lift him where most trade of danger ranged.
   Yet did you say, "Go forth." And none of this,   *175*
   Though strongly apprehended, could restrain
   The stiff-borne° action. What hath then befall'n,
   Or what hath this bold enterprise brought forth,
   More than that being which was like to be?

Lord Bardolph. We all that are engagèd° to this loss   *180*
   Knew that we ventured on such dangerous seas
   That if we wrought out life 'twas ten to one.
   And yet we ventured, for the gain proposed
   Choked the respect° of likely peril feared.
   And since we are o'erset,° venture again.   *185*
   Come, we will all put forth,° body and goods.

Morton. 'Tis more than time. And, my most noble
   lord,
   I hear for certain, and dare speak the truth:
   The gentle Archbishop of York is up
   With well-appointed pow'rs.° He is a man   *190*

---

166 **cast th' event** estimated the outcome   168 **make head** raise an
army   169 **dole** dealing out   177 **stiff-borne** determinedly carried on
180 **engagèd** bound by contract   184 **respect** consideration   185
o'erset (1) upset, capsized (2) outwagered   186 **put forth** wager
190 **well-appointed pow'rs** well-equipped armies

Who with a double° surety binds his followers.
My lord your son had only but the corpse,
But shadows and the shows of men, to fight.
For that same word "rebellion" did divide
195 The action of their bodies from their souls,
And they did fight with queasiness, constrained,
As men drink potions, that their weapons only
Seemed on our side. But for their spirits and souls,
This word "rebellion," it had froze them up
200 As fish are in a pond. But now the Bishop
Turns insurrection to religion.
Supposed sincere and holy in his thoughts,
He's followed both with body and with mind,
And doth enlarge his rising with the blood
Of fair King Richard, scraped from Pomfret°
205   stones;
Derives from heaven his quarrel and his cause;
Tells them he doth bestride a bleeding land,
Gasping for life under great Bolingbroke;°
And more and less° do flock to follow him.

Northumberland. I knew of this before; but, to speak
210   truth,
This present grief had wiped it from my mind.
Go in with me, and counsel every man
The aptest way for safety and revenge.
Get° posts and letters, and make° friends with
        speed.
215 Never so few, and never yet more need.   *Exeunt.*

191 **double** i.e., of body and soul   205 **Pomfret** Pomfret castle
(where Richard II was murdered)   208 **Bolingbroke** King Henry IV
209 **more and less** high and low   214 **Get** beget   214 **make** collect

[Scene II. *London*.]

Enter Sir John [Falstaff] alone, with his Page
bearing his sword and buckler.

Falstaff. Sirrah, you giant,° what says the doctor to
my water?°

Page. He said, sir, the water itself was a good healthy
water; but, for the party that owed° it, he might
have moe° diseases than he knew for.   5

Falstaff. Men of all sorts take a pride to gird° at me.
The brain of this foolish compounded clay, man°
is not able to invent anything that intends to
laughter more than I invent or is invented on me.
I am not only witty in myself, but the cause that   10
wit is in other men. I do here walk before thee like
a sow that hath overwhelmed all her litter but one.
If the Prince put thee into my service for any other
reason than to set me off, why then I have no judgment. Thou whoreson mandrake,° thou art fitter   15
to be worn in my cap than to wait at my heels. I
was never manned with an agate° till now, but
I will inset you neither in gold nor silver, but in
vile apparel, and send you back again to your
master, for a jewel—the juvenal,° the Prince your   20
master, whose chin is not yet fledge.° I will sooner
have a beard grow in the palm of my hand than
he shall get one off his cheek, and yet he will not

I.ii.1 **giant** (the page was played by an unusually small boy, who
probably mimicked Falstaff)   2 **water** urine   4 **owed** owned   5 **moe**
more   6 **gird** mock   7 **compounded clay, man** man, compounded of
clay   15 **mandrake** man-shaped root   17 **manned with an agate**
attended by a servingman small as a figure carved in a jewel   20
juvenal juvenile (echoing jewel)   21 **fledge** feathered

stick to say his face is a face-royal.° God may fin-
25 ish it when he will, 'tis not a hair amiss yet. He may
keep it still at a face-royal,° for a barber shall
never earn sixpence out of it; and yet he'll be crow-
ing as if he had writ° man ever since his father was
a bachelor. He may keep his own grace,° but he's
30 almost out of mine, I can assure him. What said
Master Dummelton about the satin for my short
cloak and my slops?°

Page. He said, sir, you should procure him better
assurance° than Bardolph. He would not take his
35 band° and yours; he liked not the security.

Falstaff. Let him be damned, like the glutton!° Pray
God his tongue be hotter! A whoreson Achitophel!°
A rascal, yea-forsooth knave!° To bear a gentleman in hand, and then stand upon security! The
40 whoreson smooth-pates° do now wear nothing but
high shoes,° and bunches of keys° at their girdles;
and if a man is through with them in honest taking
up, then they must stand upon security.° I had as
lief they would put ratsbane in my mouth as offer
45 to stop it with "security." I looked 'a° should have
sent me two-and-twenty yards of satin, as I am a
true knight, and he sends me "security." Well, he
may sleep in security, for he hath the horn° of
abundance, and the lightness° of his wife shines

24, 26 **face-royal** the King's face on a ten-shilling coin (the royal),
which presumably would not need the attention of a barber   28 **writ**
styled himself   29 **grace** (1) title, "your Grace," (2) favor   32 **slops**
wide breeches   34 **assurance** security (Bardolph is not Lord Bardolph, but one of Falstaff's cronies)   35 **band** bond   36 **glutton**
Dives (who in Luke 16:24 asked for water to cool his tongue)
37 **Achitophel** the counselor who betrayed Absalom (II Samuel
15–17)   38 **yea-forsooth knave** (one who swears sissy oaths like
"yea, forsooth")   40 **smooth-pates** tradesmen (who wore their hair
short, not like a nobleman's)   41 **high shoes** (sign of pride)   41 **keys**
(sign of possessions)   42–43 **if a man . . . security** after a man completes a bargain on credit with them, they suddenly demand security
45 **'a** he   48 **horn** (1) cornucopia (2) cuckold's horn   49 **lightness**
unchastity

through it. And yet cannot he see, though he have   50
his own lanthorn° to light him. Where's Bardolph?

Page. He's gone into Smithfield° to buy your worship
a horse.

Falstaff. I bought him in Paul's,° and he'll buy me a
horse in Smithfield. And I could get me but a wife   55
in the stews,° I were manned, horsed, and wived.°

Enter Lord Chief Justice [and Servant].

Page. Sir, here comes the nobleman that committed°
the Prince for striking him about Bardolph.

Falstaff. Wait close—I will not see him.

Chief Justice. What's he that goes there?   60

Servant. Falstaff, and't please your lordship.

Chief Justice. He that was in question° for the
robb'ry?

Servant. He, my lord. But he hath since done good
service at Shrewsbury, and, as I hear, is now going   65
with some charge° to the Lord John of Lancaster.

Chief Justice. What, to York? Call him back again.

Servant. Sir John Falstaff!

Falstaff. Boy, tell him I am deaf.

Page. You must speak louder; my master is deaf.   70

Chief Justice. I am sure he is—to the hearing of anything good. Go, pluck him by the elbow. I must
speak with him.

Servant. Sir John!

51 **lanthorn** lantern (in which a light shines through horn panels)
52 **Smithfield** the horse market   54 **Paul's** (unemployed men loitered
in St. Paul's cathedral seeking service)   56 **stews** brothels   56
manned, horsed, and wived (a proverb: "Who goes to Westminster
for a wife, to Paul's for a man, or to Smithfield for a horse, may
meet with a whore, a knave, and a jade")   57 **committed** i.e., to
prison (notice that the audience needed only this brief allusion to
the story about Hal striking the Lord Chief Justice)   62 **in question**
suspected   66 **charge** commission for soldiers

75 *Falstaff.* What! A young knave, and begging! Is there
     not wars? Is there not employment? Doth not the
     King lack subjects? Do not the rebels need soldiers?
     Though it be a shame to be on any side but one, it
     is worse shame to beg than to be on the worst side,
80   were it worse than the name of rebellion can tell
     how to make it.

     Servant. You mistake me, sir.

     Falstaff. Why, sir, did I say you were an honest man?
     Setting my knighthood and my soldiership aside,°
85   I had lied in my throat if I had said so.

     Servant. I pray you, sir, then set your knighthood and
     your soldiership aside and give me leave to tell you
     you lie in your throat if you say I am any other
     than an honest man.

90 *Falstaff.* I give thee leave to tell me so! I lay aside
     that which grows to me! If thou get'st any leave of
     me, hang me. If thou tak'st leave, thou wert better
     be hanged. You hunt counter.° Hence! Avaunt!

     Servant. Sir, my lord would speak with you.

95 *Chief Justice.* Sir John Falstaff, a word with you.

     Falstaff. My good lord! God give your lordship good
     time of day. I am glad to see your lordship abroad.
     I heard say your lordship was sick. I hope your
     lordship goes abroad by advice.° Your lordship,
100 though not clean past your youth, hath yet some
     smack of an age° in you, some relish of the salt-
     ness of time in you; and I most humbly beseech
     your lordship to have a reverent care of your
     health.

105 *Chief Justice.* Sir John, I sent for you before your
     expedition to Shrewsbury.

     Falstaff. And't please your lordship, I hear his Majesty

     84 **Setting . . . aside** i.e., because knights and soldiers ought not to lie
     93 **counter** in the wrong direction   99 **advice** i.e., a physician's
     advice   101 **age** (pun on "ague"; cf. IV.i.34)

is returned with some discomfort from Wales.

Chief Justice. I talk not of his Majesty. You would
not come when I sent for you.   *110*

Falstaff. And I hear, moreover, his Highness is fall'n
into this same whoreson apoplexy.

Chief Justice. Well, God mend him! I pray you, let
me speak with you.

Falstaff. This apoplexy, as I take it, is a kind of   *115*
lethargy, and't please your lordship, a kind of
sleeping in the blood, a whoreson tingling.

Chief Justice. What, tell you me of it? Be it as it is.

Falstaff. It hath it original° from much grief, from
study and perturbation of the brain. I have read the   *120*
cause of his effects in Galen.° It is a kind of deaf-
ness.

Chief Justice. I think you are fall'n into the disease,
for you hear not what I say to you.

Falstaff. Very well, my lord, very well. Rather, and't   *125*
please you, it is the disease of not listening, the
malady of not marking, that I am troubled withal.

Chief Justice. To punish you by the heels° would
amend the attention of your ears, and I care not
if I do become your physician.   *130*

Falstaff. I am as poor as Job, my lord, but not so
patient. Your lordship may minister the potion of
imprisonment to me in respect of poverty; but how
I should be your patient to follow your prescrip-
tions, the wise may make some dram° of a scruple,°   *135*
or indeed a scruple itself.

Chief Justice. I sent for you, when there were matters
against you for your life, to come speak with me.

119 **it original** its origin   121 **Galen** Greek physician (A.D. 129–199)
whose writings dominated Renaissance medical practice   128 **punish
you by the heels** put you in fetters or the stocks   135 **dram, scruple**
apothecaries' small weights

Falstaff. As I was then advised by my learned counsel
140   in the laws of this land-service,° I did not come.

Chief Justice. Well, the truth is, Sir John, you live in
       great infamy.

Falstaff. He that buckles himself in my belt cannot
       live in less.

145 *Chief Justice.* Your means are very slender and your
       waste is great.

Falstaff. I would it were otherwise. I would my means
       were greater and my waist slender.

Chief Justice. You have misled the youthful Prince.

150 *Falstaff.* The young Prince hath misled me. I am the
       fellow with the great belly,° and he my dog.

Chief Justice. Well, I am loath to gall a new-healed
       wound. Your day's service at Shrewsbury hath a
       little gilded over your night's exploit° on Gad's
155   Hill. You may thank th' unquiet time for your quiet
       o'erposting° that action.

Falstaff. My lord?

Chief Justice. But since all is well, keep it so. Wake
       not a sleeping wolf.

160 *Falstaff.* To wake a wolf is as bad as smell a fox.°

Chief Justice. What! You are as a candle, the better
       part burnt out.

Falstaff. A wassail candle,° my lord, all tallow. If I
       did say of wax,° my growth would approve the
165   truth.

140 **land-service** (a play on military service—in which Falstaff's
sword would be his "learned counsel"—as against the service of a
legal summons)   151 **belly** i.e., so large he cannot see where he is
going and therefore needs a dog to lead him (?), a reference to some
well-known beggar (?)   154 **exploit** (the robbery in *1 Henry IV*,
II.ii and iv)   155–56 **quiet o'erposting** quietly getting past   160
smell a fox be suspicious   163 **wassail candle** large candle designed
to last a whole night, as at a feast   164 **wax** a play on (1) beeswax
(2) grow

Chief Justice. There is not a white hair in your face but should have his effect of gravity.

Falstaff. His effect of gravy,° gravy, gravy.

Chief Justice. You follow the young Prince up and down like his ill angel.   *170*

Falstaff. Not so, my lord. Your ill angel° is light,° but I hope he that looks upon me will take me without weighing. And yet, in some respects, I grant, I cannot go.° I cannot tell. Virtue is of so little regard in these costermongers'° times that true valor is   *175* turned berod.° Pregnancy° is made a tapster, and hath his quick wit wasted in giving reckonings.° All the other gifts appertinent to man, as the malice of this age shapes them, are not worth a gooseberry. You that are old consider not the capacities of us   *180* that are young. You do measure the heat of our livers with the bitterness of your galls. And we that are in the vaward° of our youth, I must confess, are wags too.

Chief Justice. Do you set down your name in the   *185* scroll of youth, that are written down old with all the characters of age? Have you not a moist eye, a dry hand, a yellow cheek, a white beard, a decreasing leg, an increasing belly? Is not your voice broken, your wind short, your chin double, your   *190* wit single,° and every part about you blasted with antiquity, and will you yet call yourself young? Fie, fie, fie, Sir John!

Falstaff. My lord, I was born about three of the clock in the afternoon, with a white head and something   *195* a round belly. For my voice, I have lost it with hallowing° and singing of anthems. To approve°

168 **gravy** with pun on the sense fatty sweat   171 **ill angel** clipped coin   171 **light** (1) not due weight (2) wanton   174 **go** (1) pass for currency (2) copulate (?)   175 **costermongers'** hucksters'   176 **berod** bear-herd, one who leads tame bears   176 **Pregnancy** quickness of wit   177 **reckonings** tavern bills   183 **vaward** vanguard   191 **single** weak   197 **hallowing** (1) sanctifying (2) "halloing," shouting to hounds   197 **approve** prove

my youth further, I will not. The truth is, I am
only old in judgment and understanding; and he
200   that will caper° with me for a thousand marks, let
him lend me the money, and have at him! For the
box of the ear that the Prince gave you, he gave it
like a rude prince, and you took it like a sensible
lord. I have checked° him for it, and the young
205   lion repents, marry, not in ashes and sackcloth, but
in new silk and old sack.°

Chief Justice. Well, God send the Prince a better
companion!

Falstaff. God send the companion a better prince! I
210   cannot rid my hands of him.

Chief Justice. Well, the King hath severed you and
Prince Harry. I hear you are going with Lord John
of Lancaster against the Archbishop and the Earl
of Northumberland.

215 *Falstaff.* Yea, I thank your pretty sweet wit for it. But
look you° pray, all you that kiss my lady Peace at
home, that our armies join not in a hot day, for, by
the Lord, I take but two shirts out with me, and
I mean not to sweat extraordinarily. If it be a hot
220   day, and I brandish anything but a bottle, I would
I might never spit white° again. There is not a
dangerous action can peep out his head but I am
thrust upon it. Well, I cannot last ever. But it was
alway yet the trick of our English nation, if they
225   have a good thing, to make it too common. If ye
will needs say I am an old man, you should give
me rest. I would to God my name were not so ter-
rible to the enemy as it is. I were better to be eaten
to death with a rust than to be scoured to nothing
230   with perpetual motion.

Chief Justice. Well, be honest, be honest, and God
bless your expedition!

200 **caper** compete at dancing   204 **checked** reproved   206 **sack**
sherry   216 **look you** make sure you   221 **spit white** (1) suffer a dry
mouth from carousing (2) emit semen (?)

Falstaff. Will your lordship lend me a thousand pound to furnish me forth?

Chief Justice. Not a penny, not a penny. You are too   235
impatient to bear crosses.° Fare you well. Commend me to my cousin Westmoreland.

          [*Exeunt Chief Justice and Servant.*]

Falstaff. If I do, fillip° me with a three-man beetle.°
A man can no more separate age and covetousness than 'a can part young limbs and lechery. But the   240
gout galls the one and the pox pinches the other, and so both the degrees° prevent° my curses. Boy!

Page. Sir?

Falstaff. What money is in my purse?

Page. Seven groats° and twopence.   245

Falstaff. I can get no remedy against this consumption of the purse. Borrowing only lingers and lingers it out, but the disease is incurable. Go bear this letter to my Lord of Lancaster, this to the Prince, this to the Earl of Westmoreland, and this to old   250
Mistress Ursula, whom I have weekly sworn to marry since I perceived the first white hair of my chin. About it. You know where to find me. [*Exit Page.*] A pox of this gout! Or a gout of this pox! For the one or the other plays the rogue with my   255
great toe. 'Tis no matter if I do halt°—I have the wars for my color,° and my pension shall seem the more reasonable. A good wit will make use of anything. I will turn diseases to commodity.°   [*Exit.*]

---

236 **crosses** (1) afflictions (2) coins marked with a cross   238 **fillip** flip   238 **three-man beetle** a battering-ram carried by three men (what it would take to "fillip" Falstaff)   242 **degrees** stations in life   242 **prevent** act before   245 **groats** fourpenny coins   256 **halt** limp   257 **color** (1) pretense (2) battle flag   259 **commodity** something to sell

[Scene III. *The rebels' meeting-place.*]

Enter th' Archbishop, Thomas Mowbray
(Earl Marshal), the Lord Hastings and
[Lord] Bardolph.

Archbishop. Thus have you heard our cause and
    known our means;
  And, my most noble friends, I pray you all,
  Speak plainly your opinions of our hopes.
  And first, Lord Marshal, what say you to it?

5 *Mowbray.* I well allow the occasion° of our arms,
  But gladly would be better satisfied
  How in our means we should advance ourselves
  To look with forehead bold and big enough
  Upon the power and puissance° of the King.

10 *Hastings.* Our present musters grow upon the file°
  To five-and-twenty thousand men of choice;
  And our supplies° live largely in the hope
  Of great Northumberland, whose bosom burns
  With an incensèd fire of injuries.

Lord Bardolph. The question then, Lord Hastings,
15 standeth thus:
  Whether our present five-and-twenty thousand
  May hold up head without Northumberland?

Hastings. With him, we may.

Lord Bardolph.   Yea, marry,° there's the point.
  But if without him we be thought too feeble,
20 My judgment is, we should not step too far
  Till we had his assistance by the hand.

I.iii.5 **allow the occasion** approve the cause 9 **puissance** strength
10 **file** catalog 12 **supplies** reinforcements 18 **marry** by the Virgin
Mary (a mild oath)

For in a theme so bloody-faced as this,
Conjecture, expectation, and surmise
Of aids incertain should not be admitted.

Archbishop. 'Tis very true, Lord Bardolph, for in-
    deed   25
It was young Hotspur's case at Shrewsbury.

Lord Bardolph. It was, my lord, who lined° himself
    with hope,
Eating the air and promise of supply,
Flatt'ring himself in project of a power
Much smaller than° the smallest of his thoughts,   30
And so, with great imagination
Proper to madmen, led his powers to death
And, winking,° leaped into destruction.

Hastings. But, by your leave, it never yet did hurt
To lay down likelihoods and forms of hope.   35

Lord Bardolph. Yes, if this present quality of war.°
Indeed the instant action, a cause on foot,
Lives so in hope as in an early spring
We see th' appearing buds, which to prove fruit,
Hope gives not so much warrant as despair°   40
That frosts will bite them. When we mean to build,
We first survey the plot, then draw the model.°
And when we see the figure° of the house,
Then must we rate the cost of the erection,
Which if we find outweighs ability,   45
What do we then but draw anew the model
In fewer offices,° or at least° desist
To build at all? Much more, in this great work,
Which is almost to pluck a kingdom down
And set another up, should we survey   50
The plot of situation and the model,

27 **lined** reinforced (as in tailoring)   29–30 **in project . . . smaller than** in planning on the basis of an army that in fact was much smaller than   33 **winking** shutting his eyes   36 **Yes . . . war.** (a famous obscurity, perhaps saying: Yes, it does do hurt to plan if this planning present [i.e., represent, substitute for] quality [i.e., true substance, strength] of war)   40 **despair** (supply: "gives warrant")   42 **model** plan   43 **figure** design   47 **offices** rooms for service   47 **least** worst

Consent° upon a sure foundation,
Question surveyors, know our own estate,
How able such a work to undergo,
55 To weigh against his opposite.° Or else
We fortify in paper and in figures,
Using the names of men instead of men,
Like one that draws the model of an house
Beyond his power to build it, who, half through,
60 Gives o'er and leaves his part-created cost°
A naked subject to the weeping clouds
And waste for churlish winter's tyranny.

Hastings. Grant that our hopes, yet likely of fair birth,
Should be stillborn, and that we now possessed
65 The utmost man of expectation,
I think we are so, body strong enough
Even as we are, to equal with the King.

Lord Bardolph. What, is the King but five-and-twenty
thousand?

Hastings. To us no more, nay, not so much, Lord
Bardolph.
70 For his divisions, as the times do brawl,
Are in three heads: one power against the French,
And one against Glendower, perforce a third
Must take up us. So is the unfirm king
In three divided, and his coffers sound
75 With hollow poverty and emptiness.

Archbishop. That he should draw his several° strengths
together
And come against us in full puissance°
Need not to be dreaded.

Hastings.   If he should do so,
He leaves his back unarmed, the French and
Welsh
80 Baying him at the heels. Never fear that.

52 **Consent** agree   55 **his opposite** its opposition   60 **part-created
cost** half-realized expenditure   76 **several** separate   77 **puissance**
power

Lord Bardolph. Who is it like° should lead his forces
    hither?

Hastings. The Duke of Lancaster and Westmoreland.
    Against the Welsh, himself and Harry Monmouth.
    But who is substituted against the French,
    I have no certain notice.

Archbishop.   Let us on,   *85*
    And publish the occasion of our arms.
    The commonwealth is sick of their own choice;
    Their overgreedy love hath surfeited.
    An habitation giddy and unsure
    Hath he that buildeth on the vulgar heart.   *90*
    O thou fond many,° with what loud applause
    Didst thou beat° heaven with blessing Bolingbroke,
    Before he was what thou wouldst have him be!
    And being now trimmed° in thine own desires,
    Thou, beastly feeder, art so full of him   *95*
    That thou provok'st thyself to cast him up.
    So, so, thou common dog, didst thou disgorge
    Thy glutton bosom of the royal Richard;
    And now thou° wouldst eat thy dead vomit up,
    And howl'st to find it. What trust is in these times? *100*
    They that when Richard lived would have him die
    Are now become enamored on his grave.
    Thou° that threw'st dust upon his goodly head
    When through proud London he came sighing on
    After th' admired heels of Bolingbroke   *105*
    Criest now, "O earth, yield us that king again,
    And take thou this!" O thoughts of men accursed!
    "Past and to come seems best, things present
        worst."°

Mowbray. Shall we go draw our numbers° and set on?

Hastings. We are time's subjects, and time bids be
    gone.   *Exeunt.* *110*

81 **like** likely   91 **fond many** foolish multitude   92 **beat** assault
(with noise or prayer)   94 **trimmed** dressed   99 **thou** the multitude
(compared to a dog, as described in Proverbs 16:11)   103 **Thou** the
multitude   108 **Past . . . worst** (proverbial)   109 **draw our numbers**
assemble our troops

[ACT II

Scene I. *London*.]

*Enter Hostess of the Tavern and an Officer or
two [Fang and another, followed by Snare].*

Hostess. Master Fang, have you ent'red the action?°

Fang. It is ent'red.

Hostess. Where's your yeoman?° Is't a lusty yeoman?
Will 'a stand to't?°

5 *Fang.* Sirrah—where's Snare?°

Hostess. O Lord, ay! Good Master Snare!

Snare. Here, here.

Fang. Snare, we must arrest Sir John Falstaff.

Hostess. Yea, good Master Snare, I have ent'red him
10 and all.

Snare. It may chance cost some of us our lives, for he
will stab.

Hostess. Alas the day! Take heed of him. He stabbed
me in mine own house, and that most beastly. In
15 good faith, 'a cares not what mischief he does, if
his weapon be out. He will foin° like any devil; he
will spare neither man, woman, nor child.

II.i.1 **ent'red the action** filed the lawsuit (with a ribald second meaning) 3 **yeoman** assistant (i.e., constable) 4 **stand to't** not collapse
in the face of danger (with a ribald second meaning) 5 **Snare** (evidently hanging back) 16 **foin** thrust (with, again, a second meaning)

Fang. If I can close with him, I care not for his thrust.

Hostess. No, nor I neither. I'll be at your elbow.

Fang. And I but fist him once, and 'a come but within   20
my vice°—

Hostess. I am undone by his going. I warrant you, he's
an infinitive° thing upon my score.° Good Master
Fang, hold him sure. Good Master Snare, let him
not 'scape. 'A comes continuantly° to Pie Corner°   25
—saving° your manhoods—to buy a saddle; and he
is indited° to dinner to the Lubber's Head° in Lum-
bert° Street, to Master Smooth's the silkman. I
pray you, since my exion° is ent'red and my case
so openly known to the world, let him be brought   30
in to his answer. A hundred mark is a long one for
a poor lone woman to bear, and I have borne,°
and borne, and borne, and have been fubbed off,°
and fubbed off, and fubbed off, from this day to
that day, that it is a shame to be thought on. There   35
is no honesty in such dealing, unless a woman
should be made an ass and a beast, to bear every
knave's wrong. Yonder he comes, and that arrant
malmsey-nose° knave, Bardolph, with him. Do your
offices, do your offices. Master Fang and Master   40
Snare, do me, do me, do me your offices.

Enter Sir John and Bardolph, and the Boy.

Falstaff. How now! Whose mare's dead?° What's the
matter?

Fang. Sir John, I arrest you at the suit of Mistress
Quickly.   45

21 **vice** grip   23 **infinitive** infinite   23 **score** account at the tavern
25 **continuantly** a mix-up of "continually" and "incontinently" (Mistress Quickly speaks in a stream of malapropisms, many with indecent second meanings)   25 **Pie Corner** the cooks' quarter (with
an indecent pun)   26 **saving** no offense meant to   27 **indited** i.e., in-
vited   27 **Lubber's Head** Libbard's (i.e., Leopard's) Head   27–28
Lumbert Lombard   29 **exion** i.e., action   32 **borne** endured (with a
second, ribald sense)   33 **fubbed off** put off   39 **malmsey-nose** nose
reddened from winebibbing   42 **Whose mare's dead?** what's all the
commotion?

Falstaff. Away, varlets! Draw, Bardolph! Cut me off the villain's head. Throw the quean° in the channel.°

Hostess. Throw me in the channel! I'll throw thee the channel. Wilt thou? Wilt thou? Thou bastardly° rogue! Murder, murder! Ah, thou honeysuckle° villain! Wilt thou kill God's officers and the King's? Ah, thou honeyseed° rogue! Thou art a honeyseed, a man-queller,° and a woman-queller.

Falstaff. Keep them off, Bardolph.

Fang. A rescue!° A rescue!

Hostess. Good people, bring a rescue or two. Thou wo't, wo't thou? Thou wo't, wo't ta? Do, do, thou rogue! Do, thou hempseed!°

Page. Away, you scullion!° You rampallian!° You fustilarian!° I'll tickle your catastrophe.°

    Enter Lord Chief Justice and his Men.

Chief Justice. What is the matter? Keep the peace here, ho!

Hostess. Good my lord, be good to me. I beseech you, stand to me.°

Chief Justice. How now, Sir John! What are you brawling here?
Doth this become your place, your time and business?
You should have been well on your way to York.
Stand from him, fellow. Wherefore hang'st thou upon him?

---

47 **quean** scold   47–48 **channel** gutter   50 **bastardly** mixing "dastardly" and "bastard" (1) illegitimate (2) a sweetened wine   51 **honeysuckle** i.e., homicidal   53 **honeyseed** i.e., homicide   54 **man-queller** i.e., man-killer   56 **rescue** forcible taking of persons out of legal custody   59 **hempseed** a child destined for the gallows (but also homicide, as in line 53—Mistress Quickly is referring to the Page)   60 **scullion** kitchen wench   60 **rampallian** rampant whore   61 **fustilarian** (derived from "fustilugs," a frowsy, fat woman)   61 **catastrophe** ending   65 **stand to me** be firm for me (with a second sense)

Hostess. O my most worshipful lord, and't please your   70
Grace, I am a poor widow of Eastcheap, and he is
arrested at my suit.

Chief Justice. For what sum?

Hostess. It is more than for some, my lord, it is for
all I have. He hath eaten me out of house and   75
home; he hath put all my substance into that fat
belly of his. But I will have some of it out again,
or I will ride thee o' nights like the mare.°

Falstaff. I think I am as like to ride the mare,° if I
have any vantage of ground° to get up.   80

Chief Justice. How comes this, Sir John? What man
of good temper would endure this tempest of exclamation? Are you not ashamed to enforce a poor
widow to so rough a course to come by her own?

Falstaff. What is the gross sum that I owe thee?   85

Hostess. Marry, if thou wert an honest man, thyself
and the money too. Thou didst swear to me upon a
parcel-gilt° goblet, sitting in my Dolphin° chamber,
at the round table, by a sea-coal fire, upon Wednesday in Wheeson° week, when the Prince broke   90
thy head for liking° his father to a singing-man of
Windsor, thou didst swear to me then, as I was
washing thy wound, to marry me and make me my
lady thy wife. Canst thou deny it? Did not good-
wife Keech, the butcher's wife, come in then and   95
call me gossip° Quickly? Coming in to borrow a
mess of vinegar, telling us she had a good dish of
prawns,° whereby thou didst desire to eat some,
whereby I told thee they were ill for a green°
wound? And didst thou not, when she was gone   100
downstairs, desire me to be no more so familiarity

78 **mare** nightmare   79 **mare** female (but also the "two-legged
mare," i.e., the gallows)   80 **vantage of ground** advantage of higher
ground   88 **parcel-gilt** partly gilded   88 **Dolphin** i.e., the sign marking the room   90 **Wheeson** Whitsun   91 **liking** likening   96 **gossip**
friend (a common form of address)   98 **prawns** shrimp   99 **green**
new

with such poor people, saying that ere long they
should call me "Madam"? And didst thou not kiss
me and bid me fetch thee thirty shillings? I put thee
105 now to thy book-oath. Deny it, if thou canst.

Falstaff. My lord, this is a poor mad soul, and she
says up and down the town that her eldest son is
like you. She hath been in good case,° and the
truth is, poverty hath distracted her.° But for these
110 foolish officers, I beseech you I may have redress
against them.

Chief Justice. Sir John, Sir John, I am well acquainted
with your manner of wrenching the true cause the
false way. It is not a confident brow, nor the throng
115 of words that come with such more than impudent
sauciness from you, can thrust me from a level°
consideration. You have, as it appears to me, practiced upon° the easy-yielding spirit of this woman,
and made her serve your uses both in purse and in
120 person.

Hostess. Yea, in truth, my lord.

Chief Justice. Pray thee, peace. Pay her the debt you
owe her and unpay the villainy you have done with
her. The one you may do with sterling money, and
125 the other with current° repentance.

Falstaff. My lord, I will not undergo this sneap° without reply. You call honorable boldness impudent
sauciness. If a man will make curtsy and say nothing, he is virtuous. No, my lord, my humble duty
130 rememb'red, I will not be your suitor. I say to you,
I do desire deliverance from these officers, being
upon hasty employment in the King's affairs.

Chief Justice. You speak as having power to do
wrong. But answer in th' effect of° your reputation,
135 and satisfy the poor woman.

108 **case** situation, i.e., well-to-do   109 **distracted her** driven her mad
116 **level** straight   117–18 **practiced upon** deceived   125 **current**
(1) progressive (2) opposite of counterfeit   126 **sneap** snub   134 **in
th' effect of** so as to fulfill

Falstaff. Come hither, hostess.

    Enter a Messenger [Gower].

Chief Justice. Now, Master Gower, what news?

Gower. The King, my lord, and Harry Prince of Wales
Are near at hand. The rest the paper tells.
                    [*They draw aside.*]

Falstaff. [*To Hostess*] As I am a gentleman!   *140*

Hostess. Faith, you said so before.

Falstaff. As I am a gentleman, come, no more words
of it.

Hostess. By this heavenly ground I tread on, I must
be fain° to pawn both my plate and the tapestry   *145*
of my dining chambers.

Falstaff. Glasses, glasses, is the only drinking.° And
for thy walls, a pretty slight drollery,° or the story
of the Prodigal, or the German hunting° in waterwork,° is worth a thousand of these bed-hangers°   *150*
and these fly-bitten tapestries. Let it be ten
pound, if thou canst. Come, and 'twere not for thy
humors,° there's not a better wench in England.
Go, wash thy face, and draw° the action. Come,
thou must not be in this humor with me. Dost not   *155*
know me? Come, come, I know thou wast set on to
this.

Hostess. Pray thee, Sir John, let it be but twenty nobles.° I' faith, I am loath to pawn my plate, so God
save me, la!   *160*

Falstaff. Let it alone; I'll make other shift. You'll be
a fool still.°

---

145 **fain** obliged   147 **glasses, is the only drinking** i.e., glasses are in
fashion now, not metal tankards   148 **drollery** comic picture   149
German hunting hunting the boar   149–50 **waterwork** imitation
tapestry   150 **bed-hangers** bed-curtains   153 **humors** (1) whims (2)
general character   154 **draw** withdraw   158–59 **nobles** coins worth
six shillings eight pence   161–62 **be a fool still** always lose your
chance

Hostess. Well, you shall have it, though I pawn my
gown. I hope you'll come to supper. You'll pay me
165   all together?

Falstaff. Will I live? [*To Bardolph*] Go, with her, with
her. Hook on,° hook on!

Hostess. Will you have Doll Tearsheet meet you at
supper?

170   *Falstaff.* No more words. Let's have her.
                              Exit Hostess and Sergeant
                              [*Fang, Bardolph and others*].

Chief Justice. [*To Gower*] I have heard better news.

Falstaff. What's the news, my lord?

Chief Justice. [*Ignoring Falstaff*] Where lay the King
tonight?°

175   *Gower.* At Basingstoke, my lord.

Falstaff. I hope, my lord, all's well. What is the news,
my lord?

Chief Justice. Come all his forces back?

Gower. No. Fifteen hundred foot, five hundred horse,
180   Are marched up to my Lord of Lancaster,
Against Northumberland and the Archbishop.

Falstaff. Comes the King back from Wales, my noble
lord?

Chief Justice. [*To his men*] You shall have letters of
me presently.
185   Come, go along with me, good Master Gower.

Falstaff. My lord!

Chief Justice. What's the matter?

Falstaff. Master Gower, shall I entreat you with me to
dinner?

167 **Hook on** stick to her   174 **tonight** last night

Gower. I must wait upon my good lord here, I thank   *190*
you, good Sir John.

Chief Justice. Sir John, you loiter here too long, being
you are to take soldiers up° in counties as you go.

Falstaff. Will you sup with me, Master Gower?

Chief Justice. What foolish master taught you these   *195*
manners, Sir John?

Falstaff. Master Gower, if they become me not, he was
a fool that taught them me. This is the right° fencing grace, my lord—tap for tap, and so part fair.

Chief Justice. Now the Lord lighten° thee! Thou art   *200*
a great fool.   [*Exeunt.*]

[Scene II. *The Prince's house.*]

Enter the Prince [Henry], Poins, with others.

Prince. Before God, I am exceeding weary.°

Poins. Is't come to that? I had thought weariness durst
not have attached° one of so high blood.

Prince. Faith, it does me, though it discolors the com-
plexion° of my greatness to acknowledge it. Doth   *5*
it not show vilely in me to desire small beer?

Poins. Why, a prince should not be so loosely studied°
as to remember so weak a composition.°

Prince. Belike, then, my appetite was not princely
got,° for, by my troth, I do now remember the   *10*

193 **take soldiers up** recruit men   198 **right** correct   200 **lighten**
(1) enlighten (2) make [you] weigh less   II.ii.1 **weary** (having just
ridden from Wales)   3 **attached** arrested   4–5 **discolors the com-
plexion** causes a blush   7 **loosely studied** carelessly or wantonly applied   8 **so weak a composition** so unstable and trivial a compound
(as small beer)   10 **got** begotten

poor creature, small beer. But indeed these humble
considerations make me out of love with my greatness. What a disgrace is it to me to remember thy
name!° Or to know thy face tomorrow! Or to take
15 note how many pair of silk stockings thou hast, viz.
these, and those that were thy peach-colored ones!
Or to bear the inventory of thy shirts, as: one for
superfluity and another for use! But that the tennis-
court-keeper knows better than I; for it is a low
20 ebb of linen with thee when thou keepest not racket
there,° as thou hast not done a great while, because
the rest of thy low countries° have made a shift° to
eat up thy holland.° And God knows whether those
that bawl out the ruins of thy linen shall inherit
25 His kingdom. But the midwives say the children are
not in the fault,° whereupon the world increases,
and kindreds° are mightily strengthened.

Poins. How ill it follows, after you have labored so
hard, you should talk so idly! Tell me, how many
30 good young princes would do so, their fathers being
so sick as yours at this time is?

Prince. Shall I tell thee one thing, Poins?

Poins. Yes, faith, and let it be an excellent good thing.

Prince. It shall serve among wits of no higher breeding
35 than thine.

Poins. Go to. I stand the push° of your one thing that
you will tell.

Prince. Marry, I tell thee, it is not meet° that I should
be sad, now my father is sick. Albeit I could tell to
40 thee, as to one it pleases me, for fault of a better,

13–14 **disgrace . . . remember thy name** i.e., unlike "graceful"
courtiers who affect to forget the names of their inferiors   19–21 **it
is . . . racket there** i.e., if you have as many as two shirts, one to play
in, a second to change into, you frequent the tennis courts   22 **low
countries** Netherlands (with an obscene pun)   22 **shift** (1) con-
trivance (2) shirt   23 **holland** linen made in Holland   26 **in the fault**
share the sin (of their illegitimacy, with a pun on French, *foutre* =
to copulate)   27 **kindreds** clans   36 **push** thrust   38 **meet** fitting

to call my friend, I could be sad, and sad indeed, too.

Poins. Very hardly° upon such a subject.

Prince. By this hand, thou thinkest me as far in the
devil's book as thou and Falstaff for obduracy and　45
persistency. Let the end° try the man. But I tell
thee, my heart bleeds inwardly that my father is so
sick. And keeping such vile company as thou art
hath in reason taken from me all ostentation° of
sorrow.　50

Poins. The reason?

Prince. What wouldst thou think of me if I should
weep?

Poins. I would think thee a most princely hypocrite.

Prince. It would be every man's thought, and thou art　55
a blessed fellow to think as every man thinks. Never
a man's thought in the world keeps the roadway
better than thine. Every man would think me an
hypocrite indeed. And what accites° your most worshipful thought to think so?　60

Poins. Why, because you have been so lewd and so
much engraffed° to Falstaff.

Prince. And to thee.

Poins. By this light, I am well spoke on; I can hear it
with mine own ears. The worst that they can say　65
of me is that I am a second brother° and that I am
a proper fellow of my hands,° and those two things
I confess I cannot help. By the mass, here comes
Bardolph.

Enter Bardolph and Boy [*Page*].

43 **Very hardly** with great difficulty　46 **end** outcome　49 **ostenta-
tion** show　59 **accites** summons (a judicial term)　62 **engraffed**
grafted (like a plant)　66 **a second brother** i.e., one who inherits
nothing　67 **proper fellow of my hands** skillful with my hands as a
fighter (or as a thief?)

70 *Prince*. And the boy that I gave Falstaff. 'A had him
      from me Christian, and look if the fat villain have
      not transformed him ape.°

  Bardolph. God save your Grace.

  Prince. And yours, most noble Bardolph.

75 *Poins*. Come, you virtuous ass, you bashful fool, must
      you be blushing?° Wherefore blush you now? What
      a maidenly man-at-arms are you become! Is't such
      a matter to get a pottle-pot's° maidenhead?

  Page. 'A calls me e'en now, my lord, through a red
80   lattice,° and I could discern no part of his face
      from the window. At last I spied his eyes, and me-
      thought he had made two holes in the ale-wife's
      petticoat and so peeped through.

  Prince. Has not the boy profited?°

85 *Bardolph*. Away, you whoreson upright rabbit, away!

  Page. Away, you rascally Althaea's dream,° away!

  Prince. Instruct us, boy. What dream, boy?

  Page. Marry, my lord, Althaea dreamed she was de-
      livered of a firebrand, and therefore I call him her
90   dream.

  Prince. A crown's worth of good interpretation. There
      'tis, boy. [*Tips him.*]

  Poins. O, that this blossom could be kept from
      cankers!° Well, there is sixpence to preserve° thee.

95 *Bardolph*. And you do not make him hanged among
      you, the gallows shall have wrong.

72 **transformed him ape** dressed him fantastically   76 **blushing** red-
faced (from drinking)   78 **pottle-pot** two-quart tankard   79–80 **red
lattice** (such a window was the sign of an alehouse)   84 **profited** i.e.,
from his association with Falstaff   86 **Althaea's dream** (the dream
he describes in lines 88–90 was actually Hecuba's. The Fates told
Althaea her son would live only as long as a log on the fire remained
unconsumed. Perhaps the boy has not "profited" as much as the
Prince thought)   94 **cankers** plant-destroying worms   94 **preserve**
i.e., because Elizabethan coins bore crosses

Prince. And how doth thy master, Bardolph?

Bardolph. Well, my lord. He heard of your Grace's coming to town. There's a letter for you.

Poins. Delivered with good respect. And how doth the martlemas,° your master? 　*100*

Bardolph. In bodily health, sir.

Poins. Marry, the immortal part needs a physician, but that moves not him. Though that be sick, it dies not. 　*105*

Prince. I do allow this wen° to be as familiar with me as my dog, and he holds his place, for look you how he writes.

Poins. [*Reads*] "John Falstaff, knight"—every man must know that, as oft as he has occasion to name *110* himself. Even like those that are kin to the King, for they never prick their finger but they say, "There's some of the King's blood spilt." "How comes that?" says he that takes upon him not to conceive. The answer is as ready as a borrowed cap,° "I am the *115* King's poor cousin, sir."

Prince. Nay, they will be kin to us, or they will fetch it from Japhet.° But the letter. [*Reads*] "Sir John Falstaff, knight, to the son of the King nearest his father, Harry Prince of Wales, greeting." 　*120*

Poins. Why, this is a certificate.°

Prince. Peace! [*Reads*] "I will imitate the honorable Romans in brevity."

Poins. He sure means brevity in breath, short-winded.

[*Prince reads.*] "I commend me to thee, I commend *125* thee, and I leave thee. Be not too familiar with

101 **martlemas** i.e., a beef fattened for slaughter before winter on Martinmas Day (November 11); see pp. 208–09　106 **wen** swelling 115 **borrowed cap** (which the borrower promptly tips)　117–18 **fetch it from Japhet** i.e., fetch their ancestry from that one of Noah's sons whose offspring peopled Europe　121 **certificate** patent (in formal style)

Poins, for he misuses thy favors so much that he
swears thou art to marry his sister Nell. Repent at
idle times as thou mayst, and so farewell.

130   "Thine, by yea and no, which is as much as to
        say, as thou usest him, JACK FALSTAFF with
        my familiars, JOHN with my brothers and sis-
        ters, and SIR JOHN with all Europe."

Poins. My lord, I'll steep this letter in sack and make
135   him eat it.

Prince. That's to make him eat twenty of his words.
    But do you use me thus, Ned? Must I marry your
    sister?

Poins. God send the wench no worse fortune! But I
140   never said so.

Prince. Well, thus we play the fools with the time, and
    the spirits of the wise sit in the clouds and mock
    us. Is your master here in London?

Bardolph. Yea, my lord.

145 *Prince.* Where sups he? Doth the old boar feed in the
    old frank?°

Bardolph. At the old place, my lord, in Eastcheap.

Prince. What company?

Page. Ephesians, my lord, of the old church.°

150 *Prince.* Sup any women with him?

Page. None, my lord, but old Mistress Quickly and
    Mistress Doll Tearsheet.

Prince. What pagan° may that be?

Page. A proper gentlewoman, sir, and a kinswoman of
155   my master's.

---

146 **frank** sty (presumably a glance at the famous Boar's Head tavern)
149 **Ephesians . . . church** libertines (who had to be corrected by St.
Paul—Ephesians 5:3–8)   153 **pagan** prostitute (love-worshipper)

Prince. Even such kin as the parish heifers are to the town bull. Shall we steal upon them, Ned, at supper?

Poins. I am your shadow, my lord; I'll follow you.

Prince. Sirrah,° you boy, and Bardolph, no word to   *160* your master that I am yet come to town. There's for your silence. [*Tips them.*]

Bardolph. I have no tongue, sir.

Page. And for mine, sir, I will govern it.

Prince. Fare you well; go. [*Exeunt Bardolph and*   *165* *Page.*] This Doll Tearsheet should be some road.°

Poins. I warrant you, as common as the way between Saint Alban's and London.

Prince. How might we see Falstaff bestow himself tonight in his true colors, and not ourselves be seen?   *170*

Poins. Put on two leathern jerkins° and aprons, and wait upon him at his table as drawers.°

Prince. From a God to a bull? A heavy descension! It was Jove's case.° From a prince to a prentice? A low transformation! That shall be mine, for in   *175* everything the purpose must weigh with° the folly. Follow me, Ned.   *Exeunt.*

---

160 **Sirrah** (form of address to an inferior)   166 **road** prostitute (one to be ridden, open to all)   171 **jerkins** jackets   172 **drawers** tavern waiters   174 **Jove's case** (he transformed himself into a bull to seduce Europa)   176 **weigh with** match

[Scene III. *Northumberland's castle.*]

*Enter Northumberland, his Wife [Lady Northumber-
land], and the Wife to Harry Percy [Lady Percy].*

Northumberland. I pray thee, loving wife, and gentle
    daughter,°
    Give even way° unto my rough affairs.
    Put not you on the visage of the times
    And be like them to Percy° troublesome.

Lady Northumberland. I have given over; I will speak
5   no more.
    Do what you will, your wisdom be your guide.

Northumberland. Alas, sweet wife, my honor is at
    pawn,
    And, but° my going, nothing can redeem it.

Lady Percy. O yet, for God's sake, go not to these
    wars!
10   The time was, father, that you broke your word,
    When you were more endeared to it than now,
    When your own Percy, when my heart's dear Harry,
    Threw many a northward look to see his father
    Bring up his powers, but he did long in vain.
15   Who then persuaded you to stay at home?
    There were two honors lost, yours and your son's.
    For yours, the God of heaven brighten it!
    For his, it stuck upon him as the sun
    In the gray vault of heaven, and by his light
20   Did all the chivalry of England move
    To do brave acts. He was indeed the glass°
    Wherein the noble youth did dress themselves.

II.iii.1 **daughter** daughter-in-law   2 **Give even way** allow free pas-
sage   4 **Percy** i.e., Northumberland, "the Percy"   8 **but** except for
21 **glass** looking glass

He° had no legs that practiced not his° gait;
And speaking thick,° which nature made his blem-
    ish,
Became the accents of the valiant,   25
For those that could speak low and tardily
Would turn their own perfection to abuse,
To seem like him. So that in speech, in gait,
In diet, in affections of delight,°
In military rules, humors of blood,°   30
He was the mark and glass, copy and book,
That fashioned others. And him! O wondrous! Him!
O miracle of men! Him did you leave,
Second to none, unseconded by you,
To look upon the hideous god of war   35
In disadvantage, to abide a field°
Where nothing but the sound of Hotspur's name
Did seem defensible. So you left him.
Never, O never, do his ghost the wrong
To hold your honor more precise and nice°   40
With others than with him! Let them alone.
The Marshal and the Archbishop are strong.
Had my sweet Harry had but half their numbers,
Today might I, hanging on Hotspur's neck,
Have talked of Monmouth's° grave.

Northumberland.   Beshrew° your heart,   45
Fair daughter, you do draw my spirits from me
With new lamenting ancient oversights.
But I must go and meet with danger there,
Or it will seek me in another place
And find me worse provided.

Lady Northumberland.   O, fly to Scotland,°   50
Till that the nobles and the armèd commons
Have of their puissance° made a little taste.

23 **He** i.e., any man   23 **his** i.e., Harry Percy's   24 **thick** fast
(crowding the words)   29 **affections of delight** preferences in pleasure   30 **humors of blood** disposition   36 **abide a field** endure on a
battlefield   40 **nice** punctilious   45 **Monmouth's** Prince Hal's   45
Beshrew cursed be   50 **Scotland** i.e., far from the battle   52 **puissance** strength

Lady Percy. If they get ground and vantage of the
        King,
    Then join you with them, like a rib of steel,
55 To make strength stronger. But, for all our loves,
    First let them try themselves. So did your son;
    He was so suff'red.° So came I a widow,
    And never shall have length of life enough
    To rain° upon remembrance with mine eyes,
60 That it may grow and sprout as high as heaven,
    For recordation° to my noble husband.

Northumberland. Come, come, go in with me. 'Tis
        with my mind
    As with the tide swelled up unto his height,
    That makes a still-stand, running neither way.
65 Fain would I go to meet the Archbishop,
    But many thousand reasons hold me back.
    I will resolve for Scotland. There am I,
    Till time and vantage° crave my company.

                                    Exeunt.

[Scene IV. *Mistress Quickly's tavern.*]

Enter a Drawer or two [Francis and another].

Francis. What the devil hast thou brought there?
    Apple-johns?° Thou knowest Sir John cannot en-
    dure an apple-john.

Drawer. Mass, thou say'st true. The Prince once set
5   a dish of apple-johns before him, and told him
    there were five more Sir Johns, and, putting off his
    hat, said, "I will now take my leave of these six

---

57 **suff'red** allowed (to fight alone)   59 **rain** drop tears   61 **record-
ation** memorial   68 **vantage** profitable opportunity   II.iv.2 **Apple-
johns** (apples ripened on St. John's Day, midsummer, but eaten two
years later when withered—perhaps they remind Sir John of age or
impotency)

dry, round, old, withered knights." It ang'red him
to the heart. But he hath forgot that.

Francis. Why, then, cover,° and set them down. And   10
see if thou canst find out Sneak's noise.° Mistress
Tearsheet would fain hear some music.

Enter Will [a third Drawer].

Will. Dispatch! The room where they supped is too
hot. They'll come in straight.

Francis. Sirrah, here will be the Prince and Master   15
Poins anon, and they will put on two of our jerkins
and aprons, and Sir John must not know of it.
Bardolph hath brought word.

Drawer. By the mass, here will be old Utis.° It will
be an excellent stratagem.   20

Francis. I'll see if I can find out Sneak.　　*Exit.*

*Enter Mistress Quickly [the Hostess] and
Doll Tearsheet.*

Hostess. I' faith, sweetheart, methinks now you are in
an excellent good temperality.° Your pulsidge°
beats as extraordinarily as heart would desire, and
your color, I warrant you, is as red as any rose, in   25
good truth, la! But, i' faith, you have drunk too
much canaries,° and that's a marvelous searching
wine, and it perfumes the blood ere one can say,
"What's this?" How do you now?

Doll. Better than I was. Hem!   30

Hostess. Why, that's well said. A good heart's worth
gold. Lo, here comes Sir John.

Enter Sir John [Falstaff].

Falstaff. [*Sings*] "When Arthur first in court"°—

10 **cover** spread the tablecloth　11 **noise** band of musicians　19 **old
Utis** grand festival (*utaves* was the eighth day or "octave" of a feast)
23 **temperality** i.e., temper or temperance　23 **pulsidge** i.e., pulse
27 **canaries** Canary wine　33 **When Arthur first in court** (first line of
a ballad)

Empty the jordan!°—"And was a worthy king."—
35 How now, Mistress Doll!

Hostess. Sick of a calm,° yea, good faith.

Falstaff. So is all her sect.° And they be once in a
calm, they are sick.

Doll. A pox damn you, you muddy° rascal, is that all
40 the comfort you give me?

Falstaff. You make fat rascals,° Mistress Doll.

Doll. I make them? Gluttony and diseases make, I
make them not.

Falstaff. If the cook help to make the gluttony, you
45 help to make the diseases, Doll. We catch of you,
Doll, we catch of you. Grant that, my poor virtue,
grant that.

Doll. Yea, joy, our chains and our jewels.

Falstaff. "Your brooches, pearls, and ouches."° For
50 to serve bravely is to come halting off, you know.
To come off the breach with his pike bent bravely,
and to surgery bravely; to venture upon the charged
chambers° bravely—

Doll. Hang yourself, you muddy conger,° hang your-
55 self!

Hostess. By my troth, this is the old fashion. You
two never meet but you fall to some discord. You
are both, i' good truth, as rheumatic° as two dry
toasts.° You cannot one bear with another's con-

34 **jordan** chamber pot   36 **calm** i.e., qualm   37 **sect** prostitutes
(love-worshippers)   39 **muddy** filthy   41 **You make fat rascals** (a
rascal was a lean deer—you say or cause the lean to fat, i.e., become
bloated or to sweat as a cure for the pox)   49 **Your brooches, pearls,
and ouches** (another scrap of ballad; "ouches" are both brooches
and scabs)   52–53 **charged chambers** loaded cannon (used, like
other words in this speech, with a bawdy second meaning)   54 **conger** eel   58 **rheumatic** (she means splenetic or choleric, the hot and
dry humor—like toast)   58–59 **dry toasts** (that would scratch one
another)

firmities.° What the goodyear!° One must bear,°   60
and that must be you [*to Doll*]. You are the weaker
vessel, as they say, the emptier vessel.

Doll. Can a weak empty vessel bear such a huge full
hogshead? There's a whole merchant's venture of
Bordeaux stuff° in him. You have not seen a hulk   65
better stuffed in the hold. Come, I'll be friends
with thee, Jack. Thou art going to the wars, and
whether I shall ever see thee again or no, there is
nobody cares.

Enter Drawer.

Drawer. Sir, Ancient° Pistol's below and would speak   70
with you.

Doll. Hang him, swaggering° rascal! Let him not
come hither. It is the foul-mouthed'st rogue in
England.

Hostess. If he swagger, let him not come here. No, by   75
my faith. I must live among my neighbors. I'll no
swaggerers. I am in good name and fame with the
very best. Shut the door, there comes no swaggerers
here. I have not lived all this while to have swaggering now. Shut the door, I pray you.   80

Falstaff. Dost thou hear, hostess?

Hostess. Pray ye, pacify yourself, Sir John. There
comes no swaggerers here.

Falstaff. Dost thou hear? It is mine Ancient.

Hostess. Tilly-fally, Sir John, ne'er tell me. And your   85
ancient swagg'rer comes not in my doors. I was
before Master Tisick,° the debuty, t' other day,
and, as he said to me, 'twas no longer ago than
Wednesday last, "I' good faith, neighbor Quickly,"

59–60 **confirmities** i.e., infirmities   60 **What the goodyear!** what the
plague!   60 **bear** (1) endure (2) support   64–65 **merchant's venture
of Bordeaux stuff** shipload of wine   70 **Ancient** ensign, standard-
bearer   72 **swaggering** blustering   87 **Tisick** phthisic, consumption
(?)

90   says he—Master Dumbe, our minister, was by then
—"neighbor Quickly," says he, "receive those that
are civil, for," said he, "you are in an ill name."
Now 'a said so, I can tell whereupon. "For," says
he, "you are an honest woman, and well thought
95   on; therefore take heed what guests you receive.
Receive," says he, "no swaggering companions."°
There comes none here. You would bless you to
hear what he said. No, I'll no swagg'rers.

Falstaff. He's no swagg'rer, hostess, a tame cheater,°
100   i' faith. You may stroke him as gently as a puppy
greyhound. He'll not swagger with a Barbary hen,°
if her feathers turn back in any show of resistance.
Call him up, drawer.   [*Exit Drawer.*]

Hostess. Cheater, call you him? I will bar no honest
105   man my house, nor no cheater. But I do not love
swaggering, by my troth. I am the worse when one
says "swagger." Feel, masters, how I shake, look
you, I warrant you.

Doll. So you do, hostess.

110   *Hostess.* Do I? Yea, in very truth, do I, and 'twere
an aspen leaf. I cannot abide swagg'rers.

*Enter Ancient Pistol, [Bardolph], and Bardolph's
Boy [Page].*

Pistol. God save you, Sir John!

Falstaff. Welcome, Ancient Pistol.° Here, Pistol, I
charge° you with a cup of sack. Do you discharge°
115   upon mine hostess.

Pistol. I will discharge upon her, Sir John, with two
bullets.°

96 **companions** fellows   99 **cheater** cardsharper's decoy   101 **Barbary hen** guinea hen (whose feathers are already ruffled; also, a prostitute)   113 **Pistol** (pronounced almost like "pizzle" [= penis] hence leading to this series of obscene puns)   114 **charge** (1) toast (2) load (a pistol)   114 **discharge** go off (i.e., sound a return toast, explode like a pistol—or sexually)   117 **bullets** (an indecency)

Falstaff. She is pistol-proof, sir; you shall not hardily°
offend her.

Hostess. Come, I'll drink no proofs nor no bullets.   120
I'll drink no more than will do me good, for no
man's pleasure, I.

Pistol. Then to you, Mistress Dorothy; I will charge
you.

Doll. Charge me! I scorn you, scurvy companion.   125
What! You poor, base, rascally, cheating, lack-
linen mate! Away, you moldy rogue, away! I am
meat° for your master.

Pistol. I know you, Mistress Dorothy.

Doll. Away, you cut-purse rascal! You filthy bung,°   130
away! By this wine, I'll thrust my knife in your
moldy chaps,° and you play the saucy cuttle with
me. Away, you bottle-ale° rascal! You basket-hilt
stale juggler,° you! Since when, I pray you, sir?
God's light, with two points° on your shoulder?   135
Much!

Pistol. God let me not live but I will murder your
ruff° for this.

Falstaff. No more, Pistol; I would not have you go off
here. Discharge yourself of our company, Pistol.   140

Hostess. No, good Captain Pistol, not here, sweet
Captain.

Doll. Captain! Thou abominable damned cheater, art
thou not ashamed to be called Captain? And captains were of my mind, they would truncheon° you   145
out for taking their names upon you before you

---

118 **not hardily** by no means   128 **meat** flesh   130 **bung** pickpocket
132 **chaps** cheeks   132 **cuttle** (1) cutthroat (2) cuttlefish (that
spews out a fluid used for sauce)   133 **bottle-ale** cheap (?)   133–34
basket-hilt stale juggler doer of sword-tricks with an old-fashioned
sword with hilt shaped like a basket   135 **points** laces for tying on
armor   137–38 **murder your ruff** tear your collar   145 **truncheon**
cudgel

have earned them. You a captain! You slave, for
what? For tearing a poor whore's ruff in a bawdy
house? He a captain! Hang him, rogue! He lives
150 upon moldy stewed prunes° and dried cakes. A
captain! God's light, these villains will make the
word as odious as the word "occupy,"° which was
an excellent good word before it was ill sorted.°
Therefore captains° had need look to't.

155 *Bardolph.* Pray thee, go down, good Ancient.

Falstaff. Hark thee hither, Mistress Doll.

Pistol. Not I! I tell thee what, Corporal Bardolph, I
could tear her! I'll be revenged of her!

Page. Pray thee, go down.

160 *Pistol.* I'll see her damned first, to Pluto's damnèd
lake,° by this hand, to th' infernal deep, with
Erebus° and tortures vile also.° Hold hook and
line,° say I. Down, down, dogs! Down, faitors!°
Have we not Hiren° here?

165 *Hostess.* Good Captain Pizzle, be quiet. 'Tis very late,
i' faith. I beseek you now, aggravate° your choler.

Pistol. These be good humors, indeed! Shall pack-
horses
And hollow pampered jades° of Asia,
Which cannot go but thirty mile a day,
170 Compare with Caesars, and with Cannibals,°
And Trojan Greeks? Nay, rather damn them with

---

150 **stewed prunes** (put in the windows of brothels, "stews," as a sign)
152 **occupy** (had acquired the sense of "fornicate")   153 **ill sorted**
put in bad company   154 **captains** (Falstaff is a captain)   161 **lake**
(he means the river Styx)   162 **Erebus** passageway to Hades   162
and tortures vile also (Pistol begins to rave in his characteristic way,
spewing out garbled scraps from old declamatory plays—or, indeed,
any line that comes to his mind)   162–63 **Hold hook and line** (a
fisherman's cry)   163 **faitors** fates (?)   164 **Hiren** (Pistol applies
this name [Irene] from a play to his sword, punning on "iron")
166 **aggravate** (she means moderate)   168 **jades** nags   170 **Cannibals** (he means Hannibals)

King Cerberus,° and let the welkin° roar.
Shall we fall foul for toys?°

Hostess. By my troth, Captain, these are very bitter
words.   175

Bardolph. Be gone, good Ancient. This will grow to a
brawl anon.

Pistol. Die men like dogs! Give crowns like pins! Have
we not Hiren here?

Hostess. O' my word, Captain, there's none such here.   180
What the goodyear! Do you think I would deny
her?° For God's sake, be quiet.

Pistol. Then feed, and be fat, my fair Calipolis.
Come, give's some sack.
"*Si fortune me tormente, sperato me contento.*"°   185
Fear we broadsides? No, let the fiend give fire.
Give me some sack. And, sweetheart, lie thou there.
                              [*Lays down his sword.*]
Come we to full points° here, and are etceteras°
no things?°

Falstaff. Pistol, I would be quiet.

Pistol. Sweet knight, I kiss thy neaf.° What! We have   190
seen the seven stars.°

Doll. For God's sake, thrust him downstairs. I cannot
endure such a fustian° rascal.

Pistol. Thrust him downstairs! Know we not Galloway nags?°   195

---

172 **Cerberus** three-headed dog that guarded Hades   172 **welkin** sky
173 **toys** trivia (like Doll)   181–82 **deny her** (the Hostess evidently
thinks Pistol is calling for a special girl)   185 **Si fortune ... contento**
(a garbled proverb—"If fortune torments me, hope contents me")
188 **full points** stops, periods (closed sentences)   188 **etceteras**
(open-ended statements—with an obscene sense)   188 **no things**
(with a second meaning: women who are "naught." The line as a
whole means: Aren't we going to do anything more here?)   190 **kiss
thy neaf** kiss thy fist (a chivalric gesture)   191 **seven stars** the
Pleiades (we have made a night of it)   193 **fustian** cheap cloth or
talk   194–95 **Galloway nags** small Irish horses (bad to ride)

Falstaff. Quoit° him down, Bardolph, like a shove-
groat shilling.° Nay, and 'a do nothing but speak
nothing, 'a shall be nothing here.

Bardolph. Come, get you downstairs.

Pistol. What! Shall we have incision? Shall we im-
200   brue?°   [*Snatches up his sword.*]
Then death rock me asleep, abridge my doleful
days!
Why, then, let grievous, ghastly, gaping wounds
Untwined the Sisters Three!° Come, Atropos, I
say!

Hostess. Here's goodly stuff toward!

205 *Falstaff.* Give me my rapier, boy.

Doll. I pray thee, Jack, I pray thee, do not draw.

Falstaff. Get you downstairs!
                    [*Draws, and threatens Pistol.*]

Hostess. Here's a goodly tumult! I'll forswear keeping
house afore I'll be in these tirrits° and frights. So,
210   murder, I warrant now. Alas, alas! Put up your
naked weapons, put up your naked weapons.
      [*Falstaff drives Pistol out, Bardolph following.*]

Doll. I pray thee, Jack, be quiet. The rascal's gone.
Ah, you whoreson little valiant villain, you!

Hostess. Are you not hurt i' th' groin? Methought 'a
215   made a shrewd thrust at your belly.

                    [*Enter Bardolph.*]

Falstaff. Have you turned him out o' doors?

Bardolph. Yea, sir. The rascal's drunk. You have hurt
him, sir, i' th' shoulder.

Falstaff. A rascal! To brave° me!

196 **Quoit** pitch (with a pun on "quiet")   196–97 **shove-groat shilling**
coin used in a game like shuffleboard ("shove-ha'penny")   200 **im-
brue** shed blood   203 **Sisters Three** the Fates who spun the thread
of life, cut by the third, Atropos   209 **tirrits** (a blending of terrors
and fits?)   219 **brave** defy

Doll. Ah, you sweet little rogue, you! Alas, poor ape, 220
how thou sweat'st! Come, let me wipe thy face.
Come on, you whoreson chops.° Ah, rogue! I'
faith, I love thee. Thou art as valorous as Hector
of Troy, worth five of Agamemnon, and ten times
better than the Nine Worthies.° Ah, villain! 225

Falstaff. A rascally slave! I will toss the rogue in a
blanket.

Doll. Do, and thou dar'st for thy heart. And thou dost,
I'll canvas° thee between a pair of sheets.

[Enter Musicians.]

Page. The music is come, sir. 230

Falstaff. Let them play. Play, sirs. Sit on my knee,
Doll. A rascal bragging slave! The rogue fled from
me like quicksilver.

Doll. I' faith [*aside*] and thou followedst him like a
church. Thou whoreson little tidy Bartholomew 235
boar-pig,° when wilt thou leave fighting o' days and
foining° o' nights, and begin to patch up thine old
body for heaven?

Enter Prince and Poins [*disguised*].

Falstaff. Peace, good Doll! Do not speak like a
death's-head.° Do not bid me remember mine end.° 240

Doll. Sirrah, what humor's the Prince° of?

Falstaff. A good shallow young fellow. 'A would have
made a good pantler,° 'a would ha' chipped° bread
well.

Doll. They say Poins has a good wit. 245

222 **chops** fat-cheeked man   225 **Nine Worthies** Hector, Alexander,
Julius Caesar, Joshua, David, Judas Maccabaeus, King Arthur,
Charlemagne, Godfrey of Bouillon   229 **canvas** toss (as in a canvas)
235–36 **Bartholomew boar-pig** young male pig fattened as a special
delicacy for the Bartholomew Fair on August 24th at West Smithfield   237 **foining** thrusting (as a sword)   240 **death's-head** figure
of a skull used to remind one of mortality   240 **end** (double sense)
241 **Prince** (Doll may have spied Hal and Poins)   243 **pantler**
pantryworker   243 **chipped** chopped

Falstaff. He a good wit? Hang him, baboon! His wit's as thick as Tewksbury mustard.° There's no more conceit° in him than is in a mallet.°

Doll. Why does the Prince love him so, then?

250 *Falstaff.* Because their legs are both of a bigness, and 'a plays at quoits well, and eats conger and fennel,° and drinks off candles' ends for flap-dragons,° and rides the wild-mare° with the boys, and jumps upon joined-stools,° and swears with a good grace, and
255 wears his boots very smooth, like unto the Sign of the Leg,° and breeds no bate° with telling of discreet stories; and such other gambol° faculties 'a has, that show a weak mind and an able body, for the which the Prince admits him. For the Prince
260 himself is such another; the weight of a hair will turn scales between their avoirdupois.

Prince. Would not this nave° of a wheel have his ears cut off?

Poins. Let's beat him before his whore.

265 *Prince.* Look, whe'r° the withered elder° hath not his poll° clawed° like a parrot.

Poins. Is it not strange that desire should so many years outlive performance?

Falstaff. Kiss me, Doll.

270 *Prince.* Saturn and Venus this year in conjunction! What says th' almanac to that?

247 **Tewksbury mustard** (Tewksbury was famed for good mustard)
248 **conceit** conception   248 **mallet** i.e., a blockhead   251 **conger and fennel** eel (the eating of which was thought to make one stupid) dressed or flattered by fennel sauce   252 **flap-dragons** (flaming raisins were floated on spirit and the players tried to snap them up; or drink the liquor; here candle ends are used to fool Poins)   253 **wild-mare** seesaw   254 **joined-stools** carefully carpentered stools 255–56 **Sign of the Leg** sign over a bootmaker's   256 **bate** debate, quarrel   257 **gambol** playful   262 **nave** (1) fat hub on a cart wheel (2) pun on "knave"   265 **whe'r** whether   265 **elder** (1) old man (2) sapless tree   266 **poll** hair   266 **clawed** i.e., by Doll

Poins. And look whether the fiery Trigon,° his man,
  be not lisping to his master's old tables,° his notebook, his counsel-keeper.

Falstaff. Thou dost give me flattering busses.°   275

Doll. By my troth, I kiss thee with a most constant
  heart.

Falstaff. I am old, I am old.

Doll. I love thee better than I love e'er a scurvy young
  boy of them all.   280

Falstaff. What stuff wilt have a kirtle° of? I shall receive money o' Thursday. Shalt have a cap tomorrow. A merry song, come. 'A grows late; we'll
  to bed. Thou'lt forget me when I am gone.

Doll. By my troth, thou'lt set me a-weeping, and thou   285
  say'st so. Prove that ever I dress myself handsome
  till thy return. Well, hearken o' th' end.°

Falstaff. Some sack, Francis.

Prince. ⎱
            ⎰ Anon, anon, sir.
Poins. ⎱

                              [*Coming forward.*]

Falstaff. Ha! A bastard son of the King's? And art not   290
  thou Poins his brother?

Prince. Why, thou globe of sinful continents,° what
  a life dost thou lead!

Falstaff. A better than thou. I am a gentleman, thou
  art a drawer.   295

Prince. Very true, sir, and I come to draw you out
  by the ears.

272 **fiery Trigon** the conjunction of the three fiery signs of the
Zodiac: Aries, Leo, and Sagittarius (in Bardolph's face)   273 **tables**
tablet or engagement book (i.e., bawd, Mistress Quickly)   275 **busses**
kisses   281 **kirtle** skirt   287 **hearken o' th' end** i.e., see how it turns
out   292 **continents** (1) vast land surfaces (2) contents (3) pun on
"continence"

Hostess. O, the Lord preserve thy Grace! By my troth, welcome to London. Now, the Lord bless that sweet
300   face of thine! O Jesu, are you come from Wales?

Falstaff. Thou whoreson mad compound° of majesty, by this light° flesh and corrupt blood, thou art welcome.

Doll. How, you fat fool! I scorn you.

305 *Poins.* My lord, he will drive you out of your revenge and turn all to a merriment, if you take not the heat.

Prince. You whoreson candle-mine° you, how vilely did you speak of me now before this honest, virtu-
310   ous, civil gentlewoman!

Hostess. God's blessing of your good heart! And so she is, by my troth.

Falstaff. Didst thou hear me?

Prince. Yea, and you knew me, as you did when you
315   ran away by Gad's Hill.° You knew I was at your back, and spoke it on purpose to try my patience.

Falstaff. No, no, no, not so. I did not think thou wast within hearing.

Prince. I shall drive you then to confess the willful
320   abuse, and then I know how to handle you.

Falstaff. No abuse, Hal, o' mine honor, no abuse.

Prince. Not to dispraise me and call me pantler and bread-chipper and I know not what?

Falstaff. No abuse, Hal.

325 *Poins.* No abuse?

Falstaff. No abuse, Ned, i' th' world. Honest Ned, none. I dispraised him before the wicked, that the

---

301 **compound** mixture   302 **light** unchaste (he is referring to Doll)
308 **candle-mine** reservoir of tallow   314–15 **as . . . Gad's Hill** (the robbery of the robbers in *1 Henry IV*, II.ii and iv)

wicked might not fall in love with thee. In which
doing, I have done the part of a careful friend and
a true subject, and thy father is to give me thanks   *330*
for it. No abuse, Hal. None, Ned, none. No, faith,
boys, none.

Prince. See now, whether pure fear and entire cowardice doth not make thee wrong this virtuous
gentlewoman to close° with us. Is she of the   *335*
wicked? Is thine hostess here of the wicked? Or is
thy boy of the wicked? Or honest Bardolph, whose
zeal burns in his nose, of the wicked?

Poins. Answer, thou dead elm, answer.

Falstaff. The fiend hath pricked down° Bardolph irre-   *340*
coverable, and his face is Lucifer's privy-kitchen,
where he doth nothing but roast malt-worms.° For
the boy, there is a good angel about him, but the
devil blinds him too.

Prince. For the women?   *345*

Falstaff. For one of them, she's in hell already, and
burns° poor souls. For th' other, I owe her money,
and whether she be damned for that, I know not.

Hostess. No, I warrant you.

Falstaff. No, I think thou art not. I think thou art quit   *350*
for that.° Marry, there is another indictment upon
thee, for suffering flesh° to be eaten in thy house,
contrary to the law, for the which I think thou wilt
howl.

Hostess. All victuallers do so. What's a joint of mut-   *355*
ton° or two in a whole Lent?

Prince. You, gentlewoman—

Doll. What says your Grace?

335 **close** make peace   340 **pricked down** checked off   342 **malt-
worms** (1) weevils in beer (2) drunkards (3) the white material in
Bardolph's pimples   347 **burns** gives burning diseases to   350–51
quit for that paid off for that   352 **flesh** (1) meat (2) womanflesh
355–56 **mutton** (also meant a prostitute)

Falstaff. His Grace says that which his flesh rebels
360   against.°   *Peto knocks at door.*

Hostess. Who knocks so loud at door? Look to th'
     door there, Francis.

[*Enter Peto.*]

Prince. Peto, how now! What news?

Peto. The King your father is at Westminster,
365   And there are twenty weak and wearied posts°
     Come from the north. And as I came along
     I met and overtook a dozen captains,
     Bareheaded, sweating, knocking at the taverns,
     And asking everyone for Sir John Falstaff.

370 *Prince.* By heaven, Poins, I feel me much to blame,
     So idly to profane the precious time,
     When tempest of commotion,° like the south°
     Borne with black vapor,° doth begin to melt
     And drop upon our bare unarmèd heads.
375   Give me my sword and cloak. Falstaff, good night.
          Exeunt Prince and Poins, [*Peto, and Bardolph*].

Falstaff. Now comes in the sweetest morsel of the
     night, and we must hence and leave it unpicked.
     [*Sound of knocking.*] More knocking at the door?

[*Enter Bardolph.*]

How now! What's the matter?

380 *Bardolph.* You must away to court, sir, presently.°
     A dozen captains stay at door for you.

Falstaff. [*To the Page*] Pay the musicians, sirrah. Fare-
     well, hostess. Farewell, Doll. You see, my good
     wenches, how men of merit are sought after. The
385   undeserver may sleep when the man of action is

359–60 **His Grace . . . against** i.e., his Grace calls her a gentlewoman,
but his animal flesh rises up at the idea   365 **posts** messengers
372 **commotion** rebellion   372 **south** south wind   373 **Borne with
black vapor** laden with black clouds   380 **presently** at present, at
once

called on. Farewell, good wenches. If I be not sent
away post,° I will see you again ere I go.

Doll. I cannot speak. If my heart be not ready to
burst—well, sweet Jack, have a care of thyself.

Falstaff. Farewell, farewell.   *Exit [with Bardolph].* 390

Hostess. Well, fare thee well. I have known thee these
twenty-nine years, come peascod-time,° but an
honester and truer-hearted man—well, fare thee
well.

Bardolph. [*Within*] Mistress Tearsheet!   395

Hostess. What's the matter?

Bardolph. [*Within*] Bid Mistress Tearsheet come to
my master.

Hostess. O, run, Doll, run, run, good Doll. Come. [*To
Bardolph within*] She comes blubbered.° Yea, will 400
you come, Doll?   *Exeunt.*

387 **post** posthaste   392 **peascod-time** early summer (but there is
evidently a ribald sense, too)   400 **blubbered** disfigured with weeping

[ACT III

Scene I. *The Palace*.]

Enter the King in his nightgown,° alone.

King. [*To a Page, within*] Go, call the Earls of Surrey
and of Warwick.
But, ere they come, bid them o'erread these letters
And well consider of them. Make good speed!
How many thousand of my poorest subjects
5   Are at this hour asleep! O sleep, O gentle sleep,
Nature's soft nurse, how have I frighted thee,
That thou no more wilt weigh my eyelids down
And steep my senses in forgetfulness?
Why rather, sleep, liest thou in smoky cribs,°
10   Upon uneasy pallets° stretching thee
And hushed with buzzing night-flies° to thy
slumber,
Than in the perfumed° chambers of the great,
Under the canopies of costly state,°
And lulled with sound of sweetest melody?
15   O thou dull god, why li'st thou with the vile
In loathsome beds, and leavest the kingly couch
A watchcase° or a common 'larum-bell?°

III.i.s.d. **nightgown** dressing gown (the customary indoor garment)
9 **smoky cribs** chimneyless hovels   10 **uneasy pallets** comfortless
straw beds   11 **night-flies** nocturnal insects   12 **perfumed** (Elizabethans who could afford perfume tried to keep out fresh air)
13 **canopies of costly state** bed-curtains of those in a wealthy state
17 **watchcase** (1) sentry box (2) case of a constantly ticking watch
17 **'larum-bell** alarm-bell (hence, constantly watchful)

Wilt thou upon the high and giddy mast
Seal up the ship-boy's eyes, and rock his brains
In cradle of the rude imperious surge   20
And in the visitation of the winds,
Who take the ruffian billows by the top,
Curling their monstrous heads and hanging them
With deafing° clamor in the slippery clouds,
That, with the hurly,° death itself awakes?   25
Canst thou, O partial° sleep, give thy repose
To the wet sea-son in an hour so rude,
And in the calmest and most stillest night,
With all appliances and means to boot,°
Deny it to a king? Then happy low,° lie down!   30
Uneasy lies the head that wears a crown.

Enter Warwick, Surrey, and Sir John Blunt.

Warwick. Many good morrows to your Majesty!

King. Is it good morrow, lords?

Warwick. 'Tis one o'clock, and past.

King. Why, then, good morrow to you all, my lords.   35
Have you read o'er the letter that I sent you?

Warwick. We have, my liege.

King. Then you perceive the body of our kingdom
How foul it is, what rank° diseases grow,
And with what danger, near the heart of it.   40

Warwick. It is but as a body yet distempered,°
Which to his former strength may be restored
With good advice and little medicine.
My Lord Northumberland will soon be cooled.

King. O God, that one might read the book of fate,   45
And see the revolution of the times
Make mountains level, and the continent,°
Weary of solid firmness, melt itself

deafing deafening   25 hurly hurly-burly   26 partial not impartial
means to boot measures to further (sleep)   30 low lowborn
rank swelling   41 yet distempered as yet but sickened   47 con-
ent land surface

Into the sea! And other times to see
50 The beachy girdle of the ocean
Too wide for Neptune's hips. How chances, mocks,
And changes fill the cup of alteration
With divers liquors! O, if this were seen,
The happiest youth, viewing his progress through,
55 What perils past, what crosses° to ensue,
Would shut the book, and sit him down and die.
'Tis not ten years gone
Since Richard and Northumberland, great friends,
Did feast together,° and in two years after
60 Were they at wars. It is but eight years since
This Percy was the man nearest my soul,
Who like a brother toiled in my affairs
And laid his love and life under my foot,°
Yea, for my sake, even to the eyes of Richard
65 Gave him defiance. But which of you was by—
[*To Warwick*] You, cousin Nevil,° as I may re-
member—
When Richard, with his eye brimful of tears,
Then checked° and rated° by Northumberland,
Did speak these words, now proved a prophecy:
70 "Northumberland, thou ladder by the which
My cousin Bolingbroke ascends my throne"—
Though then, God knows, I had no such intent,
But that necessity so bowed the state
That I and greatness were compelled to kiss—
75 "The time shall come," thus did he follow it,
"The time will come that foul sin, gathering head,°
Shall break into corruption."° So went on,
Foretelling this same time's condition
And the division of our amity.

80 *Warwick.* There is a history in all men's lives,
Figuring° the nature of the times deceased,

55 **crosses** punishments   59 **Did feast together** (Shakespeare here alters history for dramatic purposes; this appears neither in Holinshed nor his own *Richard II*)   63 **under my foot** in subservience to me   66 **Nevil** (historical error for Beauchamps)   68 **checked, rated** rebuked   76 **gathering head** (1) coming to a head (2) collecting an army   70–77 **Northumberland . . . corruption** (paraphrased from *Richard II*, V.i.55ff.)   81 **Figuring** symbolizing

The which observed, a man may prophesy,
With a near aim, of the main chance of things
As yet not come to life, who in their seeds
And weak beginning lie intreasurèd.   *85*
Such things become the hatch and brood of time,
And by the necessary form of this°
King Richard might create a perfect guess
That great Northumberland, then false to him,
Would of that seed grow to a greater falseness,   *90*
Which should not find a ground to root upon,
Unless on you.

King.   Are these things then necessities?
Then let us meet them like necessities.
And that same word even now cries out on us.
They say the Bishop and Northumberland   *95*
Are fifty thousand strong.

Warwick.   It cannot be, my lord.
Rumor doth double, like the voice and echo,
The numbers of the feared. Please it your Grace
To go to bed. Upon my soul, my lord,
The powers that you already have sent forth   *100*
Shall bring this prize in very easily.
To comfort you the more, I have received
A certain instance° that Glendower is dead.
Your Majesty hath been this fortnight ill,
And these unseasoned° hours perforce must add   *105*
Unto your sickness.

King.   I will take your counsel.
And were these inward° wars once out of hand,°
We would, dear lords, unto the Holy Land.
                                          Exeunt.

87 **necessary form of this** inevitable operation of this principle of
analogy   103 **instance** proof   105 **unseasoned** unusual   107 **inward**
internal   107 **out of hand** finished

[Scene II. *Outside Justice Shallow's house.*]

Enter Justice Shallow and Justice Silence [with
Moldy, Shadow, Wart, Feeble, Bullcalf].

Shallow. Come on, come on, come on. Give me your
hand, sir, give me your hand, sir; an early stirrer, by
the rood!° And how doth my good cousin Silence?

Silence. Good morrow, good cousin Shallow.

5 *Shallow.* And how doth my cousin, your bedfellow?
And your fairest daughter and mine, my god-
daughter Ellen?

Silence. Alas, a black ousel,° cousin Shallow!

Shallow. By yea and no,° sir, I dare say my cousin
10   William is become a good scholar. He is at Oxford
still, is he not?

Silence. Indeed, sir, to my cost.

Shallow. 'A must, then, to the Inns o' Court° shortly.
I was once of Clement's Inn,° where I think they
15   will talk of mad Shallow yet.

Silence. You were called "lusty Shallow" then, cousin.

Shallow. By the mass, I was called anything. And I
would have done anything indeed too, and roundly°
too. There was I, and little John Doit of Stafford-
20   shire, and black George Barnes, and Francis Pickbone, and Will Squele,° a Cotswold° man; you had

III.ii.3 **rood** cross   8 **ousel** blackbird   9 **By yea and no** (a puritan's
oath)   13 **Inns o' Court** law schools (which functioned as universities
for the gentry)   14 **Clement's Inn** (one of the Inns of Chancery, ad-
mitting students unable to get into the Inns of Court)   18 **roundly**
fully   19–21 **Doit . . . Barnes . . . Pickbone . . . Squele** (the names
are suggestive of insignificance, a doit being a half-farthing; country
wealth [barns]; stinginess; squealing cowardice)   21 **Cotswold** (a
range of hills in Gloucestershire)

not four such swinge-bucklers° in all the Inns o'
Court again. And I may say to you we knew where
the bona-robas° were and had the best of them all
at commandment. Then was Jack Falstaff, now Sir   25
John, a boy, and page to Thomas Mowbray, Duke
of Norfolk.

Silence. This Sir John, cousin, that comes hither anon
about soldiers?

Shallow. The same Sir John, the very same. I see him   30
break Scoggin's° head at the court-gate, when 'a
was a crack° not thus high. And the very same day
did I fight with one Sampson Stockfish,° a fruiterer,
behind Gray's Inn.° Jesu, Jesu, the mad days that
I have spent! And to see how many of my old   35
acquaintance are dead!

Silence. We shall all follow, cousin.

Shallow. Certain, 'tis certain, very sure, very sure.
Death, as the Psalmist saith, is certain to all, all
shall die. How° a good yoke of bullocks at Stam-   40
ford Fair?

Silence. By my troth, I was not there.

Shallow. Death is certain. Is old Double° of your
town living yet?

Silence. Dead, sir.   45

Shallow. Jesu, Jesu, dead! 'A drew a good bow, and
dead! 'A shot a fine shoot. John a Gaunt° loved
him well and betted much money on his head.
Dead! 'A would have clapped i' th' clout at twelve
score, and carried you a forehand shaft a fourteen   50
and fourteen and a half,° that it would have done a

---

22 **swinge-bucklers** shield-beaters (i.e., blusterers)   24 **bona-robas**
high-class whores (Italian *buonaroba,* good material)   31 **Scoggin's**
(the name means a coarse joker)   32 **crack** perky boy   33 **Stockfish** a dried fish (suggestive of an impotent man)   34 **Gray's Inn**
another Inn of Court   40 **How** how much for   43 **Double** (suggests
one doubled over with age)   47 **John a Gaunt** Henry IV's father
49–51 **clapped . . . and a half** hit the bull's-eye at 240 yards, and
shot a heavy arrow (for point-blank shooting) 280 or 290 yards

man's heart good to see. How a score of ewes now?

Silence. Thereafter as they be.° A score of good ewes
may be worth ten pounds.

55 *Shallow.* And is old Double dead?

Silence. Here come two of Sir John Falstaff's men, as
I think.

Enter Bardolph and one with him.

Good morrow, honest gentlemen.

Bardolph. I beseech you, which is Justice Shallow?

60 *Shallow.* I am Robert Shallow, sir, a poor esquire° of
this county, and one of the King's justices of the
peace. What is your good pleasure with me?

Bardolph. My captain, sir, commends him to you, my
captain, Sir John Falstaff, a tall° gentleman, by
65 heaven, and a most gallant leader.

Shallow. He greets me well, sir. I knew him a good
backsword° man. How doth the good knight? May
I ask how my lady his wife doth?

Bardolph. Sir, pardon, a soldier is better accommo-
70 dated° than with a wife.

Shallow. It is well said, in faith, sir, and it is well said
indeed too. "Better accommodated"! It is good, yea,
indeed, is it. Good phrases are surely, and ever
were, very commendable. "Accommodated"! It
75 comes of *"accommodo."* Very good, a good phrase.

Bardolph. Pardon, sir. I have heard the word.
"Phrase" call you it? By this good day, I know not
the phrase, but I will maintain the word with my
sword to be a soldier-like word, and a word of ex-
80 ceeding good command, by heaven. "Accommodated," that is, when a man is, as they say, accom-

53 **Thereafter as they be** according to their condition　60 **esquire**
gentleman (ranking just below a knight)　64 **tall** brave　67 **back-
sword** stick with a hilt used by apprentices in fencing　69–70 **accommodated** provided (a "perfumed term," according to Ben Jonson)

modated; or when a man is, being, whereby 'a may
be thought to be accommodated, which is an excellent thing.

Enter Falstaff.

Shallow. It is very just.° Look, here comes good Sir   85
John. Give me your good hand, give me your worship's good hand. By my troth, you like° well and
bear your years very well. Welcome, good Sir John.

Falstaff. I am glad to see you well, good Master
Robert Shallow. Master Surecard,° as I think?   90

Shallow. No, Sir John, it is my cousin Silence, in com-
mission° with me.

Falstaff. Good Master Silence, it well befits you should
be of the peace.

Silence. Your good worship is welcome.   95

Falstaff. Fie! This is hot weather, gentlemen. Have
you provided me here half a dozen sufficient men?

Shallow. Marry, have we, sir. Will you sit?

Falstaff. Let me see them, I beseech you.

Shallow. Where's the roll? Where's the roll? Where's   100
the roll? Let me see, let me see, let me see. So, so,
so, so, so, so—so. Yea, marry, sir. Rafe Moldy!
Let them appear as I call, let them do so, let them
do so. Let me see, where is Moldy?

Moldy. Here, and't please you.   105

Shallow. What think you, Sir John? A good-limbed
fellow, young, strong, and of good friends.

Falstaff. Is thy name Moldy?

Moldy. Yea, and't please you.

Falstaff. 'Tis the more time thou wert used.   110

---

85 **just** exact   87 **like** get on   90 **Surecard** absolute winner (at cards)
91–92 **in commission** commissioned as justice of the peace

Shallow. Ha, ha, ha! Most excellent, i' faith! Things
that are moldy lack use. Very singular good! In
faith, well said, Sir John, very well said.

Falstaff. Prick him.°

115 *Moldy.* I was pricked° well enough before, and you
could have let me alone. My old dame° will be undone now for one to do her husbandry and her
drudgery. You need not to have pricked me. There
are other men fitter to go out than I.

120 *Falstaff.* Go to. Peace, Moldy, you shall go. Moldy, it
is time you were spent.

Moldy. Spent?

Shallow. Peace, fellow, peace. Stand aside. Know you
where you are? For th' other, Sir John, let me see.
125 Simon Shadow!°

Falstaff. Yea, marry, let me have him to sit under.
He's like to be a cold soldier.

Shallow. Where's Shadow?

Shadow. Here, sir.

130 *Falstaff.* Shadow, whose son art thou?

Shadow. My mother's son, sir.

Falstaff. Thy mother's son! Like enough, and thy
father's shadow. So the son° of the female is the
shadow of the male. It is often so, indeed, but
135 much° of the father's substance!

Shallow. Do you like him, Sir John?

Falstaff. Shadow will serve for summer. Prick him,
for we have a number of shadows fill up the muster-
book.

114 **Prick him** check him off   115 **pricked** (1) chosen (2) worried
(and a ribald third meaning)   116 **dame** old wife (or mother)
125 **Shadow** (1) likeness (2) shade (3) fictitious name in the muster
roll for which an officer collected pay (Falstaff jokes on all three
meanings)   133 **son** (he is punning on "sun")   135 **much** little (sar-
castic)

Shallow. Thomas Wart!   140

Falstaff. Where's he?

Wart. Here, sir.

Falstaff. Is thy name Wart?

Wart. Yea, sir.

Falstaff. Thou art a very ragged° wart.   145

Shallow. Shall I prick him, Sir John?

Falstaff. It were superfluous,° for his apparel is built
  upon his back and the whole frame stands upon
  pins. Prick him no more.

Shallow. Ha, ha, ha! You can do it,° sir! You can do   150
  it! I commend you well. Francis Feeble!

Feeble. Here, sir.

Shallow. What trade art thou, Feeble?

Feeble. A woman's tailor, sir.

Shallow. Shall I prick him, sir?   155

Falstaff. You may. But if he had been a man's tailor,
  he'd a' pricked you. Wilt thou make as many holes
  in an enemy's battle° as thou hast done in a
  woman's petticoat?

Feeble. I will do my good will, sir. You can have no   160
  more.

Falstaff. Well said, good woman's tailor! Well said,
  courageous Feeble! Thou wilt be as valiant as the
  wrathful dove or most magnanimous° mouse. Prick
  the woman's tailor well,° Master Shallow, deep,°   165
  Master Shallow.

Feeble. I would Wart might have gone, sir.

145 **ragged** having rough projections (referring to his pinned-together
clothes)   147 **superfluous** i.e., to "prick him," pin his clothes together   150 **you can do it** you know how to joke   158 **battle** battle
line   164 **magnanimous** big-spirited   165 **well, deep** (quibbles on
Shallow's name)

Falstaff. I would thou wert a man's tailor, that thou
mightst mend him and make him fit to go. I can-
170   not put him to° a private soldier that is the leader
of so many thousands.° Let that suffice, most forcible Feeble.

Feeble. It shall suffice, sir.

Falstaff. I am bound to thee, reverend Feeble. Who is
175   next?

Shallow. Peter Bullcalf o' th' green!

Falstaff. Yea, marry, let's see Bullcalf.

Bullcalf. Here, sir.

Falstaff. 'Fore God, a likely fellow! Come, prick°
180   Bullcalf till he roar again.

Bullcalf. O Lord, good my lord captain—

Falstaff. What, dost thou roar before thou art
pricked?

Bullcalf. O Lord, sir, I am a diseased man.

185   *Falstaff.* What disease hast thou?

Bullcalf. A whoreson cold, sir, a cough, sir, which I
caught with ringing in° the King's affairs upon his
coronation day, sir.

Falstaff. Come, thou shalt go to the wars in a gown.°
190   We will have away thy cold, and I will take such
order that thy friends shall ring for thee.° Is here
all?

Shallow. Here is two more called than your number.
You must have but four° here, sir. And so, I pray
195   you, go in with me to dinner.

---

170 **put him to** set him to the occupation of   171 **thousands** i.e., of
lice   179 **prick** (here the word refers to the sticking of a bull with a
goad in bullbaiting)   187 **ringing in** ringing the church bells to
celebrate   189 **gown** dressing gown   191 **ring for thee** i.e., toll your
funeral   194 **four** (he settles for three)

Falstaff. Come, I will go drink with you, but I cannot tarry dinner. I am glad to see you, by my troth, Master Shallow.

Shallow. O, Sir John, do you remember since we lay all night in the Windmill° in Saint George's Field? *200*

Falstaff. No more of that, Master Shallow.

Shallow. Ha! 'Twas a merry night. And is Jane Nightwork alive?

Falstaff. She lives, Master Shallow.

Shallow. She never could away with° me. *205*

Falstaff. Never, never, she would always say she could not abide Master Shallow.

Shallow. By the mass, I could anger° her to th' heart. She was then a bona-roba. Doth she hold her own well? *210*

Falstaff. Old, old, Master Shallow.

Shallow. Nay, she must be old. She cannot choose but be old. Certain she's old, and had Robin Nightwork by old Nightwork before I came to Clement's Inn. *215*

Silence. That's fifty-five year ago.

Shallow. Ha, cousin Silence, that thou hadst seen that that this knight and I have seen! Ha, Sir John, said I well?

Falstaff. We have heard the chimes at midnight, *220* Master Shallow.

Shallow. That we have, that we have, that we have, in faith, Sir John, we have. Our watchword was "Hem,° boys!" Come, let's to dinner, come, let's to dinner. Jesus, the days that we have seen! Come, *225* come.   *Exeunt [Falstaff and the Justices].*

200 **Windmill** (evidently a brothel) 205 **away with** put up with
208 **anger** inflame 224 **Hem** (the equivalent of "Bottoms up!")

Bullcalf. Good Master Corporate° Bardolph, stand my
friend, and here's four Harry ten shillings in French
crowns° for you. In very truth, sir, I had as lief be
230   hanged, sir, as go. And yet for mine own part, sir,
I do not care, but rather, because I am unwilling,
and, for mine own part, have a desire to stay with
my friends. Else, sir, I did not care, for mine own
part, so much.

235 *Bardolph.* Go to, stand aside.

Moldy. And, good Master Corporal Captain, for my
dame's sake, stand my friend. She has nobody to
do anything about her when I am gone, and she is
old and cannot help herself. You shall have forty,°
240   sir.

Bardolph. Go to, stand aside.

Feeble. By my troth, I care not. A man can die but
once. We owe God a death.° I'll ne'er bear a base
mind. And't be my destiny, so. And't be not, so.
245   No man's too good to serve's Prince. And let it go
which way it will, he that dies this year is quit° for
the next.

Bardolph. Well said. Th' art a good fellow.

Feeble. Faith, I'll bear no base mind.

Enter Falstaff and the Justices.

250 *Falstaff.* Come, sir, which men shall I have?

Shallow. Four of which you please.

Bardolph. Sir, a word with you. [*Aside*] I have three
pound to free Moldy and Bullcalf.

Falstaff. Go to, well.

227 **Corporate** (blunder for "corporal")   228–29 **four Harry . . .
crowns** (a country way of counting out £1: the amount of four
pieces, formerly of ten shillings' value but currently five, rendered in
five four-shilling pieces, "French crowns"; Bullcalf is offering around
$200 in today's values)   239 **forty** forty shillings (about $400 today)
243 **death** (pronounced like "debt," hence a pun)   246 **is quit** owes
nothing

Shallow. Come, Sir John, which four will you have?   255

Falstaff. Do you choose for me.

Shallow. Marry, then, Moldy, Bullcalf, Feeble, and Shadow.

Falstaff. Moldy and Bullcalf. For you, Moldy, stay at home till you are past service.° And for your part,   260
Bullcalf, grow till you come unto it. I will none of you.

Shallow. Sir John, Sir John, do not yourself wrong. They are your likeliest men, and I would have you served with the best.   265

Falstaff. Will you tell me, Master Shallow, how to choose a man? Care I for the limb, the thews,° the stature, bulk, and big assemblance° of a man? Give me the spirit, Master Shallow! Here's Wart. You see what a ragged appearance it is. 'A shall charge   270
you and discharge you with the motion of a pewterer's hammer,° come off and on swifter than he that gibbets on the brewer's bucket.° And this same half-faced fellow, Shadow. Give me this man. He presents no mark to the enemy: the foeman may   275
with as great aim level at the edge of a penknife. And for a retreat, how swiftly will this Feeble the woman's tailor run off! O, give me the spare men, and spare me the great ones. Put me a caliver° into Wart's hand, Bardolph.   280

Bardolph. Hold, Wart, traverse.° Thus, thus, thus.

Falstaff. Come, manage me your caliver. So. Very well. Go to. Very good, exceeding good. O, give me always a little, lean, old, chopped,° bald shot.°

250 **service** i.e., (1) military (2) domestic (3) bull's   267 **thews** bodily
forces   268 **assemblance** appearance   271–72 **motion of a pewterer's hammer** i.e., with a rapid tap-tap   273 **gibbets on the brewer's
bucket** hoists with the beam ("bucket") of a brewer's crane   279
caliver light musket   281 **traverse** cross over   284 **chopped** chapped
284 **shot** shooter (musketeers had to run nimbly behind the pikemen
or spearmen to reload)

285 Well said, i' faith, Wart. Th' art a good scab.° Hold, there's a tester° for thee.

Shallow. He is not his craft's master, he doth not do it right. I remember at Mile-End Green, when I lay at Clement's Inn—I was then Sir Dagonet in 290 Arthur's show°—there was a little quiver° fellow, and 'a would manage you his piece thus, and 'a would about and about, and come you in and come you in. "Rah, tah, tah," would 'a say, "Bounce," would 'a say, and away again would 'a go, and 295 again would 'a come. I shall ne'er see such a fellow.

Falstaff. These fellows would do well, Master Shallow. God keep you, Master Silence. I will not use many words with you. Fare you well, gentlemen both. I thank you. I must a dozen mile tonight. Bardolph, 300 give the soldiers coats.

Shallow. Sir John, the Lord bless you! God prosper your affairs! God send us peace! At your return visit our house, let our old acquaintance be renewed. Peradventure I will with ye to the court.

305 *Falstaff.* 'Fore God, would you would.

Shallow. Go to, I have spoke at a word.° God keep you.

Falstaff. Fare you well, gentle gentlemen. [*Exeunt Justices*]. On, Bardolph, lead the men away. 310 [*Exeunt all but Falstaff.*] As I return, I will fetch off° these justices. I do see the bottom of Justice Shallow. Lord, Lord, how subject we old men are to this vice of lying! This same starved justice hath done nothing but prate to me of the wildness of his 315 youth and the feats he hath done about Turnbull Street,° and every third word a lie, duer° paid to

---

285 **scab** i.e., wart 286 **tester** sixpence 290 **Arthur's show** (an annual archery show at Mile-End Green in which the contestants took the names of knights of the Round Table. Sir Dagonet was Arthur's fool) 290 **quiver** nimble 306 **at a word** on an impulse 310–311 **fetch off** trick 315–16 **Turnbull Street** (a red-light district) 316 **duer** more duly, regularly

the hearer than the Turk's tribute.° I do remember
him at Clement's Inn like a man made after supper
of a cheese-paring. When 'a was naked, he was, for
all the world, like a forked radish, with a head   320
fantastically carved upon it with a knife. 'A was so
forlorn that his dimensions to any thick° sight were
invisible. 'A was the very genius° of famine, yet
lecherous as a monkey, and the whores called him
mandrake.° 'A came ever in the rearward of the   325
fashion, and sung those tunes to the overscutched
huswives° that he heard the carmen whistle, and
sware they were his fancies or his goodnights.° And
now is this Vice's dagger° become a squire, and
talks as familiarly of John a Gaunt as if he had   330
been sworn brother to him, and I'll be sworn 'a
ne'er saw him but once in the Tilt-yard, and then
he° burst his head for crowding among the marshal's men. I saw it, and told John a Gaunt he beat
his own name, for you might have thrust him and   335
all his apparel into an eel-skin—the case of a treble
hautboy° was a mansion for him, a court. And now
has he land and beeves. Well, I'll be acquainted
with him, if I return, and't shall go hard but I'll
make him a philosopher's two stones° to me. If the   340
young dace° be a bait for the old pike, I see no
reason in the law of nature but I may snap at him.
Let time shape, and there an end.   [*Exit.*]

317 **than the Turk's tribute** i.e., than tribute is paid to the Turk
322 **thick** imperfect   323 **genius** spirit   325 **mandrake** forked root,
shaped like the lower half of a man   326–27 **overscutched huswives**
often-whipped whores   328 **his fancies or his goodnights** musical
improvisations of his own or goodnight songs   329 **Vice's dagger**
thin wooden dagger carried by the Vice, clown in the old morality
plays   333 **he** i.e., John of Gaunt   336–37 **treble hautboy** smallest
oboe   340 **philosopher's two stones** (i.e., twice as profitable as one
philosopher's stone which would transmute base metals to gold—
and a ribald second sense)   341 **dace** thin, small fish

[ACT IV

Scene I. *With the rebel army*.]

Enter the Archbishop [of York], Mowbray,
Hastings [and others], within the Forest of
Gaultree.

Archbishop. What is this forest called?

Hastings. 'Tis Gaultree Forest, and't shall please your
Grace.

Archbishop. Here stand, my lords, and send discover-
ers° forth
To know the numbers of our enemies.

Hastings. We have sent forth already.

5 *Archbishop.*   'Tis well done.
My friends and brethren in these great affairs,
I must acquaint you that I have received
New-dated letters from Northumberland,
Their cold intent, tenor, and substance, thus:

10 Here doth he wish his person, with such powers°
As might hold sortance with his quality,°
The which he could not levy. Whereupon
He is retired, to ripe° his growing fortunes,
To Scotland, and concludes in hearty prayers

15 That your attempts may overlive° the hazard
And fearful meeting of° their opposite.

IV.i.3 **discoverers** spies   10 **powers** armies   11 **hold sortance with
his quality** accord with his rank   13 **ripe** ripen   15 **overlive** survive
15–16 **hazard/And fearful meeting of** the fearful risk of meeting

Mowbray. Thus do the hopes we have in him touch
    ground°
And dash themselves to pieces.

               Enter Messenger.

Hastings.   Now, what news?

Messenger. West of this forest, scarcely off a mile,
In goodly form comes on the enemy,   *20*
And, by the ground they hide, I judge their number
Upon or near the rate of thirty thousand.

Mowbray. The just proportion that we gave them
    out.°
Let us sway° on and face them in the field.

Archbishop. What well-appointed° leader fronts° us
    here?   *25*

              Enter Westmoreland.

Mowbray. I think it is my Lord of Westmoreland.

Westmoreland. Health and fair greeting from our gen-
    eral,
The Prince, Lord John and Duke of Lancaster.

Archbishop. Say on, my Lord of Westmoreland, in
    peace.
What doth concern your coming?

Westmoreland.   Then, my lord,   *30*
Unto your Grace do I in chief° address
The substance of my speech. If that rebellion
Came like itself, in base and abject routs,°
Led on by bloody youth, guarded with rage,°
And countenanced° by boys and beggary,°   *35*
I say, if damned commotion° so appeared,
In his true, native and most proper shape,

17 **touch ground** (like a ship)   23 **just proportion . . . out** exact
number we allowed for   24 **sway** move   25 **well-appointed** well-
furnished   25 **fronts** confronts   31 **in chief** chiefly   33 **routs** mobs
34 **guarded with rage** trimmed with false bluster (and pun on "rag")
35 **countenanced** faced out, added to   35 **beggary** beggars   36 **commotion** rebellion

You, reverend father, and these noble lords
Had not been here, to dress the ugly form
40   Of base and bloody insurrection
With your fair honors. You, Lord Archbishop,
Whose see° is by a civil peace maintained,
Whose beard the silver hand of peace hath touched,
Whose learning and good letters° peace hath tutored,
45   Whose white investments figure° innocence,
The dove and very blessèd spirit of peace,
Wherefore do you so ill translate° yourself
Out of the speech of peace that bears such grace,
Into the harsh and boisterous tongue of war,
50   Turning your books to graves, your ink to blood,
Your pens to lances, and your tongue divine
To a loud trumpet and a point of war?°

Archbishop. Wherefore do I this? So the question
    stands.
Briefly to this end: we are all diseased,
55   And with our surfeiting and wanton° hours
Have brought ourselves into a burning fever,
And we must bleed° for it. Of which disease
Our late king, Richard, being infected, died.
But, my most noble Lord of Westmoreland,
60   I take not on me here as a physician,°
Nor do I as an enemy to peace
Troop in the throngs of military men,
But rather show awhile like fearful war,
To diet rank° minds sick of happiness
65   And purge th' obstructions which begin to stop
Our very veins of life. Hear me more plainly.
I have in equal° balance justly weighed
What wrongs our arms may do, what wrongs we
    suffer,

---

42 **see** seat, throne, hence diocese   44 **good letters** humane scholarship   45 **investments figure** vestments symbolize   47 **translate** transform (but note the extended metaphor of language in lines 48–52)   52 **point of war** bugle call   55 **wanton** self-indulgent   57 **bleed** be bled (as a purgative)   60 **I take . . . physician** I do not presume to act as the doctor (to do the bleeding; I will but "show"—line 63)   64 **rank** swollen   67 **equal** unbiased

And find our griefs° heavier than our offenses.
We see which way the stream of time doth run,   70
And are enforced from our most quiet there
By the rough torrent of occasion,
And have the summary of all our griefs,
When time shall serve, to show in articles;°
Which long ere this we offered to the King,   75
And might by no suit gain our audience.
When we are wronged and would unfold our griefs,
We are denied access unto his person
Even by those men that most have done us wrong.
The dangers of the days but newly gone,   80
Whose memory is written on the earth
With yet-appearing blood, and the examples
Of every minute's instance,° present now,
Hath put us in these ill-beseeming arms,
Not to break peace or any branch of it,   85
But to establish here a peace indeed,
Concurring both in name and quality.°

Westmoreland. When ever yet was your appeal de-
   nied?
Wherein have you been gallèd° by the King?
What peer hath been suborned to grate on° you,   90
That you should seal this lawless bloody book
Of forgèd rebellion with a seal divine?°

Archbishop. My brother general,° the commonwealth,
I make my quarrel in particular.

Westmoreland. There is no need of any such redress,   95
Or if there were, it not belongs to you.

Mowbray. Why not to him in part, and to us all
That feel the bruises of the days before,
And suffer the condition of these times

<hr>

69 **griefs** grievances   74 **articles** formal listing   83 **Of every minute's instance** proof in every minute   87 **quality** substance   89 **gallèd**
irritated   90 **suborned to grate on** set on to vex   92 **divine** (see Textual Note, p. 173)   93 **brother general** (brother in a general sense as
opposed to my brother by birth; Henry IV had executed the Archbishop's brother—*1 Henry IV,* I.iii; see Textual Note, p. 173)

100   To lay a heavy and unequal° hand
      Upon our honors?

    Westmoreland.   O, my good Lord Mowbray,
      Construe the times to their necessities,°
      And you shall say indeed, it is the time,
      And not the King, that doth you injuries.
105   Yet for your part, it not appears to me
      Either from the King or in the present time
      That you should have an inch of any ground
      To build a grief on. Were you not restored
      To all the Duke of Norfolk's signories,°
110   Your noble and right well-rememb'red father's?

    Mowbray. What thing, in honor, had my father lost,
      That need to be revived and breathed in me?
      The King that loved him, as the state stood then,
      Was force perforce° compelled to banish him.
115   And then that Henry Bolingbroke and he,
      Being mounted and both rousèd in their seats,°
      Their neighing coursers daring of° the spur,
      Their armèd staves in charge, their beavers° down,
      Their eyes of fire sparkling through sights of steel,
120   And the loud trumpet blowing them together,
      Then, then, when there was nothing could have
         stayed
      My father from the breast of Bolingbroke—
      O, when the King did throw his warder° down
      His own life hung upon the staff he threw.
125   Then threw he down himself and all their lives
      That by indictment and by dint° of sword
      Have since miscarried° under Bolingbroke.

    Westmoreland. You speak, Lord Mowbray, now you
      know not what.

---

100 **unequal** not impartial   102 **Construe . . . necessities** interpret
the present state of things according to the forces that inevitably
make them the way they are   109 **signories** lands   114 **force per-**
force willy-nilly (for the trial by battle described in lines 115–37,
see *Richard II,* I.iii)   116 **seats** saddles   117 **daring of** ready for
118 **armèd staves . . . beavers** lances at the ready, their helmet-visors
123 **warder** ceremonial baton   126 **dint** force   127 **miscarried** per-
ished

The Earl of Hereford was reputed then
In England the most valiant gentleman.   *130*
Who knows on whom Fortune would then have
    smiled?
But if your father had been victor there,
He ne'er had borne it° out of Coventry.°
For all the country in a general voice
Cried hate upon him, and all their prayers and love   *135*
Were set on Hereford, whom they doted on
And blessed and graced—and did more than° the
    King.
But this is mere digression from my purpose.
Here come I from our princely general
To know your griefs, to tell you from his Grace   *140*
That he will give you audience, and wherein
It shall appear that your demands are just,
You shall enjoy them, everything set off°
That might so much as think you enemies.

Mowbray. But he hath forced us to compel this offer,   *145*
And it proceeds from policy,° not love.

Westmoreland. Mowbray, you overween° to take it so.
This offer comes from mercy, not from fear.
For, lo, within a ken° our army lies,
Upon mine honor, all too confident   *150*
To give admittance to a thought of fear.
Our battle° is more full of names° than yours,
Our men more perfect in the use of arms,
Our armor all as strong, our cause the best.
Then reason will° our hearts should be as good.   *155*
Say you not then our offer is compelled.

Mowbray. Well, by my will we shall admit no parley.

Westmoreland. That argues but the shame of your
    offense.

A rotten° case abides no handling.

160 *Hastings.* Hath the Prince John a full commission,
       In very ample virtue° of his father,
       To hear and absolutely to determine
       Of what conditions we shall stand upon?

     Westmoreland. That is intended in the General's
          name.°
165   I muse° you make so slight a question.

     Archbishop. Then take, my Lord of Westmoreland,
          this schedule,
       For this contains our general grievances.
       Each several article herein redressed,°
       All members of our cause, both here and hence°
170   That are insinewed° to this action,
       Acquitted by a true substantial form°
       And present execution of our wills
       To us and our purposes confined,°
       We° come within our awful banks° again
175   And knit our powers to the arm of peace.

     Westmoreland. This will I show the General. Please
          you, lords,
       In sight of both our battles we may meet,
       And either end in peace—which God so frame—
       Or to the place of diff'rence° call the swords
       Which must decide it.

180 *Archbishop.*   My lord, we will do so.
                                        Exit Westmoreland.

     Mowbray. There is a thing within my bosom tells me
       That no conditions° of our peace can stand.

159 **rotten** fragile (proverbial statement)   161 **In very ample virtue**
with exactly the ample power   164 **intended in the General's name**
implicit in the King's making his son the general   165 **muse** am
puzzled   168 **Each . . . redressed** i.e., if each . . . is redressed, etc.
169 **hence** elsewhere   170 **insinewed** bound by strong sinews   171
substantial form firm formal agreement   172–173 **wills . . . confined**
demands restricted (in scope) to us and our grievances   174 **We**
i.e., then we   174 **banks** i.e., they will subside like a stream that had
been in flood   179 **diff'rence** conflict   182 **conditions** provisions in
the contract

Hastings. Fear you not that. If we can make our peace
  Upon such large terms and so absolute
  As our conditions shall consist upon,   185
  Our peace shall stand as firm as rocky mountains.

Mowbray. Yea, but our valuation° shall be such
  That every slight and false-derivèd cause,
  Yea, every idle, nice, and wanton° reason
  Shall to the King taste of this action,   190
  That, were our royal faiths martyrs in love,°
  We shall be winnowed with so rough a wind
  That even our corn shall seem as light as chaff
  And good from bad find no partition.°

Archbishop. No, no, my lord. Note this. The King is
    weary   195
  Of dainty° and such picking° grievances.
  For he hath found to end one doubt by death
  Revives two greater in the heirs of life,°
  And therefore will he wipe his tables° clean
  And keep no telltale to his memory   200
  That may repeat and history his loss
  To new remembrance. For full well he knows
  He cannot so precisely° weed this land
  As his misdoubts° present occasion.
  His foes are so enrooted with his friends   205
  That, plucking to unfix an enemy,
  He doth unfasten so and shake a friend.
  So that this land, like an offensive wife
  That hath enraged him on to offer strokes,
  As he is striking, holds his infant up   210
  And hangs resolved correction° in the arm
  That was upreared to execution.

Hastings. Besides, the King hath wasted all his rods

187 **valuation** i.e., in the King's eyes   189 **nice, and wanton** petty
and frivolous   191 **were . . . love** i.e., even if we were as faithful in
love to his royal self as martyrs   194 **partition** dividing   196 **dainty,
picking** finicky   197–98 **to end . . . life** i.e., to rid himself of one
doubtful subject by executing him creates two even more treacherous
foes in those who live on after the dead man   199 **tables** notebook
203 **precisely** thoroughly   204 **misdoubts** suspicions   211 **resolved
correction** a check on his resolution

On late offenders, that he now doth lack
215 The very instruments of chastisement.
So that his power, like to a fangless lion,
May offer,° but not hold.

Archbishop.   'Tis very true.
And therefore be assured, my good Lord Marshal,
If we do now make our atonement° well,
220 Our peace will, like a broken limb united,
Grow stronger for the breaking.

Mowbray.   Be it so.
Here is returned my Lord of Westmoreland.

Enter Westmoreland.

Westmoreland. The Prince is here at hand. Pleaseth
    your lordship
To meet his Grace just distance° 'tween our armies.

Enter Prince John [of Lancaster] and his army.

Mowbray. Your Grace of York, in God's name then,
225   set forward.

Archbishop. Before, and greet his Grace, my lord; we
    come.

[*Scene II. The same.*]°

Lancaster. You are well encount'red here, my cousin
    Mowbray.
Good day to you, gentle Lord Archbishop.
And so to you, Lord Hastings, and to all.
My Lord of York, it better showed with you
5   When that your flock, assembled by the bell,
Encircled you to hear with reverence

217 **offer** threaten   219 **atonement** becoming at one   224 **just dis-
tance** halfway   IV.ii.s.d. (notice there should be no scene division,
the action being continuous and the stage not having emptied)

Your exposition on the holy text
Than now to see you here an iron° man talking,
Cheering a rout of rebels with your drum,
Turning the word to sword and life to death.   *10*
That man that sits within a monarch's heart
And ripens in the sunshine of his favor,
Would he abuse the countenance of the King,
Alack, what mischiefs might he set abroach°
In shadow of such greatness! With you, Lord
   Bishop,   *15*
It is even so. Who hath not heard it spoken
How deep you were within the books of God?
To us the speaker in His parliament,
To us th' imagined voice of God himself,
The very opener and intelligencer°   *20*
Between the grace, the sanctities of heaven
And our dull workings.° O, who shall believe
But you misuse the reverence of your place,
Employ the countenance and grace of heaven,
As a false favorite doth his prince's name,   *25*
In deeds dishonorable? You have ta'en up,°
Under the counterfeited zeal° of God,
The subjects of His substitute,° my father,
And both against the peace of heaven and him
Have here upswarmed° them.

Archbishop.   Good my Lord of Lancaster,   *30*
I am not here against your father's peace,
But, as I told my Lord of Westmoreland,
The time misord'red doth, in common sense,°
Crowd us and crush us to this monstrous° form,
To hold our safety up. I sent your Grace   *35*
The parcels° and particulars of our grief,
The which hath been with scorn shoved from the
   court,

---

8 **iron** (1) armored (2) merciless   14 **abroach** open (like a cask)
20 **opener and intelligencer** interpreter and informant   22 **workings**
mental operations   26 **ta'en up** enlisted   27 **zeal** (with a pun on
"seal")   28 **substitute** deputy   30 **upswarmed** made (them) swarm
up   33 **in common sense** to anybody's senses   34 **monstrous** un-
natural   36 **parcels** small parts

Whereon this Hydra° son of war is born,
Whose dangerous eyes may well be charmed asleep
40 With grant of our most just and right desires,
And true obedience, of this madness cured,
Stoop tamely to the foot of majesty.

Mowbray. If not, we ready are to try our fortunes
To the last man.

Hastings.   And though we here fall down,
45 We have supplies to second° our attempt.
If they miscarry, theirs° shall second them,
And so success° of mischief shall be born
And heir from heir shall hold this quarrel up
Whiles England shall have generation.°

Lancaster. You are too shallow, Hastings, much too
50 shallow,
To sound° the bottom of the after-times.

Westmoreland. Pleaseth your Grace to answer them
directly
How far forth you do like their articles.

Lancaster. I like them all, and do allow them well,
55 And swear here, by the honor of my blood,
My father's purposes have been mistook,
And some about him have too lavishly°
Wrested° his meaning and authority.
My lord, these griefs shall be with speed redressed.
60 Upon my soul, they shall. If this may please you,
Discharge your powers unto their several counties,
As we will ours. And here between the armies
Let's drink together friendly and embrace,
That all their eyes may bear those tokens home
65 Of our restorèd love and amity.

Archbishop. I take your princely word for these re-
dresses.

---

38 **Hydra** many-headed monster   45 **supplies to second** reinforcements to back up   46 **theirs** i.e., their supplies   47 **success** succession   49 **generation** offspring   51 **sound** measure the depth of
57 **lavishly** loosely   58 **Wrested** twisted

Lancaster. I give it you, and will maintain my word.
  And thereupon I drink unto your Grace.
                                        [*He drinks.*]

Hastings. Go, Captain, and deliver to the army
  This news of peace. Let them have pay, and part.°   *70*
  I know it will well please them. Hie thee, Captain.
                                        [*Exit Officer.*]

Archbishop. To you, my noble Lord of Westmoreland.
                                        [*He drinks.*]

Westmoreland. I pledge your Grace, and, if you knew
      what pains
  I have bestowed to breed this present peace,
  You would drink freely. But my love to ye   *75*
  Shall show itself more openly hereafter.

Archbishop. I do not doubt you.

Westmoreland.   I am glad of it.
  Health to my lord and gentle cousin, Mowbray.

Mowbray. You wish me health in very happy season,
  For I am, on the sudden, something° ill.   *80*

Archbishop. Against° ill chances men are ever merry,
  But heaviness foreruns the good event.

Westmoreland. Therefore be merry, coz, since sudden
      sorrow
  Serves to say thus, "Some good thing comes to-
      morrow."

Archbishop. Believe me, I am passing° light in spirit.   *85*

Mowbray. So much the worse, if your own rule be
      true.   *Shout* [*within*].

Lancaster. The word of peace is rend'red. Hark, how
      they shout!

Mowbray. This had been cheerful after victory.

---

70 **part** depart   80 **something** somewhat   81 **Against** expecting   85
passing surpassingly

Archbishop. A peace is of the nature of a conquest,
90   For then both parties nobly are subdued,
And neither party loser.

Lancaster.   Go, my lord,
And let our army be dischargèd too.
                              [*Exit Westmoreland.*]
And, good my lord, so please you, let our trains°
March by us, that we may peruse the men
We should have coped withal.°

95 *Archbishop.*   Go, good Lord Hastings,
And, ere they be dismissed, let them march by.
                              [*Exit Hastings.*]

Lancaster. I trust, lords, we shall lie tonight together.

Enter Westmoreland.

Now cousin, wherefore stands our army still?

Westmoreland. The leaders, having charge from you
      to stand,
100   Will not go off until they hear you speak.

Lancaster. They know their duties.

Enter Hastings.

Hastings. My lord, our army is dispersed already.
    Like youthful steers unyoked, they take their
      courses
    East, west, north, south, or, like a school broke up,
105   Each hurries toward his home and sporting-place.°

Westmoreland. Good tidings, my Lord Hastings, for
      the which
    I do arrest thee, traitor, of high treason.
    And you, Lord Archbishop, and you, Lord Mow-
      bray,
    Of capital° treason I attach° you both.

93 **our trains** those who follow us   95 **coped withal** been matched
with   105 **sporting-place** playground   109 **capital** punishable by
death   109 **attach** arrest

Mowbray. Is this proceeding just and honorable?   *110*

Westmoreland. Is your assembly so?

Archbishop. [*To Prince John*] Will you thus break
  your faith?

Lancaster.   I pawned° thee none.
  I promised you redress of these same grievances
  Whereof you did complain, which, by mine honor,
  I will perform with a most Christian care.   *115*
  But for you, rebels, look to taste the due
  Meet for rebellion and such acts as yours.
  Most shallowly did you these arms commence,
  Fondly° brought here and foolishly sent hence.
  Strike up our drums, pursue the scatt'red stray.   *120*
  God, and not we, hath safely fought today.
  Some guard these traitors to the block of death,
  Treason's true bed and yielder up of breath.

                              [*Exeunt.*]

[Scene III. *The same.*]°

Alarum. Enter Falstaff [*and Coleville, meeting*].

                    Excursions.°

Falstaff. What's your name, sir? Of what condition°
  are you, and of what place?

Coleville. I am a knight, sir, and my name is Coleville
  of the Dale.°

Falstaff. Well, then, Coleville is your name, a knight   *5*
  is your degree, and your place the Dale. Coleville
  shall be still your name, a traitor your degree, and

112 **pawned** pledged   119 **Fondly** foolishly   IV.iii.s.d. (again, there
should be no scene division; see Textual Note, p. 174)   s.d. **Excur-
sions** brief combats   1 **condition** rank   4 **Dale** deep place

the dungeon your place, a place deep enough. So
shall you be still Coleville of the Dale.

10 *Coleville.* Are not you Sir John Falstaff?

Falstaff. As good a man as he, sir, whoe'er I am. Do
ye yield, sir, or shall I sweat for you? If I do sweat,
they are the drops of thy lovers,° and they weep for
thy death. Therefore rouse up fear and trembling,
15 and do observance to my mercy.

Coleville. I think you are Sir John Falstaff, and in
that thought yield me.

Falstaff. I have a whole school° of tongues in this
belly of mine, and not a tongue of them all speaks
20 any other word but my name. And I had but a belly
of any indifferency,° I were simply the most active
fellow in Europe. My womb,° my womb, my womb
undoes° me. Here comes our general.

Enter [Prince] John [of Lancaster], Westmore-
land, [Blunt,] and the rest. Retreat [sounded].

Lancaster. The heat° is past, follow no further now.
25 Call in the powers, good cousin Westmoreland.
                              [*Exit Westmoreland.*]
Now, Falstaff, where have you been all this while?
When everything is ended, then you come.
These tardy tricks of yours will, on my life,
One time or other break some gallows' back.

30 *Falstaff.* I would be sorry, my lord, but it should be
thus. I never knew yet but rebuke and check was
the reward of valor. Do you think me a swallow,
an arrow, or a bullet? Have I, in my poor and old
motion, the expedition of thought? I have speeded
35 hither with the very extremest inch of possibility.
I have found'red° nine score and odd posts,° and

---

13 **drops of thy lovers** teardrops of those who love you   18 **school**
multitude (he is saying "my belly proclaims my identity as loudly as
a multitude")   21 **indifferency** undistinguished quality   22 **womb**
belly   23 **undoes** unmans   24 **heat** hot fighting   36 **found'red**
lamed   36 **posts** post-horses (Falstaff is, after all, heavy)

here, travel-tainted as I am, have, in my pure and
immaculate valor, taken Sir John Coleville of the
Dale, a most furious knight and valorous enemy.
But what of that? He saw me, and yielded, that I   40
may justly say, with the hook-nosed fellow of
Rome, "There, cousin,° I came, saw, and over-
came."

Lancaster. It was more of his courtesy than your de-
serving.   45

Falstaff. I know not. Here he is, and here I yield him.
And I beseech your Grace, let it be booked with
the rest of this day's deeds, or, by the Lord, I will
have it in a particular ballad else,° with mine own
picture on the top on't, Coleville kissing my foot. 50
To the which course if I be enforced, if you do not
all show like gilt twopences° to° me, and I in the
clear sky of fame o'ershine you as much as the full
moon doth the cinders of the element,° which show
like pins' heads to her, believe not the word of the 55
noble. Therefore let me have right, and let desert
mount.

Lancaster. Thine's too heavy to mount.

Falstaff. Let it shine, then.

Lancaster. Thine's too thick to shine.   60

Falstaff. Let it do something, my good lord, that may
do me good, and call it what you will.

Lancaster. Is thy name Coleville?

Coleville. It is, my lord.

Lancaster. A famous rebel art thou, Coleville.   65

Falstaff. And a famous true subject took him.

Coleville. I am, my lord, but as my betters are

42 **There, cousin** (a gross familiarity to Prince John; the Folio reads
"their Caesar")   49 **particular ballad else** special broadside ballad
otherwise   52 **gilt twopences** (silver twopenny pieces, if gilded,
could pass for gold half crowns)   52 **to** in comparison to   54 **cinders of the element** stars

That led me hither. Had they been ruled by me,
You should have won them dearer than you have.

70 *Falstaff.* I know not how they sold themselves. But
thou, like a kind fellow, gavest thyself away gratis,
and I thank thee for thee.

Enter Westmoreland.

Lancaster. Now, have you left pursuit?

Westmoreland. Retreat is made° and execution
stayed.°

75 *Lancaster.* Send Coleville with his confederates
To York, to present° execution.
Blunt, lead him hence, and see you guard him sure.
        [*Exeunt Blunt and others with Coleville.*]
And now dispatch° we toward the court, my lords.
I hear the King my father is sore sick.
80 Our news shall go before us to his Majesty,
Which, cousin, you shall bear to comfort him,
And we with sober speed will follow you.

Falstaff. My lord, I beseech you give me leave to go
Through Gloucestershire. And when you come to
court,
85 Stand° my good lord in your good report.

Lancaster. Fare you well, Falstaff. I, in my condition,°
Shall better speak of you than you deserve.
        [*Exeunt all but Falstaff.*]

Falstaff. I would you had the wit. 'Twere better than
your dukedom. Good faith, this same young sober-
90 blooded boy doth not love me, nor a man cannot
make him laugh. But that's no marvel, he drinks
no wine. There's never none of these demure boys
come to any proof,° for thin drink doth so over-
cool their blood, and making many fish-meals, that

---

74 **Retreat is made** the order for retreat has been given   74 **stayed**
halted   76 **present** immediate   78 **dispatch** hurry   85 **Stand** act as
86 **condition** present state of mind (but Falstaff takes his meaning as
"rank")   93 **come to any proof** stand much testing

they fall into a kind of male green-sickness,° and   95
then, when they marry, they get° wenches. They
are generally fools and cowards, which some of us
should be too, but for inflammation.° A good
sherris-sack° hath a twofold operation in it. It
ascends me into the brain, dries me there all the   100
foolish and dull and cruddy° vapors which environ
it, makes it apprehensive,° quick, forgetive,° full
of nimble, fiery, and delectable shapes, which, delivered o'er to the voice, the tongue, which is the
birth, becomes excellent wit.° The second property   105
of your excellent sherris is the warming of the
blood, which, before cold and settled, left the liver°
white and pale, which is the badge of pusillanimity
and cowardice. But the sherris warms it and makes
it course from the inwards to the parts extremes. It   110
illumineth the face, which as a beacon gives warning to all the rest of this little kingdom, man, to
arm, and then the vital commoners and inland
petty spirits° muster me all to their captain, the
heart, who, great and puffed up with this retinue,   115
doth any deed of courage, and this valor comes of
sherris. So that skill in the weapon is nothing without sack, for that sets it a-work, and learning a
mere hoard of gold kept by a devil, till sack com-
mences it° and sets it in act and use. Hereof comes   120
it that Prince Harry is valiant, for the cold blood
he did naturally inherit of his father, he hath, like
lean, sterile, and bare land, manured,° husbanded,
and tilled with excellent endeavor of drinking good
and good store of fertile sherris, that he is become   125
very hot and valiant. If I had a thousand sons, the
first humane principle I would teach them should

5 **green-sickness** anemia common to young girls   96 **get** beget
8 **inflammation** i.e., of the spirits with liquor   99 **sherris-sack** sherry
vine from the Jerez district in Spain; "sack" is from the French, *sec,*
ry)   101 **cruddy** curded   102 **apprehensive** quick to take in
02 **forgetive** begetting, procreative   105 **wit** intelligence   107 **liver**
seat of the passions, including courage)   113–14 **vital . . . spirits**
luids within the body that give it life and motion)   119–20 **com-
ences it** gives it a university degree (licensing it to act)   123 **man-
red** tilled by hand

be to forswear thin potations and to addict themselves to sack.

Enter Bardolph.

130   How now, Bardolph?

Bardolph. The army is discharged all and gone.

Falstaff. Let them go. I'll through Gloucestershire,
and there will I visit Master Robert Shallow,
Esquire. I have him already temp'ring° between
135   my finger and my thumb, and shortly will I seal°
with him. Come away.   [*Exeunt.*]

[Scene IV. *Westminster.*]

*Enter the King, Warwick, Kent, Thomas Duke
of Clarence, Humphrey [Duke] of Gloucester,
[and others].*

King. Now, lords, if God doth give successful end
To this debate that bleedeth at our doors,
We will our youth lead on to higher fields
And draw no swords but what are sanctified.°
5   Our navy is addressed,° our power° collected,
Our substitutes in absence well invested,°
And everything lies level° to our wish.
Only, we want° a little personal strength
And pause us, till these rebels, now afoot,
10   Come underneath the yoke of government.

Warwick. Both which we doubt not but your Majesty
Shall soon enjoy.

134 **temp'ring** softening (like sealing wax)   135 **seal** (1) squeeze (2)
close the deal   IV.iv.4 **sanctified** i.e., in a Crusade   5 **addressed** a
the ready   5 **power** army   6 **invested** clothed (with authority
7 **level** according   8 **want** lack

King.   Humphrey, my son of Gloucester,
Where is the Prince your brother?

Gloucester. I think he's gone to hunt, my lord, at
Windsor.

King. And how accompanied?

Gloucester.   I do not know, my lord.   *15*

King. Is not his brother, Thomas of Clarence, with
him?

Gloucester. No, my good lord, he is in presence° here.

Clarence. What would my lord and father?

King. Nothing but well to thee, Thomas of Clarence.
How chance thou art not with the Prince thy
brother?   *20*
He loves thee, and thou dost neglect him, Thomas;
Thou hast a better place in his affection
Than all thy brothers. Cherish it, my boy,
And noble offices thou mayst effect
Of mediation, after I am dead,   *25*
Between his greatness and thy other brethren.
Therefore omit him not, blunt not his love,
Nor lose the good advantage of his grace
By seeming cold or careless of his will.
For he is gracious,° if he be observed.°   *30*
He hath a tear for pity and a hand
Open as day for meeting charity.
Yet notwithstanding, being incensed, he's flint,
As humorous° as winter and as sudden
As flaws congealèd° in the spring of day.   *35*
His temper, therefore, must be well observed.
Chide him for faults, and do it reverently,
When you perceive his blood inclined to mirth,
But, being moody, give him time and scope,
Till that his passions, like a whale on ground,   *40*

17 **presence** i.e., the royal presence   30 **gracious** full of royal grace
30 **observed** respected   34 **humorous** given to whims   35 **flaws congealèd** snowstorms turned to sleet

Confound° themselves with working.° Learn this,
    Thomas,
And thou shalt prove a shelter to thy friends,
A hoop of gold to bind thy brothers in,
That the united vessel of their blood,
45   Mingled with venom of suggestion°—
As, force perforce,° the age will pour it in—
Shall never leak, though it do work as strong
As aconitum° or rash gunpowder.

Clarence. I shall observe him with all care and love.

50 *King.* Why art thou not at Windsor with him, Thomas?

Clarence. He is not there today. He dines in London.

King. And how accompanied? Canst thou tell that?

Clarence. With Poins and other his continual fol-
    lowers.

King. Most subject is the fattest° soil to weeds,
55   And he, the noble image of my youth,
Is overspread with them. Therefore my grief
Stretches itself beyond the hour of death.
The blood weeps from my heart when I do shape
In forms imaginary th' unguided days
60   And rotten times that you shall look upon
When I am sleeping with my ancestors.
For when his headstrong riot hath no curb,
When rage° and hot blood are his counselors,
When means and lavish manners° meet together,
65   O, with what wings shall his affections° fly
Towards fronting° peril and opposed decay!

Warwick. My gracious lord, you look beyond° him
    quite.
The Prince but studies his companions

---

41 **Confound** defeat   41 **working** acting out   45 **suggestion** insinua-
tions   46 **force perforce** willy-nilly   48 **aconitum** wolfsbane (a poison)   54 **fattest** richest   63 **rage** passion   64 **lavish manners** loose
behavior   65 **affections** desires   66 **fronting** confronting   67 **look
beyond** misjudge, i.e., you look further into the future than the
evidence warrants

Like a strange tongue, wherein, to gain the lan-
  guage,
'Tis needful that the most immodest word   *70*
Be looked upon and learned, which once attained,
Your Highness knows, comes to no further use
But to be known and hated. So, like gross terms,
The Prince will in the perfectness of time
Cast off his followers, and their memory   *75*
Shall as a pattern or a measure live,
By which his Grace must mete° the lives of others,
Turning past evils to advantages.

King. 'Tis seldom when the bee doth leave her comb
  In the dead carrion.° Who's here? Westmoreland?   *80*

                    Enter Westmoreland.

Westmoreland. Health to my sovereign, and new hap-
  piness
Added to that that I am to deliver.
Prince John your son doth kiss your Grace's hand.
Mowbray, the Bishop Scroop, Hastings and all
Are brought to the correction of your law.   *85*
There is not now a rebel's sword unsheathed,
But Peace puts forth her olive everywhere.
The manner how this action hath been borne
Here at more leisure may your Highness read,
With every course° in his particular.   *90*

King. O Westmoreland, thou art a summer bird,
  Which ever in the haunch° of winter sings
  The lifting up of day.

                    Enter Harcourt.

                Look, here's more news.

Harcourt. From enemies, heavens keep your Majesty,
  And, when they stand against you, may they fall   *95*
As those that I am come to tell you of!
The Earl Northumberland and the Lord Bardolph,

---

77 **mete** measure, judge   79–80 **'Tis seldom ... carrion** i.e., the bee
who has created sweetness in rottenness rarely abandons it   90
course occurrence   92 **haunch** back portion

With a great power of English and of Scots,
Are by the shrieve° of Yorkshire overthrown.
100 The manner and true order of the fight
This packet, please it you, contains at large.

King. And wherefore should these good news make
    me sick?
Will Fortune never come with both hands full,
But write her fair words still° in foulest letters?
105 She either gives a stomach° and no food—
Such are the poor, in health—or else a feast
And takes away the stomach—such are the rich
That have abundance and enjoy it not.
I should rejoice now at this happy news,
110 And now my sight fails, and my brain is giddy.
O me! Come near me. Now I am much ill.

Gloucester. Comfort, your Majesty!

Clarence.   O my royal father!

Westmoreland. My sovereign lord, cheer up yourself,
    look up.

Warwick. Be patient, Princes. You do know these fits
115 Are with his Highness very ordinary.
Stand from him, give him air, he'll straight° be well.

Clarence. No, no, he cannot long hold out these pangs.
Th' incessant care and labor of his mind
Hath wrought the mure° that should confine it in
120 So thin that life looks through and will break out.

Gloucester. The people fear me,° for they do observe
Unfathered° heirs and loathly° births off nature.
The seasons change their manners, as° the year
Had found some months asleep and leaped them
    over.

99 **shrieve** sheriff   104 **still** ever   105 **stomach** appetite   116 **straight**
straightway   119 **wrought the mure** worked the wall   121 **fear me**
make me fear   122 **Unfathered** supernaturally begotten   122 **loathly**
monstrous   123 **as** as if

Clarence. The river° hath thrice flowed,° no ebb be-
  tween,   *125*
 And the old folk, time's doting chronicles,
 Say it did so a little time before
 That our great-grandsire, Edward,° sicked and died.

Warwick. Speak lower, Princes, for the King recovers.

Gloucester. This apoplexy will certain be his end. *130*

King. I pray you, take me up, and bear me hence
 Into some other chamber. Softly, pray.
      [*They bear him to another
        part of the stage.*]

[Scene V. *The same.*]°

[*King.*] Let there be no noise made, my gentle friends,
 Unless some dull and favorable° hand
 Will whisper music to my weary spirit.

Warwick. Call for the music in the other room.

King. Set me the crown upon my pillow here. *5*

Clarence. His eye is hollow, and he changes° much.

Warwick. Less noise, less noise!

    Enter [Prince] Harry.

Prince.   Who saw the Duke of Clarence?

Clarence. I am here, brother, full of heaviness.

---

125 **river** Thames 125 **flowed** flooded 128 **Edward** Edward III
IV.v.s.d. (the stage is not emptied, the King being lifted onto a bed
and moved to the inner stage or another part of the outer stage, and
the Quarto and the Folio indicate no scene division; the conventional
nineteenth-century scene division is superfluous) 2 **dull and favor-
able** drowsy and kindly 6 **changes** i.e., changes color

Prince. How now! Rain° within doors, and none
    abroad!
10   How doth the King?

Gloucester. Exceeding ill.

Prince.   Heard he the good news yet?
    Tell it him.

Gloucester. He altered much upon the hearing it.

Prince. If he be sick with joy, he'll recover without
    physic.

Warwick. Not so much noise, my lords. Sweet Prince,
15   speak low.
    The King your father is disposed to sleep.

Clarence. Let us withdraw into the other room.

Warwick. Will't please your Grace to go along with
    us?

Prince. No, I will sit and watch here by the King.
                    [Exeunt all but Prince Hal.]
20   Why doth the crown lie there upon his pillow,
    Being so troublesome a bedfellow?
    O polished perturbation! Golden care!
    That keep'st the ports° of slumber open wide
    To many a watchful night! Sleep with it now!
25   Yet not so sound and half so deeply sweet
    As he whose brow with homely biggen° bound
    Snores out the watch of night. O majesty!
    When thou dost pinch thy bearer, thou dost sit
    Like a rich armor worn in heat of day,
30   That scald'st with safety.° By his gates of breath°
    There lies a downy feather which stirs not.
    Did he suspire,° that light and weightless down
    Perforce must move. My gracious lord, my father!
    This sleep is sound indeed. This is a sleep

9 **Rain** i.e., tears   23 **ports** city gates (as the eyes are to the mind)
26 **biggen** nightcap   30 **scald'st with safety** scorches while it protects
30 **gates of breath** i.e., lips   32 **suspire** breathe

That from this golden rigol° hath divorced　　35
So many English kings. Thy due from me
Is tears and heavy sorrows of the blood,
Which nature, love, and filial tenderness
Shall, O dear father, pay thee plenteously.
My due from thee is this imperial crown,　　40
Which, as immediate from° thy place and blood,
Derives° itself to me. [*Puts on the crown.*] Lo,
　　where it sits,
Which God shall guard. And put the world's whole
　　strength
Into one giant arm, it shall not force
This lineal° honor from me. This from thee　　45
Will I to mine leave, as 'tis left to me.　　　*Exit.*

King. [*Waking*] Warwick! Gloucester! Clarence!

　　　Enter Warwick, Gloucester, Clarence.

Clarence. Doth the King call?

Warwick. What would your Majesty? How fares your
　　Grace?

King. Why did you leave me here alone, my lords?　　50

Clarence. We left the Prince my brother here, my
　　liege,
Who undertook to sit and watch by you.

King. The Prince of Wales! Where is he? Let me see
　　him.
He is not here.

Warwick. This door is open. He is gone this way.　　55

Gloucester. He came not through the chamber where
　　we stayed.

King. Where is the crown? Who took it from my pil-
　　low?

Warwick. When we withdrew, my liege, we left it here.

---

35 **rigol** circle　41 **as immediate from** i.e., as nothing is between me
and　42 **Derives** flows down　45 **lineal** inherited (as against taken)

   King. The Prince hath ta'en it hence. Go, seek him
      out.

60   Is he so hasty that he doth suppose
    My sleep my death?
    Find him, my Lord of Warwick, chide him hither.
                     [Exit Warwick.]
    This part° of his conjoins with my disease
    And helps to end me. See, sons, what things you
      are!

65   How quickly nature falls into revolt
    When gold becomes her object!
    For this the foolish overcareful fathers
    Have broke their sleep with thoughts,
    Their brains with care, their bones with industry.

70   For this they have engrossèd° and piled up
    The cank'red° heaps of strange-achievèd° gold;
    For this they have been thoughtful° to invest
    Their sons with arts° and martial exercises.
    When, like the bee, culling from every flower

75   The virtuous sweets, our thighs packed with wax,
    Our mouths with honey, we bring it to the hive,
    And, like the bees, are murdered for our pains.
    This bitter taste yields his engrossments°
    To the ending father.

              Enter Warwick.

80   Now, where is he that will not stay so long
    Till his friend sickness hath determined° me?

   Warwick. My lord, I found the Prince in the nex
      room,
    Washing with kindly° tears his gentle cheeks,
    With such a deep demeanor° in great sorrow

85   That tyranny, which never quaffed but blood,
    Would, by beholding him, have washed his knife
    With gentle eye-drops. He is coming hither.

---

63 part act **70 engrossèd** bought up **71 cank'red** (1) rusting (
malignant **71 strange-achievèd** hard-won **72 thoughtful** caref
73 arts i.e., liberal arts **78 yields his engrossments** his accumulatio
yield **81 determined** ended **83 kindly** natural **84 deep demean**
intense manner

King. But wherefore did he take away the crown?

        Enter [Prince] Harry.

Lo, where he comes. Come hither to me, Harry.
Depart the chamber, leave us here alone.   *90*
        Exeunt [Warwick and the others].

Prince. I never thought to hear you speak again.

King. Thy wish was father, Harry, to that thought.
I stay too long by thee,° I weary thee.
Dost thou so hunger for mine empty chair
That thou wilt needs invest thee with my honors   *95*
Before thy hour be ripe? O foolish youth!
Thou seek'st the greatness that will overwhelm thee.
Stay but a little, for my cloud of dignity
Is held from falling with so weak a wind°
That it will quickly drop. My day is dim.   *100*
Thou hast stol'n that which after some few hours
Were thine without offense, and at my death
Thou hast sealed up° my expectation.
Thy life did manifest thou lov'dst me not,
And thou wilt have me die assured of it.   *105*
Thou hid'st a thousand daggers in thy thoughts,
Which thou hast whetted on thy stony heart,
To stab at half an hour of my life.
What! Canst thou not forbear me half an hour?
Then get thee gone and dig my grave thyself,   *110*
And bid the merry bells ring to thine ear
That thou art crownèd, not that I am dead.
Let all the tears that should bedew my hearse
Be drops of balm° to sanctify thy head.
Only compound° me with forgotten dust.   *115*
Give that which gave thee life unto the worms.
Pluck down my officers, break my decrees,
For now a time is come to mock at form.°
Harry the Fifth is crowned. Up, vanity!
Down, royal state! All you sage counselors, hence!   *120*

---

93 **by thee** (1) with thee (2) in thy opinion   99 **wind** i.e., breath
103 **sealed up** confirmed   114 **balm** coronation oil   115 **Only compound** just mix   118 **form** order

And to the English court assemble now,
From every region, apes of idleness!
Now, neighbor confines,° purge you of your scum.
Have you a ruffian that will swear, drink, dance,
125 Revel the night, rob, murder, and commit
The oldest sins the newest kind of ways?
Be happy, he will trouble you no more.
England shall double gild his treble guilt,
England shall give him office, honor, might,
130 For the fifth Harry from curbed license plucks
The muzzle of restraint, and the wild dog
Shall flesh° his tooth on every innocent.
O my poor kingdom, sick with civil blows!
When that my care could not withhold thy riots,
135 What wilt thou do when riot is thy care?
O, thou wilt be a wilderness again,
Peopled with wolves, thy old inhabitants.

Prince. O, pardon me, my liege! But for my tears,
The moist impediments unto my speech,
140 I had forestalled this dear° and deep rebuke
Ere you with grief had spoke and I had heard
The course of it so far. There is your crown,
And He that wears the crown immortally
Long guard it yours. If I affect° it more
145 Than as your honor and as your renown,
Let me no more from this obedience° rise,
Which my most inward true and duteous spirit
Teacheth, this prostrate and exterior bending.
God witness with me, when I here came in,
And found no course° of breath within your
150   Majesty,
How cold it struck my heart. If I do feign,
O, let me in my present wildness die
And never live to show th' incredulous world
The noble change that I have purposèd.
155 Coming to look on you, thinking you dead,

123 **neighbor confines** nearby regions   132 **flesh** sink in flesh   140
dear heartfelt   144 **affect** desire   146 **obedience** low curtsy   150
course occurrence

And dead almost, my liege, to think you were,
I spake unto this crown as having sense,
And thus upbraided it: "The care on thee depend-
　　ing
Hath fed upon the body of my father.
Therefore, thou best of gold art worst of gold.   160
Other, less fine in carat,° is more precious,
Preserving life in medicine potable,°
But thou, most fine, most honored, most renowned,
Hast eat thy bearer up." Thus, my most royal liege,
Accusing it, I put it on my head,   165
To try with it, as with an enemy
That had before my face murdered my father,
The quarrel of a true inheritor.
But if it did infect my blood with joy,
Or swell my thoughts to any strain° of pride,   170
If any rebel or vain spirit of mine
Did with the least affection of a welcome
Give entertainment to the might of it,
Let God forever keep it from my head
And make me as the poorest vassal is   175
That doth with awe and terror kneel to it.

King. O my son,
God put it in thy mind to take it hence,
That thou mightst win the more thy father's love,
Pleading so wisely in excuse of it!   180
Come hither, Harry, sit thou by my bed,
And hear, I think, the very latest° counsel
That ever I shall breathe. God knows, my son,
By what bypaths and indirect crooked ways
I met° this crown, and I myself know well   185
How troublesome it sat upon my head.
To thee it shall descend with better quiet,
Better opinion, better confirmation,
For all the soil° of the achievement goes
With me into the earth. It seemed in me   190

161 **carat** (with pun on "charact," character)   162 **medicine potable**
gold in solution (prescribed as medicine)   170 **strain** musical theme
(i.e., feeling)   182 **latest** last   185 **met** i.e., as one meets one's fate
189 **soil** dirt

But as an honor snatched with boisterous° hand,
And I had many living to upbraid
My gain of it by their assistances,
Which daily grew to quarrel and to bloodshed
195 Wounding supposèd peace. All these bold fears°
Thou seest with peril I have answered,
For all my reign hath been but as a scene
Acting that argument.° And now my death
Changes the mood,° for what in me was purchased°
200 Falls upon thee in a more fairer sort,
So thou the garland wear'st successively.°
Yet, though thou stand'st more sure than I could
         do,
Thou art not firm enough, since griefs are green.°
And all my friends, which thou must make thy
         friends,
205 Have but their stings and teeth newly ta'en out,
By whose fell° working I was first advanced
And by whose power I well might lodge a fear
To be again displaced. Which to avoid,
I cut them off, and had a purpose now
210 To lead out many to the Holy Land,
Lest rest and lying still might make them look
Too near° unto my state. Therefore, my Harry,
Be it thy course to busy giddy minds
With foreign quarrels, that action, hence borne
         out,°
215 May waste the memory of the former days.
More would I, but my lungs are wasted so
That strength of speech is utterly denied me.
How I came by the crown, O God forgive,
And grant it may with thee in true peace live!

220 *Prince.* My gracious liege,
   You won it, wore it, kept it, gave it me.

---

191 **boisterous** rough   195 **fears** things causing fear   198 **argument**
plot (in a play)   199 **mood** (punning on "mode")   199 **purchased** (a
legal term: acquired by deed rather than inheritance)   201 **successively** by hereditary succession   203 **green** fresh and growing   206
fell fierce   211–212 **look/Too near** (1) examine (2) aspire too closely
214 **hence borne out** carried on elsewhere

Then plain and right must my possession be,
Which I with more than with a common pain°
'Gainst all the world will rightfully maintain.

Enter [Prince John of] Lancaster [and Warwick].

King. Look, look, here comes my John of Lancaster.   225

Lancaster. Health, peace, and happiness to my royal
   father!

King. Thou bring'st me happiness and peace, son
   John,
But health, alack, with youthful wings is flown
From this bare, withered trunk. Upon thy sight
My worldly business makes a period.   230
Where is my Lord of Warwick?

Prince.   My Lord of Warwick!

King. Doth any name particular belong
Unto the lodging where I first did swoon?

Warwick. 'Tis called "Jerusalem,"° my noble lord.

King. Laud° be to God! Even there my life must end.   235
It hath been prophesied to me many years
I should not die but "in Jerusalem,"
Which vainly I supposed the Holy Land.
But bear me to that chamber; there I'll lie.
In that "Jerusalem" shall Harry die.   *[Exeunt.]*   240

---

223 **pain** effort (and note the formal rhymes)   234 **Jerusalem**
(Holinshed states correctly that the "Jerusalem chamber" is in Westminster Abbey, not Westminster Palace; Shakespeare leaves the
setting of IV.iv and v ambiguous until this line—see the stage direction at IV.iv.1)   235 **Laud** praise

[ACT V

Scene I. *Justice Shallow's home*.]

Enter Shallow, Falstaff, and Bardolph [and Page].

Shallow. By cock and pie,° sir, you shall not away
   tonight. What, Davy, I say!

Falstaff. You must excuse me, Master Robert Shallow.

Shallow. I will not excuse you. You shall not be ex-
5   cused. Excuses shall not be admitted. There is no
   excuse shall serve. You shall not be excused. Why,
   Davy!

   [*Enter Davy.*]

Davy. Here, sir.

Shallow. Davy, Davy, Davy, Davy, let me see, Davy.
10   Let me see, Davy, let me see. Yea, marry, William
   cook, bid him come hither. Sir John, you shall not
   be excused.

Davy. Marry, sir, thus, those precepts° cannot be
   served. And, again, sir, shall we sow the headland°
15   with wheat?

Shallow. With red wheat,° Davy. But for William cook
   —are there no young pigeons?

V.i.1 **By cock and pie** (a mild oath)   13 **precepts** orders   14 **head-land** unploughed strip between two ploughed fields   16 **red wheat** (sown in late August)

Davy. Yes, sir. Here is now the smith's note° for shoeing and plow-irons.

Shallow. Let it be cast° and paid. Sir John, you shall 　20
not be excused.

Davy. Now, sir, a new link to the bucket° must needs be had. And, sir, do you mean to stop any of William's wages, about the sack he lost the other day at Hinckley Fair?° 　25

Shallow. 'A shall answer it. Some pigeons, Davy, a couple of short-legged hens, a joint of mutton, and any pretty little tiny kickshaws,° tell William cook.

Davy. Doth the man of war stay all night, sir?

Shallow. Yea, Davy. I will use him well. A friend i' 　30
th' court is better than a penny in purse. Use his men well, Davy, for they are arrant knaves and will backbite.

Davy. No worse than they are backbitten,° sir, for they have marvelous foul linen. 　35

Shallow. Well conceited,° Davy. About thy business, Davy.

Davy. I beseech you, sir, to countenance° William Visor of Woncot against Clement Perkes o' th' hill.

Shallow. There is many complaints, Davy, against that 　40
Visor. That Visor is an arrant knave, on my knowledge.

Davy. I grant your worship that he is a knave, sir, but yet, God forbid, sir, but a knave should have some countenance at his friend's request. An honest 　45
man, sir, is able to speak for himself, when a knave is not. I have served your worship truly, sir, this eight years—and I cannot once or twice in a quar-

---

18 **note** bill　20 **cast** checked　22 **link to the bucket** chain link for the yoke　25 **Hinckley Fair** (held August 26, thirty miles northeast of Stratford)　28 **kickshaws** fancy things (French, *quelquechoses*)　34 **backbitten** i.e., with lice　36 **conceited** conceived　38 **countenance** show favor to

ter bear out° a knave against an honest man, I have
50   but a very little credit with your worship. The knave
is mine honest friend, sir. Therefore, I beseech you,
let him be countenanced.

Shallow. Go to, I say he shall have no wrong. Look
about,° Davy! [*Exit Davy.*] Where are you, Sir
55   John? Come, come, come, off with your boots. Give
me your hand, Master Bardolph.

Bardolph. I am glad to see your worship.

Shallow. I thank thee with my heart, kind Master Bardolph. [*To the Page*] And welcome, my tall fellow.
60   Come, Sir John.

Falstaff. I'll follow you, good Master Robert Shallow.
[*Exit Shallow.*] Bardolph, look to our horses.
[*Exeunt Bardolph and Page.*] If I were sawed into
quantities,° I should make four dozen of such
65   bearded hermits' staves as Master Shallow. It is a
wonderful thing to see the semblable coherence° of
his men's spirits and his. They, by observing him,
do bear themselves like foolish justices. He, by
conversing with them, is turned into a justice-like
70   servingman. Their spirits are so married in conjunction with the participation of society° that they
flock together in consent,° like so many wild geese.
If I had a suit to Master Shallow, I would humor
his men with the imputation of being near their
75   master. If to his men, I would curry° with Master
Shallow that no man could better command his
servants. It is certain that either wise bearing° or
ignorant carriage is caught, as men take diseases,
one of another. Therefore let men take heed of
80   their company.° I will devise matter enough out of
this Shallow to keep Prince Harry in continual
laughter the wearing out of six fashions, which is

49 **bear out** help out   53–54 **Look about** look sharp!   64 **quantities**
lengths   66 **semblable coherence** visible similarity   71 **society** association   72 **in consent** unanimously   75 **curry** i.e., curry favor
77 **bearing** behavior   79–80 **take heed of their company** (ironical,
coming from Falstaff)

four terms,° or two actions,° and 'a shall laugh
without intervallums.° O, it is much that a lie with
a slight oath and a jest with a sad brow will do with   85
a fellow that never had the ache in his shoulders! O,
you shall see him laugh till his face be like a wet
cloak ill laid up!°

Shallow. [*Within*] Sir John!

Falstaff. I come, Master Shallow. I come, Master Shal-   90
low.   [*Exit.*]

[Scene II. *London.*]

*Enter the Earl of Warwick and the
Lord Chief Justice [meeting].*

Warwick. How now, my Lord Chief Justice! Whither
away?

Chief Justice. How doth the King?

Warwick. Exceeding well. His cares are now all ended.

Chief Justice. I hope, not dead.

Warwick.   He's walked the way of nature,
And to our° purposes he lives no more.   5

Chief Justice. I would his Majesty had called me with
him.
The service that I truly° did his life
Hath left me open to all injuries.

Warwick. Indeed I think the young king loves you not.

83 **terms** court sessions (four in the year)   83 **actions** lawsuits
84 **intervallums** intersessions   88 **ill laid up** put away wrinkled
V.ii.5 **our** i.e., living men's as contrasted to God's   7 **truly** faithfully

10 *Chief Justice.* I know he doth not, and do arm myself
  To welcome the condition of the time,
  Which cannot look more hideously upon me
  Than I have drawn it in my fantasy.

  *Enter [Prince] John [of Lancaster], Thomas
  [of Clarence], and Humphrey [of Gloucester].*

Warwick. Here come the heavy issue° of dead Harry.
15 O that the living Harry had the temper°
  Of he,° the worst of these three gentlemen!
  How many nobles then should hold their places
  That must strike° sail to spirits of vile sort!

Chief Justice. O God, I fear all will be overturned!

Lancaster. Good morrow, cousin Warwick, good mor-
20 row.

Gloucester. ⎫
         ⎬ Good morrow, cousin.
Clarence. ⎭

Lancaster. We meet like men that had forgot to speak.

Warwick. We do remember, but our argument°
  Is all too heavy to admit much talk.

Lancaster. Well, peace be with him that hath made us
25 heavy.

Chief Justice. Peace be with us, lest we be heavier.

Gloucester. O, good my lord, you have lost a friend
  indeed,
  And I dare swear you borrow not that face
  Of seeming sorrow—it is sure your own.

Lancaster. Though no man be assured what grace to
30 find,
  You stand in coldest expectation.
  I am the sorrier. Would 'twere otherwise.

____

14 **heavy issue** grieving sons   15 **temper** temperament   16 **he** i.e.,
whoever is   18 **strike** lower (i.e., submit to pirates)   23 **argument**
situation

Clarence. Well, you must now speak Sir John Falstaff
  fair,
  Which swims against your stream of quality.°

Chief Justice. Sweet Princes, what I did, I did in
  honor,   35
  Led by th' impartial conduct of my soul,
  And never shall you see that I will beg
  A ragged and forestalled remission.°
  If truth and upright innocency fail me,
  I'll to the King my master that is dead,   40
  And tell him who hath sent me after him.

Warwick. Here comes the Prince.

Enter the Prince [as King Henry the Fifth] and Blunt.

Chief Justice. Good morrow, and God save your
  Majesty!

King. This new and gorgeous garment, majesty,
  Sits not so easy on me as you think.   45
  Brothers, you mix your sadness with some fear.
  This is the English, not the Turkish court.
  Not Amurath° an Amurath succeeds,
  But Harry Harry. Yet be sad, good brothers,
  For, by my faith, it very well becomes you.   50
  Sorrow so royally in you appears°
  That I will deeply° put the fashion on
  And wear it in my heart. Why then, be sad,
  But entertain no more of it, good brothers,
  Than a joint burden laid upon us all.   55
  For me, by heaven, I bid you be assured,
  I'll be your father and your brother too.
  Let me but bear your love, I'll bear your cares.
  Yet weep that Harry's dead, and so will I,
  But Harry lives, that shall convert those tears   60
  By number into hours of happiness.

34 **swims . . . quality** goes against the current of your disposition
and rank   38 **ragged and forestalled remission** beggarly and already
prevented pardon   48 **Amurath** Amurath IV of Turkey strangled
his brothers on his accession in 1574   51 **appears** (they are wearing
black, he royal red)   52 **deeply** (1) solemnly (2) within

Brothers. We hope no otherwise from your Majesty.

King. You all look strangely on me. [*To the Chief
    Justice*] And you most.
    You are, I think, assured I love you not.

65 *Chief Justice.* I am assured, if I be measured rightly,
    Your Majesty hath no just cause to hate me.

King. No?
    How might a prince of my great hopes forget
    So great indignities you laid upon me?
70   What! Rate,° rebuke, and roughly send to prison
    Th' immediate heir of England! Was this easy?°
    May this be washed in Lethe,° and forgotten?

Chief Justice. I then did use the person° of your
    father.
    The image of his power lay then in me.
75   And, in th' administration of his law,
    Whiles I was busy for the commonwealth,
    Your Highness pleasèd to forget my place,
    The majesty and power of law and justice,
    The image of the King whom I presented,
80   And struck me in my very seat of judgment.
    Whereon, as an offender to your father,
    I gave bold way to my authority
    And did commit° you. If the deed were ill,
    Be you contented, wearing now the garland,
85   To have a son set your decrees at nought?
    To pluck down justice from your awful° bench?
    To trip the course of law and blunt the sword
    That guards the peace and safety of your person?
    Nay, more, to spurn at your most royal image
90   And mock your workings in a second body?°
    Question your royal thoughts. Make the case yours.

---

70 **Rate** berate   71 **easy** unimportant (the legend was well known;
see above, note to I.ii.57–58, below, pp. 175 and 184, and the Signet
Classic edition of *1 Henry IV*, pp. 192–200)   72 **Lethe** the river
of forgetfulness in Hades   73 **use the person** act in the character
83 **commit** send to prison   86 **awful** causing awe   90 **in a second
body** (i.e., one who uses your person, line 73)

Be now the father and propose° a son:
Hear your own dignity so much profaned,
See your most dreadful laws so loosely slighted,
Behold yourself so by a son disdained,   95
And then imagine me taking your part
And in your power soft silencing your son.
After this cold considerance,° sentence me,
And, as you are a king, speak in your state°
What I have done that misbecame my place,   100
My person, or my liege's sovereignty.

King. You are right, Justice, and you weigh this well.
Therefore still bear the balance and the sword.
And I do wish your honors may increase,
Till you do live to see a son of mine   105
Offend you—and obey you—as I did.
So shall I live to speak my father's words:
"Happy am I, that have a man so bold
That dares do justice on my proper° son,
And not less happy, having such a son   110
That would deliver up his greatness so
Into the hands of justice." You did commit me.
For, which, I do commit into your hand
Th' unstainèd sword that you have used to bear,
With this remembrance,° that you use the same   115
With the like bold, just, and impartial spirit
As you have done 'gainst me. There is my hand.
You shall be as a father to my youth.
My voice shall sound as you do prompt mine ear,
And I will stoop and humble my intents   120
To your well-practiced wise directions.
And, Princes all, believe me, I beseech you,
My father is gone wild° into his grave,
For in his tomb lie my affections,°
And with his spirits° sadly I survive,   125
To mock the expectation of the world,
To frustrate prophecies, and to raze° out

92 **propose** put the case of (legal term)   98 **cold considerance** cool
consideration   99 **state** station   109 **proper** own   115 **remembrance**
entry in the records (legal term)   123 **wild** uncivilized   124 **affections** appetites   125 **spirits** character (based on his humors)
127 **raze** erase

Rotten opinion, who hath writ me down
After my seeming.° The tide of blood in me
130   Hath proudly flowed in vanity till now.
Now doth it turn and ebb back to the sea,
Where it shall mingle with the state of floods°
And flow henceforth in formal majesty.
Now call we our high court of parliament.
135   And let us choose such limbs of noble counsel
That the great body of our state may go
In equal rank with the best-governed nation;
That war, or peace, or both at once, may be
As things acquainted and familiar to us,
140   In which you, father, shall have foremost hand.
Our coronation done, we will accite,°
As I before rememb'red,° all our state.°
And, God consigning° to my good intents,
No prince nor peer shall have just cause to say,
145   God shorten Harry's happy life one day!
                              Exit [with the rest].

[Scene III. *Justice Shallow's home.*]

*Enter Sir John [Falstaff], Shallow, Silence, Davy,
Bardolph, Page.*

Shallow. Nay, you shall see my orchard, where, in an
   arbor, we will eat a last year's pippin° of mine own
   graffing,° with a dish of caraways,° and so forth.
   Come, cousin Silence. And then to bed.

129 **my seeming** the way I seem outwardly   132 **state of floods**
majesty of the ocean   141 **accite** summon   142 **rememb'red** noted
(cf. line 115)   142 **state** great men of the land   143 **consigning**
signing ratification (legal term; notice Hal's knowledge of different
"languages")   V.iii.2 **pippin** type of apple   3 **graffing** grafting
3 **caraways** caraway seeds

Falstaff. 'Fore God, you have here a goodly dwelling   5
    and a rich.

Shallow. Barren, barren, barren. Beggars all, beggars
    all, Sir John. Marry, good air. Spread, Davy,
    spread, Davy. Well said, Davy.

Falstaff. This Davy serves you for good uses. He is   10
    your servingman and your husband.°

Shallow. A good varlet,° a good varlet, a very good
    varlet, Sir John. By the mass, I have drunk too
    much sack at supper. A good varlet. Now sit down,
    now sit down. Come, cousin.   15

Silence. Ah, sirrah, quoth-a,° we shall
    [*Sings*] Do nothing but eat, and make good cheer,
        And praise God for the merry year,
        When flesh° is cheap and females dear,
        And lusty lads roam here and there   20
            So merrily,
        And ever among so merrily.

Falstaff. There's a merry heart! Good Master Silence,
    I'll give you a health for that anon.

Shallow. Give Master Bardolph some wine, Davy.   25

Davy. Sweet sir, sit, I'll be with you anon. Most sweet
    sir, sit. Master page, good master page, sit. [*Makes
    them sit down, at another table.*] Proface!° What
    you want° in meat, we'll have in drink. But you
    must bear,° the heart's all.   [*Exit.*]   30

Shallow. Be merry, Master Bardolph, and, my little
    soldier there, be merry.

Silence. [*Sings*] Be merry, be merry, my wife has all,
            For women are shrews, both short
                and tall.
            'Tis merry in hall when beards wag
                all,   35

11 **husband** housemanager   12 **varlet** servant   16 **quoth-a** said he
19 **flesh** meat (with a ribald second sense)   28 **Proface!** (a dinner
welcome)   29 **want** lack   30 **bear** endure

And welcome merry Shrovetide.°
Be merry, be merry.

Falstaff. I did not think Master Silence had been a
man of this mettle.

40 *Silence.* Who, I? I have been merry° twice and once
ere now.

Enter Davy.

Davy. [*To Bardolph*] There's a dish of leather-coats°
for you.

Shallow. Davy!

45 *Davy.* Your worship! [*To Bardolph*] I'll be with you
straight.—A cup of wine, sir?

Silence. [*Sings*] A cup of wine that's brisk and fine,
                And drink unto the leman° mine,
                And a merry heart lives long-a.

50 *Falstaff.* Well said, Master Silence.

Silence. [*Sings*] And we shall be merry, now comes in
the sweet o' the night.

Falstaff. Health and long life to you, Master Silence.

Silence. [*Sings*] Fill the cup, and let it come,
                I'll pledge you a mile° to th'
55   bottom.

Shallow. Honest Bardolph, welcome. If thou want'st
anything, and wilt not call, beshrew° thy heart. [*To
the Page*] Welcome, my little tiny thief, and welcome indeed too. I'll drink to Master Bardolph,
60 and to all the cabileros° about London.

Davy. I hope to see London once ere I die.

Bardolph. And I might see you there, Davy—

36 **Shrovetide** period of feasting just before Lent   40 **merry** tipsy
(?)   42 **leather-coats** russet apples   48 **leman** sweetheart   55 **pledge
you a mile** drink in one draught though it were a mile deep
57 **beshrew** cursed be   60 **cabileros** cavaliers

Shallow. By the mass, you'll crack° a quart together,
   ha! Will you not, Master Bardolph?

Bardolph. Yea, sir, in a pottle-pot.°   65

Shallow. By God's liggens,° I thank thee. The knave
   will stick by thee, I can assure thee that. 'A will not
   out,° 'a. 'Tis true bred.

Bardolph. And I'll stick by him, sir.
                         One knocks at door.

Shallow. Why, there spoke a king. Lack nothing. Be   70
   merry. Look who's at door there, ho! Who knocks?
                              [Exit Davy.]

Falstaff. [*To Silence, seeing him drinking*] Why, now
   you have done me right.°

Silence. [*Kneels, drinks and sings*] Do me right,
                       And dub me
                           knight.°   75
                       Samingo.°

  Is't not so?

Falstaff. 'Tis so.

Silence. Is't so? Why then, say an old man can do
   somewhat.   80

                [Enter Davy.]

Davy. And't please your worship, there's one Pistol
   come from the court with news.

Falstaff. From the court! Let him come in.

                Enter Pistol.

  How now, Pistol!

Pistol. Sir John, God save you!   85

---

63 **crack** split, share   65 **pottle-pot** two-quart tankard   66 **By God's
liggens** (an oath of unknown meaning, possibly because Shallow is
tipsy)   68 **out** pass out   73 **done me right** i.e., pledged to my
pledge   75 **knight** (drinking a deep draught while kneeling entitled
one to be called "knight")   76 **Samingo** Monsieur Mingo, the hero
of the song

Falstaff. What wind blew you hither, Pistol?

Pistol. Not the ill wind which blows no man to good.
Sweet knight, thou art now one of the greatest men
in this realm.

90 *Silence.* By'r lady, I think 'a be, but goodman Puff°
of Barson.

Pistol. Puff!°
Puff i' thy teeth, most recreant coward base!
Sir John, I am thy Pistol and thy friend,
95 And helter-skelter have I rode to thee,
And tidings do I bring and lucky joys
And golden times and happy news of price.

Falstaff. I pray thee now, deliver them like a man of
this world.°

100 *Pistol.* A foutra° for the world and worldlings base!
I speak of Africa° and golden joys.

Falstaff. O base Assyrian° knight, what is thy news?
Let King Cophetua° know the truth thereof.

Silence. [*Sings*] "And Robin Hood, Scarlet, and John."

105 *Pistol.* Shall dunghill curs confront the Helicons?°
And shall good news be baffled?°
Then, Pistol, lay thy head in Furies' lap.

Shallow. Honest gentleman, I know not your breeding.

110 *Pistol.* Why then, lament therefore.°

Shallow. Give me pardon, sir. If, sir, you come with
news from the court, I take it there's but two ways,
either to utter them, or conceal them. I am, sir,
under the King, in some authority.

90 **but goodman Puff** except for yeoman Puff (whose name suggests
a shape and size as "great" as Falstaff's) 92 **Puff** swaggerer
98–99 **man of this world** ordinary man 100 **foutra** (French, *foutre*
accompanied by an indecent gesture) 101 **Africa** (where the gold
comes from) 102 **Assyrian** pun on "ass" (?) (Falstaff adopts Pistol's
style in hopes of communicating with him) 103 **Cophetua** African
king in a famous ballad 105 **Helicons** poets (?) 106 **baffled** treated
shamefully 110 **therefore** for that

Pistol. Under which king, Besonian?° Speak, or die.   *115*

Shallow. Under King Harry.

Pistol.   Harry the Fourth, or Fifth?

Shallow. Harry the Fourth.

Pistol.   A foutra for thine office!°
Sir John, thy tender lambkin now is king.
Harry the Fifth's the man. I speak the truth.
When Pistol lies, do this,° and fig me, like   *120*
The bragging Spaniard.

Falstaff. What, is the old king dead?

Pistol. As nail in door. The things I speak are just.

Falstaff. Away, Bardolph! Saddle my horse. Master
Robert Shallow, choose what office thou wilt in the   *125*
land, 'tis thine. Pistol, I will double-charge° thee
with dignities.

Bardolph. O joyful day!
I would not take a knighthood for my fortune.

Pistol. What! I do bring good news.°   *130*

Falstaff. Carry Master Silence to bed. Master Shallow,
my Lord Shallow—be what thou wilt, I am fortune's steward! Get on thy boots! We'll ride all
night! O sweet Pistol! Away, Bardolph! [*Exit
Bardolph.*] Come, Pistol, utter more to me, and   *135*
withal devise something to do thyself good. Boot,
boot, Master Shallow. I know the young king is
sick for me. Let us take any man's horses;° the
laws of England are at my commandment. Blessed
are they that have been my friends, and woe to my   *140*
Lord Chief Justice!

115 **Besonian** beggarly recruit   117 **thine office** (the King's death
terminated Shallow's appointment)   120 **do this** (make an insulting
gesture, the "fig," by putting the thumb between the index and third
fingers)   126 **double-charge** twice-load (a pistol)   130 **What! . . .
news** (a knighthood is evidently not enough for Pistol or perhaps he
is responding to Silence's sudden collapse)   138 **take any man's
horses** i.e., "press" them (for they are on the King's service)

Pistol. Let vultures vile seize on his lungs also!
　"Where is the life that late I led?"° say they.
　Why, here it is. Welcome these pleasant days!
　　　　　　　　　　　　　Exit [with the rest].

[Scene IV. *London.*]

*Enter Beadle° and three or four Officers [with
　Hostess Quickly and Doll Tearsheet].*

Hostess. No, thou arrant knave, I would to God that
　I might die, that I might have thee hanged.° Thou
　hast drawn my shoulder out of joint.

Beadle. The constables have delivered her over to
5　me, and she shall have whipping-cheer,° I warrant
　her. There hath been a man or two killed about°
　her.

Doll. Nut-hook,° nut-hook, you lie. Come on, I'll tell
　thee what, thou damned tripe-visaged° rascal, and
10　the child I go with do miscarry, thou wert better
　thou hadst struck thy mother, thou paper-faced°
　villain.

Hostess. O the Lord, that Sir John were come! I
　would make this a bloody day to somebody. But
15　I pray God the fruit of her womb miscarry!°

Beadle. If it do, you shall have a dozen of cushions
　again. You have but eleven° now. Come, I charge

---

143 **Where ... led** scrap of an old song   V.iv.s.d. **Beadle** parish officer (who punished petty offenders)   2 **hanged** i.e., for murdering
me   5 **whipping-cheer** hospitality of the whip   6 **about** (1) because
of, or (2) in the presence of   8 **Nut-hook** (slang for the "catchpole"
carried by beadles)   9 **tripe-visaged** pock-marked   11 **paper-faced**
thin and pale   15 **miscarry** (she goes along with Doll's threat)
17 **eleven** (Doll having used one to simulate pregnancy)

you both go with me, for the man is dead that you
and Pistol beat amongst you.

Doll. I'll tell you what, you thin man in a censer,° I   20
will have you as soundly swinged° for this—you
blue-bottle° rogue, you filthy famished correctioner,
if you be not swinged, I'll forswear half-kirtles.°

Beadle. Come, come, you she-knight-errant, come.

Hostess. O God, that right should thus overcome   25
might!° Well, of sufferance° comes ease.

Doll. Come, you rogue, come. Bring me to a justice.

Hostess. Ay, come, you starved bloodhound.

Doll. Goodman death, goodman bones!

Hostess. Thou atomy,° thou!   30

Doll. Come, you thin thing! Come, you rascal!°

Beadle. Very well.   [*Exeunt.*]

[Scene V. *London.*]

Enter Strewers of rushes.

First Strewer. More rushes, more rushes!°

Second Strewer. The trumpets have sounded twice.

Third Strewer. 'Twill be two o'clock ere they come
from the coronation. Dispatch, dispatch.   [*Exeunt.*]

---

20 **thin man in a censer** figure of a man stamped on the lid of a pan
for burning incense (?)   21 **swinged** beaten   22 **blue-bottle** (beadles,
like modern policemen, wore blue coats)   23 **half-kirtles** skirts
25–26 **O God . . . might!** (a typical Quickly blunder)   26 **of sufferance** out of suffering (but "sufferance" means tolerance)   30 **atomy**
atom (does she mean "anatomy," "cadaver"?)   31 **rascal** lean deer
V.v.1 **rushes** (the usual floor covering; here, strewn in the streets)

*Trumpets sound, and the King and his Train pass
over the stage. After them enter Falstaff, Shallow,
Pistol, Bardolph, and the Boy.*

5 *Falstaff.* Stand here by me, Master Shallow. I will
   make the King do you grace.° I will leer° upon him
   as 'a comes by, and do but mark the countenance
   that he will give me.

   Pistol. God bless thy lungs, good knight.

10 *Falstaff.* Come here, Pistol, stand behind me. [*To
   Shallow*] O, if I had had time to have made new
   liveries,° I would have bestowed the thousand
   pound I borrowed of you. But 'tis no matter; this
   poor show doth better. This doth infer° the zeal I
15 had to see him.

   Pistol. It doth so.

   Falstaff. It shows my earnestness of affection—

   Pistol. It doth so.

   Falstaff. My devotion—

20 *Pistol.* It doth, it doth, it doth.

   Falstaff. As it were, to ride day and night, and not to
   deliberate, not to remember, not to have patience
   to shift me°—

   Shallow. It is best, certain.

25 *Falstaff.* But to stand stained with travel, and sweat-
   ing with desire to see him, thinking of nothing else,
   putting all affairs else in oblivion, as if there were
   nothing else to be done but to see him.

   Pistol. 'Tis *"semper idem,"*° for *"obsque hoc nihil
30 est."*° 'Tis all in every part.°

---

6 do you grace show you favor   **6 leer** glance slyly (instead of
reverently bowing his head)   **12 liveries** servants' uniforms   **14 infer**
imply   **23 shift me** change my clothes   **29 semper idem** ever the
same   **29–30 obsque hoc nihil est** without this, nothing (both
phrases are mottoes, the second garbled)   **30 all in every part** absolute (another motto)

Shallow. 'Tis so, indeed.

Pistol. My knight, I will inflame thy noble liver,°
And make thee rage.
Thy Doll, and Helen of thy noble thoughts,
Is in base durance and contagious° prison,   35
Haled thither by most mechanical° and dirty hand.
Rouse up revenge from ebon° den with fell
    Alecto's° snake,
For Doll is in. Pistol speaks nought but truth.

Falstaff. I will deliver her.

Pistol. There roared the sea, and trumpet clangor
    sounds.   40

[*Trumpets sound.*] *Enter the King and his Train*
    [*including the Lord Chief Justice*].

Falstaff. God save thy Grace, King Hal, my royal Hal!

Pistol. The heavens thee guard and keep, most royal
    imp° of fame!

Falstaff. God save thee, my sweet boy!

King. My Lord Chief Justice, speak to that vain man.   45

Chief Justice. Have you your wits? Know you what
    'tis you speak?

Falstaff. My king! My Jove! I speak to thee, my heart!

King. I know thee not,° old man. Fall to thy prayers.
How ill white hairs becomes a fool and jester!
I have long dreamt of such a kind of man,   50
So surfeit-swelled, so old, and so profane,
But, being awaked, I do despise my dream.
Make less thy body hence,° and more thy grace.
Leave gormandizing. Know the grave doth gape
For thee thrice wider than for other men.   55

32 **liver** seat of the passions (love as well as rage)   35 **contagious**
pestilential   36 **mechanical** working-class   37 **ebon** black   37 **Alecto**
one of the Furies   43 **imp** (1) scion (2) graft (in falconry or gardening—that which adds to)   48 **I know thee not** (see Matthew 25:10–
12)   53 **hence** henceforth

Reply not to me with a fool-born° jest.
Presume not that I am the thing I was,
For God doth know, so shall the world perceive,
That I have turned away my former self.
60   So will I those that kept me company.
When thou dost hear I am as I have been,
Approach me, and thou shalt be as thou wast,
The tutor and the feeder of my riots.
Till then, I banish thee, on pain of death,
65   As I have done the rest of my misleaders,
Not to come near our person by ten mile.
For competence of life° I will allow you,
That lack of means enforce you not to evils.
And, as we hear you do reform yourselves,
70   We will, according to your strengths and qualities,
Give you advancement. Be it your charge, my lord,
To see performed the tenor of my word.
Set on.   [*Exeunt the King and his Train.*]

Falstaff. Master Shallow, I owe you a thousand pound.

75   *Shallow.* Yea, marry, Sir John, which I beseech you
to let me have home with me.

Falstaff. That can hardly be, Master Shallow. Do not
you grieve at this. I shall be sent for in private to
him. Look you, he must seem thus to the world.
80   Fear not your advancements; I will be the man yet
that shall make you great.

Shallow. I cannot perceive how, unless you give me
your doublet and stuff me out with straw. I beseech
you, good Sir John, let me have five hundred of my
85   thousand.

Falstaff. Sir, I will be as good as my word. This that
you heard was but a color.°

Shallow. A color° that I fear you will die° in, Sir John.

---

56 **fool-born** (note the pun)   67 **competence of life** allowance for
necessaries   87 **color** pretense   88 **color** (punning on "choler," and
"collar," i.e., noose)   88 **die** (punning on "dye")

Falstaff. Fear no colors.° Go with me to dinner. Come,
  Lieutenant° Pistol. Come, Bardolph. I shall be sent   90
  for soon at night.°

  *Enter [Lord Chief] Justice and Prince John [of
  Lancaster, and Officers].*

Chief Justice. Go, carry Sir John Falstaff to the Fleet.°
  Take all his company along with him.

Falstaff. My lord, my lord—

Chief Justice. I cannot now speak. I will hear you
  soon.   95
  Take them away.

Pistol. "Si fortuna me tormenta, spero contenta."°

  Exeunt [all but Prince John and the Chief Justice].

Lancaster. I like this fair proceeding of the King's.
  He hath intent his wonted° followers
  Shall all be very well provided for,   100
  But all are banished till their conversations
  Appear more wise and modest to the world.

Chief Justice. And so they are.

Lancaster. The King hath called his parliament, my
  lord.

Chief Justice. He hath.   105

Lancaster. I will lay odds that, ere this year expire,
  We bear our civil swords° and native fire
  As far as France. I heard a bird so sing,
  Whose music, to my thinking, pleased the King.
  Come, will you hence?   [*Exeunt.*]   110

---

89 **colors** enemy flags (a proverb)   90 **Lieutenant** (note the promo-
tion)   91 **soon at night** at early evening   92 **Fleet** prison for distinguished prisoners temporarily detained for inquiry ("I will hear
you soon"—line 95)   97 **Si fortuna . . . contenta** if fortune torments
me, hope contents me   99 **wonted** customary   107 **civil swords**
i.e., swords presently used in civil war

EPILOGUE°

[Spoken by a Dancer]

First my fear,° then my curtsy, last my speech. My
fear is your displeasure; my curtsy my duty; and my
speech to beg your pardons. If you look for a good
speech now, you undo° me, for what I have to say
5 is of mine own making, and what indeed I should say
will, I doubt,° prove mine own marring. But to the
purpose, and so to the venture. Be it known to you,
as it is very well, I was lately here in the end of a displeasing play,° to pray your patience for it and to
10 promise you a better. I meant indeed to pay you with
this, which, if like an ill venture° it come unluckily
home, I break,° and you, my gentle creditors, lose.
Here I promised you I would be and here I commit
my body to your mercies. Bate me some° and I will
15 pay you some and, as most debtors do, promise you
infinitely, and so I kneel down before you, but, indeed, to pray for the Queen.

If my tongue cannot entreat you to acquit me, will
you command me to use my legs? And yet that were
20 but light payment, to dance out of your debt. But a
good conscience will make any possible satisfaction,
and so would I. All the gentlewomen here have forgiven me.° If the gentlemen will not, then the gentlemen do not agree with the gentlewomen, which was
25 never seen in such an assembly.

One word more, I beseech you. If you be not too
much cloyed with fat meat, our humble author will

Epilogue (evidently, as in *Midsummer Night's Dream*, a mingling of
epilogues: the first paragraph is for one occasion, the second and
third for another, and epilogues for any occasion could be built up
out of separate parts)   **1 fear** stage fright (pretended)   **4 undo** ruin
6 doubt fear   **8–9 displeasing play** (unidentified)   **11 venture** i.e.,
business venture   **12 break** (1) break my promise (2) go bankrupt
14 Bate me some forgive part of my debt   **22–23 have forgiven me**
(perhaps the Epilogue was spoken by the Page)

continue the story, with Sir John in it,° and make you
merry with fair Katharine of France. Where, for anything I know, Falstaff shall die of a sweat, unless   *30*
already 'a be killed with your hard opinions, for Old-
castle° died martyr, and this is not the man. My
tongue is weary. When my legs are too, I will bid you
good night.

        [End with a dance.]

        F I N I S

28 **Sir John in it** (but Falstaff does not appear in *Henry V*)
31–32 **Oldcastle** (Sir John Oldcastle was the name of the Prince's
boon companion in the source play, *The Famous Victories of Henry
V*, and, evidently, in Shakespeare's first versions of the *Henry IV*
plays. *Old.* appears as a speech tag at Quarto *2 Henry IV* I.ii.125.
[See also the Signet Classic edition of *Part One*, I.ii.43–44 and
pp. 181–208.] In this Epilogue, Shakespeare is saying his Falstaff
is not the historical Oldcastle, executed in 1417 and honored by
Protestant chroniclers as a Lollard martyr [though Catholic chroniclers said he was a drunkard and a robber]. The name was probably
removed from Shakespeare's plays at the behest of Oldcastle's de-
scendant, Lord Cobham—who was promptly nicknamed by the
Essex faction Sir John Falstaff).

Textual Note

Henry IV [*Part Two*] comes to us in two—or really, three—texts: the Folio of 1623 and the Quarto of 1600; the Quarto, however, occurs in two forms, the second (Qb) a modification of the first, evidently to admit a scene (III.i) omitted in Qa. The researches of a number of scholars[1] have now converged to give us a history of these three texts.

Shakespeare wrote the play in late 1597 or early 1598, and from his manuscript (called "foul papers") the Chamberlain's Men had a transcript made to serve as the promptbook for performances. In 1600, possibly to forestall pirating, the company sold the publication rights to *Much Ado About Nothing* and *2 Henry IV*, which were then entered in the Stationers' Register on August 23. The foul papers were sent to the printshop of Valentine Simmes for publication in quarto form. While there, perhaps while the copy was being cast off into page-length units for the compositors, the sheets containing Act III, scene i were misplaced (perhaps mixed into the sheets of *Much Ado*, which were in the same handwriting). At this point, the deputy of the Bishop of London, whose task it was to censor the play, read the manuscript and ordered the deletion of eight short passages that might conceivably compare Elizabeth to Richard II or otherwise tend to rebellion. He did not, however, see and censor the longer and more important references to Richard in Act III,

[1] Notably J. Dover Wilson, Matthias Shaaber, James McManaway, and John H. Smith.

scene i, for the sheets containing that scene had been mislaid. In due course, Simmes and his men finished and issued the first quarto version of *2 Henry IV*, Qa, and turned to work on *Much Ado*. But then someone discovered a scene was missing, and Simmes had to put aside *Much Ado* and, at some cost to himself, correct his error by resetting two leaves as four to accommodate the omitted scene. Simmes then issued this second version of the Quarto, Qb.

Shakespeare's acting company, meanwhile, was using a transcript of the foul papers for their prompt copy and altering it to indicate their stage-practices: removing profanity, omitting mute characters, revising stage business, and so on. There is, of course, no way to tell whether Shakespeare agreed to these changes or whether they simply accumulated over the years. Further, at some point, the prompt copy itself may have been recopied—perhaps for a collector of plays, perhaps preparatory to printing the Folio; if so, the copyist was probably someone used to working with play texts, who systematically took out colloquial and vulgar expressions, improved the punctuation, and rewrote the stage directions. The Folio text of the play was then set up either directly from the altered prompt copy or indirectly through a transcript of it.

Thus, Qa (supplemented by III.i from Qb) comes closest to Shakespeare's original words and imagined staging—though often in the form of "bunched" stage directions (simply an initial listing at the beginning of a scene of the characters who will appear in it). The Folio suggests alterations in staging that Shakespeare may (or may not) have participated in, and it supplies eight passages the censor removed, but for the most part the Folio is authoritative only to correct obvious blunders or otherwise help in deciphering the oddly punctuated quarto text. Accordingly, I have modernized spelling and punctuation, regularized the speech-tags and the printing of prose and verse, and supplied the Globe act and scene divisions used in standard reference books, but otherwise I have followed the quartos closely, with a few exceptions.

The eight passages I have supplied from the Folio that

do not appear in Qa or Qb are: I.i.166–79, *You cast . . . to be?* I.i.189–209, *The gentle . . . follow him.* I.iii.21–24, *Till we . . . admitted.* I.iii.36–55, *Yes, if . . . Or else.* I.iii.85–108, *Let us . . . worst.* II.iii.23–45, *He had . . . grave.* IV.i.55–79, *And with . . . wrong.* IV.i.101–37, *O, my . . . the King.* The Folio also includes many small expansions, some of a word or two, others of whole sentences or phrases. I have included the longer ones, but not those so short as likely to be mere compositors' expansions. Finally, the list of characters appearing at the end of the Folio text I have here reproduced at the beginning.

Occasionally I have adopted certain readings that do not appear in the quartos; these readings are listed in the following, with the accepted reading first in italics, the rejected reading second in roman. Since, in almost all these cases, I have used the Folio reading instead of the quartos', unless otherwise indicated, the accepted reading is from the Folio (F), the rejected from quarto Qa.

Induction   36 *Where* When   40s.d. *Rumor* [ed.] Rumours

I.i.96 *say so* [Q omits]   161 *Lord Bardolph* Vmfr[evile]   162 *Morton* Bard. [Mour. at line 163]   164 *Lean on your* Leaue on you 166–79 [Q omits; F, with editorial *brought* from "bring" at line 178]   189–209 [Q omits]

I.ii.40 *smooth* smoothy   51 *Where's Bardolph* [after "through it" in Q]   52 *into* in   100 *hath* haue   101 *an age* [ed.] an ague [Q] age [F]   179 *this age shapes them, are* his age shapes the one 211–12 *and Prince Harry* [Q omits]

I.iii.s.d. [Q includes a mute character, Fauconbridge]   21–24 [Q omits]   26 *case* [ed.] cause [F, Q]   36–55 [Q omits]   71 *Are* And 79 *He . . . Welsh* French and Welch he leaues his/back vnarmde, they   85–108 [Q omits]   109 *Mowbray* Bish.

II.i.14 *and that* [Q omits]   21 *vice* view   25 *continuantly* continually   44 *Sir John* [Q omits]   151 *tapestries* tapestrie   175 *Basingstoke* Billingsgate

II.ii.s.d. *Poins, with* [ed.] Poynes, sir Iohn Russel, with   15 *viz.* with 16 *ones* once   22 *thy* the   22 *made a shift to* [Q omits]   79 *e'en now* [ed.] enow [Q] euen now [F]   89 *rabbit* rabble   125–33 [Q and F give to Poins]   132 *familiars* family

II.iii.11 *endeared* endeere   23–44 [Q omits]

II.iv.12s.d. [occurs after line 18, Q; F omits]   13 Will Dra[wer] [Q; F omits]   178 *Die men* Men   226 *A* Ah   273 *master's* master 286 *so* to

III.i.26 *thy* them [Qb]   81 *nature of* natures or [Qb]

III.ii.1 *come on.* [Qa] come on sir [Qb]   114 *Falstaff. Prick him.* Iohn prickes him. [as stage direction, Q]   147 *his* [Q omits] 296 *would* [ed.] will [F] wooll [Q]   308 *Exeunt* [ed.] exit   309–43 [Q assigns this speech to Shallow]   323 *invisible* [ed.] inuincible [Q, F]   325 *ever* ouer

IV.i.s.d. *Mowbray, Hastings* Mowbray, Bardolfe, Hastings   12 *could* ["would" in some copies of Q]   30 *Then, my lord* [omitted in some copies of Q]   36 *appeared* [ed.] appeare   45 *figure* ["figures" in some copies of Q]   55–79 [Q omits] After line 92, line omitted: And consecrate commotions bitter edge. [appears in some copies of Q] After line 93, line omitted: To brother borne an houshold cruelty [appears in some copies of Q, but it seems probable that Shakespeare had marked on his ms. that both these lines were to be deleted]   101–37 [Q omits]   114 *force* [ed.] forc'd [F]   178 *And* [ed.] At [Q, F]   183 *not that. If* [ed.] not, that if [F, Q]

IV.ii.1 [notice that there should be no scene division, the action being continuous, and the stage not having emptied. The stage direction at IV.i.224 follows Q]   8 *Than* That   19 *imagined* [ed.] imagine [Q, F]   24 *Employ* Imply   48 *this* his   67–71 [as in F; Q assigns 67–68 to Bishop, 69–71 to Prince]   117 *and such acts as yours* [Q omits]   122 *these traitors* this traitour

IV.iii.1 [as at IV.ii.1, there should be no scene division]

IV.iv.33 *he's* he is   52 *Canst thou tell that?* [Q omits]   77 *others* other   104 *write* wet   104 *letters* termes   120 *and will break out* [Q omits]   132 *Softly, pray* [Q omits]

IV.v.1 [as at IV.ii.1, there should be no scene division]   13 *altered* vttred [Q, some copies]   49 *How fares your Grace?* [Q omits]   60–61 [one line in Q]   74 *culling* toling   75–79 [text follows F] Our thigh, packt with waxe our mouthes with hony,/We bring it to the hiue: and like the bees,/Are murdred for our paines, this bitter taste/Yeelds his engrossements to the ending father [Q]   79s.d. at line 81 in Q   81 *hath* hands   107 *Which* Whom   160 *worst of* worse then   161 *is* [Q omits]   177 *O my son* [Q omits]   178 *it* [Q omits]   204 *my* [ed.] thy [Q,F]   220 *My gracious liege* [Q omits]

V.i.24 *the other day* [Q omits]   25 *Hinckley* Hunkly   50 *but a very* [Q omits]

V.ii.s.d. *Enter the Earl of Warwick and the Lord Chief Justice.* Enter Warwike, duke Humphrey, L. chiefe Iustice, Thomas Clarence, Prince, Iohn Westmerland   46 *mix* mixt

V.iii.5–6 *a, a* [Q omits]   35 *wag* wags   129 *knighthood* Knight

V.iv.s.d. *Beadle* Sincklo [Q, and so in the Q speech-tags for this scene; Sincklo was a small-part actor in Shakespeare's company]

V.v.25 *Falstaff* [Q omits]   30 *all* [Q omits]

The Sources of *Henry IV, Part Two*

As was his custom in the histories, Shakespeare developed *Henry IV* [*Part Two*] from several sources. Chiefly, he used his favorite, Raphael Holinshed's *Chronicles of England, Scotland, and Ireland* (probably the 1587 edition), and an old, anonymous play, *The Famous Victories of Henry V* (performed before 1588, but the earliest extant printing is of 1598). Almost certainly, he drew a few details from Samuel Daniel's long narrative poem, *The First Four Books of the Civil Wars between the Two Houses of Lancaster and York* (1595). He may also have looked at Edward Hall's earlier chronicle, more moralistic than Holinshed's, *The Union of the Two Noble and Illustre Famelies of Lancastre and Yorke* (1548) or John Stow's *The Chronicles of England* (1580). The story of the Prince's giving the Lord Chief Justice a box on the ear and being sent to prison for it was first printed in Sir Thomas Elyot's *Boke Named the Governour* (1531), though the story was widely retold and much stressed in the *Famous Victories*.

Shakespeare took from the *Famous Victories* (reprinted in the Signet Classic edition of *1 Henry IV*) the broad outlines of the comic sections of Parts One and Two and the battles of *Henry V*. The old play was strong on Hal's roistering and his swaggering companions, and, though it has neither Pistol nor Mistress Quickly, it does offer a crude prototype of Falstaff in "Jockey" or "Sir John Oldcastle" (see p. 169), though he is no more than a tadpole compared to Shakespeare's full-blown conception. Holinshed,

Daniel, and the other sources were used for the portrait of Henry IV as a king sick in body and soul and also for facts about the various rebellions and battles.

Shakespeare saved from his chronicle sources even small details if they fitted his theme, the failure to fit into a larger order because of a selfish appetite for food, drink, words, or power. Thus, he dutifully recounted from Holinshed the drinking between the armies, the Archbishop's preoccupation with his articles, and the floods that mark Henry IV's death. At the same time, he altered large patterns of history where it suited his purpose. Of these changes, one stands out particularly. Shakespeare attributes the "betrayal" of the rebels to Prince John as well as to Westmoreland, though Holinshed had painted Westmoreland as the sole author of the strategy. Obviously, to understand the play fully, we must be able to account for such a marked and faintly discrediting change.

It is interesting, too, to see how Shakespeare's style of thought differs from his contemporaries'. One can see it by examining three episodes from Shakespeare's play in which he does follow his sources fairly closely. They are rich moments in the Shakespearean world: the scene of the King's death with Hal's precipitate taking of the crown; the coronation scene with the rejection of Falstaff; the forgiving of the Lord Chief Justice. Holinshed (pp. 182–84) sees the first with the eye of a political reporter, interested in events and statecraft, while Daniel sees the King's death in terms of the psychology of the noble classes (pp. 185–89). The anonymous author of the *Famous Victories* pleased his broader public with the almost folkloric regeneration of a prodigal son (see Signet Classic *1 Henry IV*, pp. 181–208). Reading *2 Henry IV* IV.v, V.v, and V.ii against these parts of the sources, one experiences not only Shakespeare's fusing of popular and courtly traditions but also that special transmuting touch which was his alone.

from *Chronicles of England, Scotland, and Ireland*

[A New Conspiracy Against Henry IV]

But at the same time, to his further disquieting, there was a conspiracy put in practice against him at home by the Earl of Northumberland, who had conspired with Richard Scroop, Archbishop of York, Thomas Mowbray, Earl Marshal, son to Thomas Duke of Norfolk, who for the quarrel betwixt him and King Henry had been banished (as ye have heard), the Lords Hastings, Falconbridge, Bardolph, and divers others. It was appointed that they should meet all together with their whole power upon Yorkswold, at a day assigned, and that the Earl of Northumberland should be chieftain, promising to bring with him a great number of Scots. The Archbishop, accompanied with the Earl Marshal, devised certain articles of such matters, as it was supposed that not only the commonalty of the realm but also the nobility found themselves grieved with, which articles they showed first unto such of their adherents as were near about them and after sent them abroad to their friends further off, assuring them that for redress of such oppressions they would shed the last drop of blood in their bodies, if need were.

The Archbishop, not meaning to stay after he saw himself accompanied with a great number of men that came flocking to York to take his part in this quarrel, forthwith discovered his enterprise, causing the articles aforesaid to be set up in the public streets of the city of York and upon the gates of the monasteries, that each man might understand the cause that moved him to rise in arms against the King, the reforming whereof did not yet appertain unto him. Hereupon knights, esquires, gentlemen, yeomen, and other of the commons as well of the city, towns, and countries about, being allured either for desire of change or else for desire to see a reformation in such things as were mentioned in the articles, assembled together in great numbers. And the Archbishop, coming forth amongst them clad in armor, encouraged, exhorted and by all means he could pricked them forth to take the enterprise in hand and manfully to continue in their begun purpose, promising forgiveness of sins to all them whose hap it was to die in the quarrel. And thus not only all the citizens of York but all other in the countries about that were able to bear weapon came to the Archbishop and the Earl Marshal. Indeed, the respect that men had to the Archbishop caused them to like the better of the cause, since the gravity of his age, his integrity of life and incomparable learning with the reverent aspect of his amiable personage moved all men to have him in no small estimation.

The King, advertised of these matters, meaning to prevent them, left his journey into Wales and marched with all speed toward the north parts. Also, Ralph Neville, Earl of Westmoreland, that was not far off, together with the Lord John of Lancaster, the King's son, being informed of this rebellious attempt, assembled together such power as they might make, and together with those which were appointed to attend on the said Lord John to defend the borders against the Scots (as the Lord Henry Fitzhugh, the Lord Ralph Evers, the Lord Robert Umfreville, and others) made forward against the rebels, and coming into a plain within the forest of Gaultree, caused their standards to be pitched down in like sort as the Archbishop had pitched his, over against them, being far stronger in number of people than the other, for (as some write) there were of the rebels at the least twenty thousand men.

When the Earl of Westmoreland perceived the force of

the adversaries, and that they lay still and attempted not to come forward upon him, he subtly devised how to quell their purpose and forthwith dispatched messengers unto the Archbishop to understand the cause, as it were, of that great assembly, and for what cause (contrary to the King's peace) they came so in armor. The Archbishop answered that he took nothing in hand against the King's peace, but that whatsoever he did tended rather to advance the peace and quiet of the commonwealth than otherwise. And where he and his company were in arms, it was for fear of the King, to whom he could have no free access by reason of such a multitude of flatterers as were about him. And therefore he maintained that—his purpose—to be good and profitable, as well for the King himself as for the realm, if men were willing to understand a truth. And herewith he showed forth a scroll in which the articles were written whereof before ye have heard.

The messengers, returning to the Earl of Westmoreland, showed him what they had heard and brought from the Archbishop. When he had read the articles, he showed in word and countenance outwardly that he liked of the Archbishop's holy and virtuous intent and purpose, promising that he and his would prosecute the same in assisting the Archbishop, who, rejoicing hereat, gave credit to the Earl and persuaded the Earl Marshal (against his will, as it were) to go with him to a place appointed for them to commune together. Here, when they were met with like number on either part, the articles were read over, and, without any more ado, the Earl of Westmoreland and those that were with him agreed to do their best to see that a reformation might be had according to the same.

The Earl of Westmoreland, using more policy than the rest, "Well," said he, "then our travel is come to the wished end; and where our people have been long in armor, let them depart home to their wonted trades and occupations. In the meantime, let us drink together in sign of agreement that the people on both sides may see it and know that it is true that we be light at a point." They had no sooner shaken hands together but that a knight was sent straightways from the Archbishop to bring word to the people that there was peace concluded, commanding each man to lay aside his arms and to resort home to their houses. The people, beholding such tokens of peace as shaking of hands and drinking together of the lords in loving manner, they, being already wearied with the unaccustomed travail of war, brake up their field and returned homewards. But, in the meantime, whilst the people of the Archbishop's side withdrew away, the number of the contrary part increased, according to order given by the Earl of Westmoreland. And yet the Archbishop perceived not that he was deceived until the Earl of Westmoreland arrested both him and the Earl Marshal with diverse other. Thus saith Walsingham.

But others write somewhat otherwise of this matter, affirming that the Earl of Westmoreland, indeed, and the Lord Ralph Evers procured the Archbishop and the Earl Marshal to come to a communication with them upon a ground just in the midway betwixt both the armies, where the Earl of Westmoreland in talk declared to them how perilous an enterprise they had taken in hand so to raise the people and to move war against the King, advising them therefore to submit themselves without further delay unto the King's mercy and his son the Lord John, who was present there in the field with banners spread, ready to try the matter by dint of sword if they refused this counsel. And therefore he willed them to remember themselves well, and, if they would not yield and crave the King's pardon, he bade them do their best to defend themselves.

Hereupon as well the Archbishop as the Earl Marshal submitted themselves unto the King and to his son the Lord John that was there present and returned not to their army. Whereupon their troops scaled [i.e., came away in small groups] and fled their ways, but, being pursued, many were taken, many slain, and many spoiled of that that they had about them and so permitted to go their ways.

Howsoever the matter was handled, true it is that the Archbishop and the Earl Marshal were brought to Pomfret to the King, who in this meanwhile was advanced thither with his power, and from thence he went to York, whither the prisoners were also brought, and there beheaded the morrow after Whitsunday in a place without the city, that is to understand, the Archbishop himself, the Earl Marshal, Sir John Lampley, and Sir Robert Plumpton. Unto all which persons though indemnity were promised, yet was the same to none of them at any hand performed. By the issue hereof, I mean the death of the foresaid, but specially of the Archbishop, the prophecy of a sickly canon of Bridlington in Yorkshire fell out to be true, who darkly enough foretold this matter and the unfortunate event thereof in these words hereafter following, saying:

> *Pacem tractabunt, sed fraudem subter arabunt,*
>   *Pro nulla marca, salvabitur ille hierarcha.*
> [They will treat for peace but foster secret deceit; nor shall that great priest be saved for all his distinction—Holinshed's marginal translation]

The Archbishop suffered death very constantly, insomuch as the common people took it he died a martyr, affirming that certain miracles were wrought as well in the field where he was executed as also in the place where he was buried. And immediately upon such bruits, both men and women began to worship his dead carcass, whom they loved so much when he was alive, till they were forbidden by the King's friends, and for fear gave over to visit the place of his sepulture. The Earl Marshal's body, by the King's leave, was buried in the cathedral church, many lamenting his destiny. But his head was set on a pole aloft on the walls for a certain space, till by the King's permission (after the same had suffered many a hot, sunny day and many a wet shower of rain) it was taken down and buried together with the body.

After the King, accordingly as seemed to him good, had ransomed and punished by grievous fines the citizens of York (which had borne armor on their Archbishop's side against him), he departed from York with an army of thirty and seven thousand fighting men furnished with all provision necessary, marching northwards against the Earl of Northumberland. At his coming to Durham, the Lord Hastings, the Lord Falconbridge, Sir John Coleville of the Dale, and Sir John Griffith, being convicted of the conspiracy, were there beheaded.

[Just Before the Death of Henry IV]

In this year [1411] and upon the twelfth day of October, were there three floods in the Thames, the one following upon the other and no ebbing in between, which thing no man then living could remember the like to be seen.

[The Death of King Henry IV]

In this fourteenth and last year of King Henry's reign, a council was holden in the Whitefriars in London, at the which, among other things, order was taken for ships and galleys to be builded and made ready and all other things necessary to be provided for a voyage which he meant to make into the Holy Land, there to recover the city of Jerusalem from the infidels. For it grieved him to consider the great malice of Christian princes, that were bent upon a mischievous purpose to destroy one another, to the peril of their own souls, rather than to make war against the enemies of the Christian faith, as in conscience (it seemed to him) they were bound. He held his Christmas this year at Eltham, being sore vexed with sickness, so that it was thought sometime that he had been dead. Notwithstanding, it pleased God that he somewhat recovered his strength again, and so passed that Christmas with as much joy as he might.

The morrow after Candlemas day began a Parliament, which he had called at London, but he departed this life before the same Parliament was ended, for now that his provisions were ready and that he was furnished with sufficient treasure, soldiers, captains, victuals, munitions, tall ships, strong galleys, and all things necessary for such a royal journey as he pretended to take into the Holy Land, he was eftsoons taken with a sore sickness—which was not a leprosy stricken by the hand of God (saith Master Hall), as foolish friars imagined, but a very apoplexy of the which he languished till his appointed hour, and had none other grief nor malady, so that what man ordaineth, God altereth at his good will and pleasure, not giving place more to the prince than to the poorest creature living, when He seeth His time to dispose of him this way or that, as to His omnipotent power and Divine Providence seemeth expedient.

During this last sickness, he caused his crown (as some write) to be set on a pillow at his bed's head, and suddenly his pangs so sore troubled him that he lay as though all his vital spirits had been from him departed. Such as were about him, thinking verily that he had been departed, covered his face with a linen cloth.

The Prince, his son, being hereof advertised, entered into the chamber, took away the crown, and departed. The father, being suddenly revived out of that trance, quickly perceived the lack of his crown, and, having knowledge that the Prince his son had taken it away, caused him to come before his presence, requiring of him what he meant, so to misuse himself. The Prince with a good audacity answered, "Sir, to mine and all men's judgments, you seemed dead in this world, wherefore I, as your next heir apparent, took that as mine own and not as yours."

"Well, fair son," said the King with a great sigh, "what right I had to it, God knoweth."

"Well," said the Prince, "if you die king, I will have the garland and trust to keep it with the sword against all mine enemies, as you have done."

"Then," said the King, "I commit all to God, and remember you to do well." With that he turned himself in his bed and shortly after departed to God in a chamber of the Abbot's of Westminster called "Jerusalem". . . . he was so suddenly and grievously taken, that such as were about him feared lest he would have died presently, wherefore to relieve him (if it were possible) they bare him into a chamber that was next at hand, belonging to the Abbot of Westminster, where they laid him on a pallet before the fire and used all remedies to revive him. At length, recovering his speech and understanding, and perceiving himself in a strange place which he knew not, he willed to know if the chamber had any particular name, whereunto answer was made that it was called "Jerusalem." "Then," said the King, "lauds be given to the Father of Heaven, for now I know that I shall die here in this chamber, according to the prophecy of me declared, that I should depart this life in Jerusalem."

Whether this was true that so he spake, as one that gave too much credit to foolish prophecies and vain tales, or whether it was feigned, as in such cases it commonly happeneth, we leave it to the advised reader to judge.

[The Coronation of Henry V]

He was crowned the ninth of April, being Passion Sunday, which was a sore, ruggie, and tempestuous day, with wind, snow and sleet, that men greatly marveled thereat, making divers interpretations what the same might signify. But the King even at first appointing with himself to show that in his person princely honors should change public manners, he determined to put on him the shape of a new man. For whereas aforetime he had made himself a companion unto misruly mates of dissolute order and life, he now banished them all from his presence (but not unrewarded or else unpreferred), inhibiting them upon a great pain not once to approach, lodge, or sojourn within ten miles of his court or presence; and in their places he chose men of gravity, wit, and high policy, by whose wise counsel he might at all times rule to his honor and dignity, calling to mind how once, to high offense of the King his father, he had with his fist stricken the Chief Justice for sending one of his minions (upon desert) to prison, when the Justice stoutly commanded himself also straight to ward, and he (then Prince) obeyed. The King after expelled him out of his Privy Council, banished him the court, and made the Duke of Clarence (his younger brother) President of Council in his stead.

SAMUEL DANIEL

from *The First Four Books of the Civil Wars between the Two Houses of Lancaster and York*

The Third Book

115

But now the King retires him to his peace,
A peace much like a feeble sick man's sleep
(Wherein his waking pains do never cease
Though seeming rest his closed eyes doth keep),
For, O, no peace could ever so release
His intricate turmoils and sorrows deep,
But that his cares kept waking all his life
Continue on till death conclude the strife.

116

Whose herald sickness, being sent before
With full commission to denounce his end,
And pain, and grief, enforcing more and more,
Besieged the hold that could not long defend,
And so consumed all that emboldening store
Of hot gain-striving blood that did contend,
Wearing the wall so thin that now the mind
Might well look through, and his frailty find.

117

When, lo, as if the vapors vanished were,
Which heat of boiling blood and health did breed
(To cloud the sense that nothing might appear
Unto the thought, that which it was indeed),
The lightened soul began to see more clear
How much it was abused, and notes with heed
The plain discovered falsehood open laid
Of ill persuading flesh that so betrayed.

118

And lying on his last afflicted bed
Where death and conscience both before him stand,
The one holding out a book, wherein he read
In bloody lines the deeds of his own hand;
The other shows a glass, which figured
An ugly form of foul corrupted sand—
Both bringing horror in the highest degree
With what he was, and what he straight should be.

119

Which seeing, all confused, trembling with fear,
He lay awhile, as overthrown in spirit,
At last commands some that attending were
To fetch the crown and set it in his sight,
On which with fixed eye and heavy cheer
Casting a look, "O God," saith he, "what right
I had to thee my soul doth now conceive—
Thee, which with blood I got, with horror leave.

120

"Wert thou the cause my climbing care was such
To pass those bounds nature and law ordained?
Is this that good which promised so much,
And seemed so glorious ere it was attained?
Wherein was never joy but gave a touch
To check my soul to think how thou were gained,
And now, how do I leave thee unto mine,
Which it is dread to keep, death to resign?"

121

With this the soul, rapt wholly with the thought
Of such distress, did so attentive weigh
Her present horror, whilst, as if forgot,
The dull, consumed body senseless lay,
And now as breathless quite, quite dead is thought,
When, lo, his son comes in, and takes away
The fatal crown from thence, and out he goes
As if unwilling longer time to lose.

122

And whilst that sad confused soul doth cast
Those great accounts of terror and distress,
Upon this counsel it doth light at last
How she might make the charge of horror less,
And finding no way to acquit that's past,
But only this, to use some quick redress
Of acted wrong, with giving up again
The crown to whom it seemed to appertain.

123

Which found, lightened with some small joy she lies,
Rouses her servants that dead-sleeping lay
(The members of her house) to exercise
One feeble duty more during her stay;
And, opening those dark windows, he espies
The crown for which he looked was borne away,
And, all aggrieved with the unkind offense,
He caused him bring it back that took it thence.

124

To whom (excusing his presumptuous deed
By the supposing him departed quite)
He said, "O son, what needs thee make such speed
Unto that care, where fear exceeds thy right,
And where his sin whom thou shalt now succeed
Shall still upbraid thy inheritance of might,
And if thou canst live, and live great from woe
Without this careful travail—let it go."

125

"Nay, father, since your fortune did attain
So high a stand, I mean not to descend,"
Replies the Prince, "as if what you did gain
I were of spirit unable to defend.
Time will appease them well that now complain,
And ratify our interest in the end.
What wrong hath not continuance quite outworn?
Years make that right which never was so born."

126

"If so, God work his pleasure," said the King,
"And, O, do thou contend with all thy might
Such evidence of virtuous deeds to bring,
That well may prove our wrong to be our right,
And let the goodness of the managing
Rase out the blot of foul attaining quite,
That discontent may all advantage miss
To wish it otherwise than now it is.

127

"And since my death my purpose doth prevent
Touching this sacred war I took in hand
(An action wherewithal my soul had meant
T'appease my God and reconcile my land)
To thee is left to finish my intent,
Who, to be safe, must never idly stand,
But some great actions entertain thou still
To hold their minds who else will practice ill.

128

"Thou hast not that advantage by my reign
To riot it (as they whom long descent
Hath purchased love by custom), but with pain
Thou must contend to buy the world's content.
What their birth gave them, thou hast yet to gain
By thine own virtues and good government,

And that unless thy worth confirm the thing
Thou canst not be the father to a king.

129

"Nor art thou born in those calm days, where rest
Hath brought a sleepy, sluggish security,
But in tumultuous times, where minds addressed
To factions are inured to mutiny,
A mischief not by force to be suppressed
Where rigor still begets more enmity.
Hatred must be beguiled with some new course
Where states are strong, and princes doubt their force."

130

This and much more, affliction would have said
Out of the experience of a troublous reign,
For which his high desires had dearly paid
The interest of an ever-toiling pain,
But that this all-subduing power here stayed
His faltering tongue and pain r'inforced again
And cut off all the passages of breath
To bring him quite under the state of death.

Commentaries

Critical essays on *2 Henry IV* tend to focus on three topics: the rightness or wrongness of Prince John's trick on the rebels; the character of Falstaff and Hal's rejection of him; the relation of Part Two to Part One. Since two of these topics concern Part One as well as Part Two, they are frequently discussed in essays on Part One. The reader should consult the Commentaries in the Signet Classic edition of *1 Henry IV* as well as those reprinted here.

Of these, Hazlitt gives the traditional view of the rejection of Falstaff, a view which A. C. Bradley greatly expanded in *Oxford Lectures on Poetry*. Freud and Philip Williams present two modern approaches to Falstaff. Freud's is psychological, an analysis of our response to Falstaff, while Williams considers Falstaff a mythic figure, a Lord of Misrule who must be banished to cleanse the land (a view developed at greater length in C. L. Barber's excellent and readily available book, *Shakespeare's Festive Comedy*). Harold Jenkins wittily summarizes the view of those who consider Parts One and Two a single ten-act play and presents cogent arguments to the contrary.

WILLIAM HAZLITT

from *Characters of Shakespear's Plays*

Henry IV in Two Parts

If Shakespear's fondness for the ludicrous sometimes
led to faults in his tragedies (which was not often the
case) he has made us amends by the character of Falstaff.
This is perhaps the most substantial comic character that
ever was invented. Sir John carries a most portly presence
in the mind's eye; and in him, not to speak it profanely,
"we behold the fullness of the spirit of wit and humor
bodily." We are as well acquainted with his person as his
mind, and his jokes come upon us with double force and
relish from the quantity of flesh through which they make
their way, as he shakes his fat sides with laughter, or
"lards the lean earth as he walks along." Other comic
characters seem, if we approach and handle them, to
resolve themselves into air, "into thin air"; but this is
embodied and palpable to the grossest apprehension: it
lies "three fingers deep upon the ribs," it plays about the
lungs and the diaphragm with all the force of animal
enjoyment. His body is like a good estate to his mind,
from which he receives rents and revenues of profit and
pleasure in kind, according to its extent, and the richness
of the soil. Wit is often a meager substitute for pleasurable
sensation; an effusion of spleen and petty spite at the comforts of others, from feeling none in itself. Falstaff's wit is
an emanation of a fine constitution; an exuberance of good
humor and good nature; an overflowing of his love of

From *Characters of Shakespear's Plays,* by William Hazlitt. 2nd ed.
London: Taylor & Hessey, 1818. One long quotation in the essay has been
replaced by a citation.

laughter and good-fellowship; a giving vent to his heart's ease, and overcontentment with himself and others. He would not be in character if he were not so fat as he is; for there is the greatest keeping in the boundless luxury of his imagination and the pampered self-indulgence of his physical appetites. He manures and nourishes his mind with jests, as he does his body with sack and sugar. He carves out his jokes, as he would a capon or a haunch of venison, where there is *cut and come again;* and pours out upon them the oil of gladness. His tongue drops fatness, and in the chambers of his brain "it snows of meat and drink." He keeps up perpetual holiday and open house, and we live with him in a round of invitations to a rump and dozen. —Yet we are not to suppose that he was a mere sensualist. All this is as much in imagination as in reality. His sensuality does not engross and stupefy his other faculties, but "ascends me into the brain, clears away all the dull, crude vapors that environ it, and makes it full of nimble, fiery, and delectable shapes." His imagination keeps up the ball after his senses have done with it. He seems to have even a greater enjoyment of the freedom from restraint, of good cheer, of his ease, of his vanity, in the ideal exaggerated description which he gives of them, than in fact. He never fails to enrich his discourse with allusions to eating and drinking, but we never see him at table. He carries his own larder about with him, and he is himself "a tun of man." His pulling out the bottle in the field of battle is a joke to show his contempt for glory accompanied with danger, his systematic adherence to his Epicurean philosophy in the most trying circumstances. Again, such is his deliberate exaggeration of his own vices, that it does not seem quite certain whether the account of his hostess's bill, found in his pocket, with such an out-of-the-way charge for capons and sack with only one half-penny-worth of bread, was not put there by himself as a trick to humor the jest upon his favorite propensities, and as a conscious caricature of himself. He is represented as a liar, a braggart, a coward, a glutton, etc., and yet we are not offended but delighted with him; for he is all these as much to amuse others as to gratify himself. He openly assumes all these characters to show the humorous part of them. The unrestrained indulgence of his own ease, appetites, and convenience, has neither malice nor hypocrisy in it. In a word, he is an actor in himself almost as much as upon the stage, and we no more object to the character of Falstaff in a moral point of view than we should think of bringing an excellent comedian, who should represent him to the life, before one of the police offices. We only consider the number of pleasant lights in which he puts certain foibles (the more pleasant as they are opposed to the received rules and necessary restraints of society) and do not trouble ourselves about the consequences resulting from them, for no mischievous consequences do result. Sir John is old as well as fat, which gives a melancholy retrospective tinge to the character; and by the disparity between his inclinations and his capacity for enjoyment, makes it still more ludicrous and fantastical.

The secret of Falstaff's wit is for the most part a masterly presence of mind, an absolute self-possession, which nothing can disturb. His repartees are involuntary suggestions of his self-love; instinctive evasions of everything that threatens the career of his triumphant jollity and self-complacency. His very size floats him out of all his difficulties in a sea of rich conceits; and he turns round on the pivot of his convenience with every occasion and at a moment's warning. His natural repugnance to every unpleasant thought or circumstance, of itself makes light of objections, and provokes the most extravagant and licentious answers in his own justification. His indifference to truth puts no check upon his invention, and the more improbable and unexpected his contrivances are, the more happily does he seem to be delivered of them, the anticipation of their effect acting as a stimulus to the gaiety of his fancy. The success of one adventurous sally gives him spirits to undertake another: he deals always in round numbers, and his exaggerations and excuses are "open, palpable, monstrous as the father that begets them." His dissolute carelessness of what he says discovers itself in the first dialogue with the Prince.

"*Falstaff.* By the lord, thou say'st true, lad; and is not
    mine hostess of the tavern a most sweet wench?

P. Henry. As the honey of Hibla, my old lad of the
    castle, and is not a buff-jerkin a most sweet robe of
    durance?

Falstaff. How now, how now, mad wag, what in thy
    quips and thy quiddities? what a plague have I to do
    with a buff-jerkin?

P. Henry. Why, what a pox have I to do with mine host-
    ess of the tavern?"

In the same scene he afterwards affects melancholy,
from pure satisfaction of heart, and professes reform, because it is the farthest thing in the world from his thoughts.
He has no qualms of conscience, and therefore would as
soon talk of them as of anything else when the humor
takes him.

"*Falstaff.* But Hal, I pr'ythee trouble me no more with
    vanity. I would to God thou and I knew where a com-
    modity of good names were to be bought: an old lord
    of council rated me the other day in the street about
    you, sir; but I mark'd him not, and yet he talked very
    wisely, and in the street too.

P. Henry. Thou didst well, for wisdom cries out in the
    street, and no man regards it.

Falstaff. O, thou hast damnable iteration, and art indeed
    able to corrupt a saint. Thou hast done much harm
    unto me, Hal; God forgive thee for it. Before I knew
    thee, Hal, I knew nothing, and now I am, if a man
    should speak truly, little better than one of the wicked.
    I must give over this life, and I will give it over, by the
    lord; an I do not, I am a villain. I'll be damn'd for
    never a king's son in Christendom.

P. Henry. Where shall we take a purse tomorrow, Jack?

Falstaff. Where thou wilt, lad, I'll make one; an I do
    not, call me villain, and baffle me.

P. Henry. I see good amendment of life in thee, from
    praying to purse-taking.

Falstaff. Why, Hal, 'tis my vocation, Hal. 'Tis no sin for
    a man to labor in his vocation."

Of the other prominent passages, his account of his pretended resistance to the robbers, "who grew from four men in buckram into eleven" as the imagination of his own valor increased with his relating it, his getting off when the truth is discovered by pretending he knew the Prince, the scene in which in the person of the old king he lectures the prince and gives himself a good character, the soliloquy on honor, and description of his new-raised recruits, his meeting with the chief justice, his abuse of the Prince and Poins, who overhear him, to Doll Tearsheet, his reconciliation with Mrs. Quickly who has arrested him for an old debt, and whom he persuades to pawn her plate to lend him ten pounds more, and the scenes with Shallow and Silence, are all inimitable. Of all of them, the scene in which Falstaff plays the part, first, of the King, and then of Prince Henry, is the one that has been the most often quoted. We must quote it once more in illustration of our remarks. [And Hazlitt quotes *1 Henry IV*, II.iv.380–461—ed.]

One of the most characteristic descriptions of Sir John is that which Mrs. Quickly gives of him when he asks her "What is the gross sum that I owe thee?"

> "*Hostess.* Marry, if thou wert an honest man, thyself, and the money too. Thou didst swear to me upon a parcel-gilt goblet, sitting in my Dolphin-chamber, at the round table, by a sea-coal fire on Wednesday in Whitsunweek, when the Prince broke thy head for likening his father to a singing man of Windsor; thou didst swear to me then, as I was washing thy wound, to marry me, and make me my lady thy wife. Canst thou deny it? Did not goodwife Keech, the butcher's wife, come in then, and call me gossip Quickly? coming in to borrow a mess of vinegar; telling us, she had a good dish of prawns; whereby thou didst desire to eat some; whereby I told thee, they were ill for a green wound? And didst thou not, when she was gone down stairs, desire me to be no more so familiarity with such poor people; saying, that ere long they should call me madam? And didst thou not kiss me, and bid me fetch

thee thirty shillings? I put thee now to thy book-oath;
deny it, if thou canst."

This scene is to us the most convincing proof of
Falstaff's power of gaining over the good will of those
he was familiar with, except indeed Bardolph's somewhat
profane exclamation on hearing the account of his death,
"Would I were with him, wheresoe'er he is, whether in
heaven or hell."

One of the topics of exulting superiority over others
most common in Sir John's mouth is his corpulence and
the exterior marks of good living which he carries about
him, thus "turning his vices into commodity." He accounts
for the friendship between the Prince and Poins, from
"their legs being both of a bigness"; and compares Justice
Shallow to "a man made after supper of a cheese-paring."
There cannot be a more striking gradation of character
than that between Falstaff and Shallow, and Shallow and
Silence. It seems difficult at first to fall lower than the
squire; but this fool, great as he is, finds an admirer and
humble foil in his cousin Silence. Vain of his acquaintance
with Sir John, who makes a butt of him, he exclaims,
"Would, cousin Silence, that thou had'st seen that which
this knight and I have seen!"—"Aye, Master Shallow, we
have heard the chimes at midnight," says Sir John. To
Falstaff's observation "I did not think Master Silence had
been a man of this mettle," Silence answers, "Who, I? I
have been merry twice and once ere now." What an idea
is here conveyed of a prodigality of living? What good
husbandry and economical self-denial in his pleasures?
What a stock of lively recollections? It is curious that
Shakespear has ridiculed in Justice Shallow, who was "in
some authority under the King," that disposition to un-
meaning tautology which is the regal infirmity of
later times, and which, it may be supposed, he acquired
from talking to his cousin Silence, and receiving no answers.

"*Falstaff.* You have here a goodly dwelling, and a rich.
Shallow. Barren, barren, barren; beggars all, beggars all;

> Sir John: marry, good air. Spread Davy, spread Davy.
> Well said, Davy.
> *Falstaff.* This Davy serves you for good uses.
> *Shallow.* A good varlet, a good varlet, a very good varlet.
> By the mass, I have drank too much sack at supper.
> A good varlet. Now sit down, now sit down. Come,
> cousin."

The true spirit of humanity, the thorough knowledge of the stuff we are made of, the practical wisdom with the seeming fooleries in the whole of the garden scene at Shallow's countryseat, and just before in the exquisite dialogue between him and Silence on the death of old Double, have no parallel anywhere else. In one point of view, they are laughable in the extreme; in another they are equally affecting, if it is affecting to show *what a little thing is human life,* what a poor forked creature man is!

The heroic and serious part of these two plays founded on the story of Henry IV is not inferior to the comic and farcical. The characters of Hotspur and Prince Henry are two of the most beautiful and dramatic, both in themselves and from contrast, that ever were drawn. They are the essence of chivalry. We like Hotspur the best upon the whole, perhaps because he was unfortunate. —The characters of their fathers, Henry IV and old Northumberland, are kept up equally well. Henry naturally succeeds by his prudence and caution in keeping what he has got; Northumberland fails in his enterprise from an excess of the same quality, and is caught in the web of his own cold, dilatory policy. Owen Glendower is a masterly character. It is as bold and original as it is intelligible and thoroughly natural. The disputes between him and Hotspur are managed with infinite address and insight into nature. We cannot help pointing out here some very beautiful lines, where Hotspur describes the fight between Glendower and Mortimer.

> —"When on the gentle Severn's sedgy bank,
> In single opposition hand to hand,
> He did confound the best part of an hour

In changing hardiment with great Glendower:
Three times they breath'd, and three times did they drink,
Upon agreement, of swift Severn's flood;
Who then affrighted with their bloody looks,
Ran fearfully among the trembling reeds,
And hid his crisp head in the hollow bank,
Blood-stained with these valiant combatants."

The peculiarity and the excellence of Shakespear's poetry is, that it seems as if he made his imagination the handmaid of nature and nature the plaything of his imagination. He appears to have been all the characters and in all the situations he describes. It is as if either he had had all their feelings or had lent them all his genius to express themselves. There cannot be stronger instances of this than Hotspur's rage when Henry IV forbids him to speak of Mortimer, his insensibility to all that his father and uncle urge to calm him, and his fine abstracted apostrophe to honor, "By heaven methinks it were an easy leap to pluck bright honor from the moon," etc. After all, notwithstanding the gallantry, generosity, good temper, and idle freaks of the madcap Prince of Wales, we should not have been sorry, if Northumberland's force had come up in time to decide the fate of the battle at Shrewsbury; at least, we always heartily sympathize with Lady Percy's grief, when she exclaims,

"Had my sweet Harry had but half their numbers,
  Today might I (hanging on Hotspur's neck)
  Have talked of Monmouth's grave."

The truth is, that we never could forgive the Prince's treatment of Falstaff; though perhaps Shakespear knew what was best, according to the history, the nature of the times, and of the man. We speak only as dramatic critics. Whatever terror the French in those days might have of Henry V, yet, to the readers of poetry at present, Falstaff is the better man of the two. We think of him and quote him oftener.   [1817]

SIGMUND FREUD

from *Jokes and Their Relation to the Unconscious*

[Freud is pursuing the distinctions between wit, the comic, and humor, suggesting that the pleasure of humor comes from suddenly discovering we do not have to make an expenditure in emotion that we had expected to make. His view of Falstaff contrasts interestingly with Dr. Johnson's, quoted in the Signet Classic *1 Henry IV*.]

The grandiose humorous effect of a figure like that of the fat knight Sir John Falstaff rests on an economy in contempt and indignation. We recognize him as an undeserving gormandizer and swindler, but our condemnation is disarmed by a whole number of factors. We can see that he knows himself as well as we do; he impresses us by his wit, and, besides this, his physical misproportion has the effect of encouraging us to take a comic view of him instead of a serious one, as though the demands of morality and honor must rebound from so fat a stomach. His doings are on the whole harmless, and are almost excused by the comic baseness of the people he cheats. We admit that the poor fellow has a right to try to live and enjoy himself like anyone else, and we almost pity him because in the chief situations we find him a plaything in the hands of someone far his superior. So we

From *Jokes and their relation to the Unconscious* by Sigmund Freud. Newly translated from the German and edited by James Strachey. New York: W. W. Norton & Co., Inc.; London: Routledge & Kegan Paul, Ltd., 1960. Copyright © 1960 by James Strachey. Reprinted by permission of the publishers.

cannot feel angry with him and we add all that we economize in indignation with him to the comic pleasure which he affords us apart from this. Sir John's own humor arises in fact from the superiority of an ego which neither his physical nor his moral defects can rob of its cheerfulness and assurance.   [1905]

PHILIP WILLIAMS

The Birth and Death of Falstaff Reconsidered

In "Falstaff No Martyr," a paper read at a recent meeting of the South Atlantic Modern Language Association,
Prof. Allan Gilbert said:

> Perhaps the most striking lack of the critics for many
> years and to no small extent at present is failure to con-
> sider the question: What are the proper limits of literary
> interpretation? Art is universal, we are told. But that
> hardly means that anything can be brought into the ex-
> position of a speech or character. The middle ages . . .
> had a formula for exegesis. . . . Ridiculous enough, in our
> eyes, are some of their interpretations. But we may ad-
> mire their clarity. A medieval preacher must have re-
> alized when he went over from the literal Samson to the
> allegorical Christ. But for a modern going from Falstaff,
> a fat man trying to run, to Falstaff the spirit of humanity,
> there is no post to mark the boundary. Do we have de-
> duction straight from the play, or do we have the critic's
> fancy? Or, the boundaries of interpretation can be dif-
> ferently considered. Academics as we are here, we lay
> some importance on detailed study, even of the single
> word. How far can we go in allowing critics the very ut-
> most from every word, from insisting on its absolute
> connection with every other word in the play? Or if they
> take the play just as something to be put on the stage,
> played so rapidly that a hearer cannot stop to reflect but

From *Shakespeare Quarterly*, VIII (1957), pp. 359–65. Reprinted by
permission of *Shakespeare Quarterly*, The Shakespeare Association of
America, Inc.

must rely on a hurried impression, a total rather than a
detailed effect, how far can we trust such an impression
as adequate?

These are difficult questions, and I profess no answers.
But a recent book on Shakespeare by the distinguished
Lecturer in English at Christ Church, Oxford, and the review of that book by an even more distinguished American
scholar, afford a convenient case on which to speculate.
I refer to Mr. J. I. M. Stewart's *Character and Motive in
Shakespeare,* and "A Freudian Detective's Shakespeare,"
the long review of it by Prof. E. E. Stoll. The subject for
consideration here can conveniently be limited to Stewart's
final chapter, "The Birth and Death of Falstaff."

In this chapter, Stewart first discusses the inadequacies
of the familiar critical approaches, and then, by drawing
freely on the formulations of psychology and anthropology,
offers what seems to him a more satisfactory interpretation. The objections to his predecessors are tightly argued
and cogently expressed; but the book is a thin one, and
there is room for little documentation of the author's own
critical insights. Having canvassed the interpretations of
Falstaff from Morgann to Dover Wilson, Mr. Stewart presents his own contribution:

> I suggest that Hal, by a displacement common enough
> in the evolution of ritual, kills Falstaff instead of killing
> the king, his father. In a sense Falstaff *is* his father; cer-
> tainly a father-substitute in the psychologist's word; and
> this makes the theory of a vicarious sacrifice the more
> colorable.

For Prof. Stoll, this is arrant nonsense. He writes:

> And Falstaff. Whether in the hands of [Mr. Stewart]
> he or Leontes is the more astounding the reader shall
> now judge for himself. After repeating many of the
> vagaries of Maurice Morgann and his followers on the
> subject, Mr. Stewart ends up by making him symbolical,
> the victim of a fertility ritual, as in *The Golden Bough.*
> (After Freud Frazer, but Sir James, I trust, would of
> this have none; and again we can determine what Shake-

speare's conception was *not*.) There is something "atavic" about the final rejection of him on the stage (to many of us now unacceptable) as there is, the critic thinks, also about the blinding of Gloucester, which reminds him (as possibly nobody else in the world) of Uranus castrated by his son Cronus (so long before Oedipus!) with the scythe. Similarly, the rejection is thought to be like the primeval religious rite of killing the king, and thus is made more acceptable. . . . But why, even if Shakespeare and the audience thus "instinctively" anticipated Freud and Frazer, Hal, the hero of Agincourt-to-be, should engage in a "vicarious sacrifice" of his real father, whose death he has mourned, does not satisfactorily appear. Nor does any reason why that should have reconciled the Elizabethan (however it may be with us) to the comic fat man's ignominious, though not unmerited, end.

And all this at Oxford, the Oxford of Arnold, Raleigh, the late illustrious Bradley, Ker, and Mackail!

It must be emphasized that Mr. Stewart does not claim uniqueness for his interpretation. "I hope it will be clear," he writes, "that what I am . . . concerned with is the *multiple* significance of the Falstaff story. To assert that Falstaff is the sacrificial object in a fertility ritual is not in the least to deny that he is (a good deal less remotely indeed) the Riot of a Morality [as Dover Wilson would have it]." Nor does Mr. Stewart deny that Falstaff "is" Prof. Stoll's braggart soldier, or Prof. Draper's down-and-out military man. His primary concern is why we, in the theater if not in the study, accept the rejection and death as inevitable and right.

If we turn to the plays themselves, do we find that what Shakespeare wrote can possibly permit Mr. Stewart's startling interpretation, which proposes that instead of killing his real father, Hal kills Falstaff, a father-substitute; and that this killing is necessary before a diseased land can regain its health under a virile young king? Is this "deduction straight from the play," or is it "the critic's fancy"?

The antagonism between Prince Hal and his king-father is an important, and obvious, theme in these plays, from the forward-looking scene near the end of *Richard II* in which King Henry asks for news about his "unthrifty" son and adds, "If any plague hang over us 'tis he," to the deathbed scene near the end of *Henry IV, Part Two,* in which the King sums up the antagonism between father and son with the charge, "Thy life did manifest thou lovedst me not." Embedded in this antagonism are latent parricidal impulses, and King Henry IV is haunted by the vision of being slain by the son he has publicly rejected and whom he at times hates. For him, Hal is his "nearest and dearest enemy." When, at the battle of Shrewsbury, Hal rescues the king from Douglas, Henry is almost surprised:

> Thou has redeem'd thy lost opinion,
> And show'd thou makest some tender of my life.

Hal's reply is curious, suggesting as it does that thoughts of his father's death had indeed not been absent from his mind:

> O God, they did me too much injury
> That ever said I hearkened for your death.
> If it were so, I might have let alone
> The insulting hand of Douglas over you
> Which would have been as speedy in your end
> As all the poisonous potions in the world,
> And saved the treacherous labor of your son.

When on his deathbed, Henry awakes to find the crown gone, taken by his son, the theme of parricide receives long and detailed statement:

> This part of his conjoins with my disease
> And helps to end me. See, sons, what things you are!
> How quickly nature falls into revolt
> When gold becomes her object!
> For this the foolish overcareful fathers
> Have broke their sleep with thoughts, their brains with care,
> Their bones with industry;
> For this they have engrossed and piled up

The cankered heaps of strange-achieved gold;
For this they have been thoughtful to invest
Their sons with arts and martial exercises:
When like the bee, culling from every flower
The virtuous sweets,
Our thighs packed with wax, our mouths with honey,
We bring it to the hive, and, like the bees,
Are murdered for our pains.

Hal then reenters, saying that he never thought to hear the King speak again. "Thy wish was father, Harry, to that thought," says the King, who then continues the parricide theme:

Thou hid'st a thousand daggers in thy thoughts
Which thou hast whetted on thy stony heart
To stab at half an hour of my life.

In Hal's reply to these charges, he shifts the parricidal impulse from himself to the crown: It is not I but the crown who kills my father:

I spake unto this crown as having sense,
And thus unbraided it: "The care on thee depending
Hath fed upon the body of my father. . . .
[And] eat thy bearer up." Thus most royal liege
Accusing it, I put it on my head,
To try with it, as with an enemy
That had before my face murdered my father.

In the corresponding scene in *The Famous Victories of Henry V,* based on hints found in the chronicles, Hal appears before the sick king with a drawn dagger. Shakespeare subtilizes his crude source, putting the daggers in Hal's mind rather than in his hand, but the overtones in both scenes are the same: parricide.

As a result of this antagonism between father and son, it is to be expected, the psychologist would say, that the son seeks a father-substitute. Given the character of the real father—sin-ridden, punctilious, lean, and cold—he would go further and predict what the father image would be: it would be, of course, a Falstaff, the opposite of the real father in all those qualities that the Prince resents, and yet like enough the real father to make the identification possible. Falstaff, without a son of his own, has found that son in Hal; and Hal, rejecting and rejected by his real father, has found Falstaff. It is right, the psychologist would add, that the ambivalent feeling of love-hate toward the real father be transferred to the father image, and this psychological insight may, in part at least, explain Hal's paradoxical attitude toward Falstaff.

Falstaff's role as father to Hal is unobtrusively developed throughout the plays, but in certain scenes the father-son relationship receives explicit statement. Falstaff's possessive paternalism is fully revealed in the rejection scene. "God save thy Grace, King Hal, my royal Hal!/God save thee, my sweet boy!" are the words with which the old knight greets the newly crowned king. This overt statement has been carefully prepared for.

Perhaps most important because of its initial position is the great tavern scene in Part One where, in the play impromptu, Falstaff becomes Hal's father. Hal commands him to "stand for my father," and the father ruffian complies willingly. Is it romanticizing this scene to sense with what satisfaction Sir John says, "That thou art my son" (and so on)? I think not. Then comes the ominous word "depose." Hal becomes king, replacing Falstaff on the joint-stool throne. Comic, yes; but we have here acted out the major theme of the *Henry IV* plays. "When thou art king," introduced by Falstaff in his second speech in Part One, and echoed again and again by King Henry, runs like a refrain through the plays. The image of Falstaff as king-father being deposed by his prince-son is printed indelibly on our minds, and we are prepared for the rejection scene where the symbolic act of the play impromptu is literally enacted. In making the play impromptu deal with the father-son relationship, Shakespeare has again significantly deviated from his source, for in *The Famous Victories* the subject is Hal's encounter with the Chief Justice.

To emphasize the dual father roles of Falstaff and

Henry IV, Shakespeare makes them parallel characters. Both Falstaff and Henry are mistaken for dead by Hal, who then reveals a curious mixture of grief and satisfaction over the supposedly dead bodies. Hal "robs" both Falstaff and Henry while they sleep: Falstaff of a tavern reckoning, Henry IV of the crown. The deaths of both Falstaff and Henry are surrounded by the aura of folklore and superstition: Falstaff passing to Arthur's bosom "just between twelve and one, even at the turning of the tide"; Henry IV dying in the Jerusalem Chamber after the river had "thrice flowed, no ebb between." In Part Two, the King's apostrophe to sleep is structurally balanced by Falstaff's apostrophe to sack. The cumulative effect of these and other parallels is to define the equivalency of their twin roles of father to the young prince.

But the most striking parallel between Falstaff and King Henry leads to the second part of Stewart's thesis. Much has been written about what happens to Falstaff in Part Two. It has been suggested that he is degraded, that his wit fails, that Shakespeare grows tired of him, that he becomes, somehow, an unsympathetic character. But the truth is, I think, that like Henry IV he grows old. In Part One, although his age and white hairs are not neglected, it is Falstaff's size that receives the greatest emphasis. In Part Two, although his girth has not decreased (in spite of Falstaff's claim to the contrary), the emphasis shifts to his age and infirmities. And Falstaff's growing old, his physical decay, parallels what happens to King Henry IV, who, in Part Two, also grows suddenly old and sick. In most of the historical scenes, and in many of the comic scenes, the infirmities of the King are stressed. The garden imagery of *Richard II* has been superseded by the imagery of disease, and Richard's prediction (that Henry quotes)

> The time will come that foul sin, gathering head,
> Shall break into corruption

becomes literally true. Under the guilt-ridden, infirm, old king, England itself has become diseased.

> The body of our kingdom,
> How foul it is, what rank diseases grow
> And with what danger, near the heart of it,

says the King, who is acutely aware that his own infirmities are reflected in the land he rules. Nor is he alone in making this primitive connection.

Do we not find here, surprising as it may at first appear, a classic example of a situation that anthropologists—and poets—have so thoroughly investigated—the wasteland? Under the rule of an infirm and guilty king, England has become diseased, and before regeneration can come—as it so obviously does under King Henry V—sacrificial rites must be performed. The penitential pilgrimage to the Holy Land, by which Henry hoped to expiate his guilt in Richard's murder, was never undertaken. On his deathbed, Henry is fully aware that his death is necessary to remove that stain from the succession. "And now my death," he says to Hal, "changes the mode." Hal too senses that the death of the king-father expiates past sins, but when he says

> My father has gone wild into his grave,
> For in his tomb lie my affections [that is, my sins]

he is speaking only half the truth. Into Henry's grave went the guilt of Richard's murder, but another grave, a more momentous sacrifice, is needed to bring regeneration to a wasted land.

In more ways than one, Falstaff is the only sufficient object for the sacrifice. Not only his person (and all that person symbolizes) but also his relationship to Hal marks him as the inevitable choice.

Dover Wilson long ago detected the sacrificial and symbolic quality in Falstaff. Commenting on the epithet "Martlemas" that Poins once employs, Wilson explains:

> Martlemas, or the feast of St. Martin, on 11 November, was in those days of scarce fodder the season at which most of the beasts had to be killed off and salted

for the winter, and therefore the season for great banquets of fresh meat. Thus it had been for centuries, long before the coming of Christianity. In calling him a "Martlemas" Poins is at once likening Falstaff's enormous proportions to the prodigality of fresh-killed meat which the feast brought, and acclaiming his identity with Riot and Festivity in general.

To this, Mr. Stewart would add:

> But such festivals commemorate more than the need to reduce stock against a winter season. They commemorate a whole mythology of the cycle of the year, and of the sacrifices offered to secure a new fertility on the earth. . . . Perhaps we glimpse here a further reason why the rejection of Falstaff is inevitable—not merely traditionally and moralistically inevitable but symbolically inevitable as well. And this may be why, when in the theater, we do not really rebel against the rejection; why we find a fitness too in its being sudden and catastrophic. . . . For the killing carries something of the ritual suggestion, the obscure *pathos,* of death in tragedy. . . . And Falstaff is in the end the dethroned and sacrificed king, the scapegoat as well as the sweet beef. For Falstaff . . . so fit a sacrifice . . . to lard the lean, the barren earth, is of that primitive and magical world upon which all art, even with a profound unconsciousness, draws.

If Falstaff is ritually slain by Hal, if his death is necessary for the regeneration of a diseased land, we should expect to find further corroboration in the structure and imagery of the plays. One example from each category will have here to suffice. It is significant, in terms of the structure of *Henry V,* that Hal does not "assume the port of Mars," does not become the hero-king, until *after* the death of Falstaff. He is uncomfortable in his new role of king in the last scenes of *Henry IV, Part Two,* and in the early scenes of *Henry V* there is much talk of his miraculous transformation, but it is only talk. Then, in Act II, scene 3, comes Falstaff's death, and Henry V's next words are:

> Once more unto the breach, dear friends, once more;
> Or close the wall up with our English dead!
> . . . On, on, you noblest English,
> Whose blood is fet from fathers of war proof!
> Fathers that, like so many Alexanders,
> Have in these parts from morn to even fought,
> And sheathed their swords for lack of argument.

For the first time, Henry V becomes in word and deed the national hero, the mirror of all Christian kings.

With a single image drawn from the rich storehouse of classic myth, Shakespeare sometimes found that he could present the essence of his play, a statement of its theme in miniature. In the first play of this tetralogy, *Richard II,* he accomplished this, for the whole play is contained in Richard's lines,

> Down, down I come like glistering Phaeton,
> Wanting the manage of unruly steeds.

And he may, I think, have accomplished the same thing in the rejection scene with Falstaff's climactic line,

> My King, my Jove, I speak to thee my heart!

For Hal is Falstaff's Jove, the son who deposes his king-father, old Saturn. It is only at this appropriate moment that Falstaff calls Hal Jove. He has never done so before, but Hal himself has made the identification. "It was Jove's case," he says as he dons the leather jerkin disguise to spy on Falstaff and Doll—Saturn and Venus as he calls them.

And for a final bit of evidence, not from the plays and yet not without significance: It is reassuring to note how often the critics have slipped unconsciously into the metaphor of making Falstaff a king and his rejection a dethronement or sacrifice. A. C. Bradley, who wrote, "[Shakespeare] created so extraordinary a being, and fixed him so firmly on his intellectual throne, that when he sought to dethrone him he could not," is only one of many whose intuitive understanding of the situation is revealed in the metaphors they chose to describe it. Even Stoll himself has written: "The King casts [Falstaff] off, but morally, officially, it is to his credit. The poet's hand here is a bit heavy, but he would simply convey to the audience that as King of England, Henry has broken with the past." Is it Shakespeare's hand that is heavy, or the hand of Hal as he runs bad humors on the knight and kills his heart?

In the final analysis, Stoll's own approach to Falstaff and Stewart's are curiously similar: both attempt to explain Falstaff by discovering his ancestors. Stoll found them in the *milites gloriosi* of Latin comedy; Stewart finds them in those ritually slain kings whose diverse histories and lingering traditions are so copiously recorded in *The Golden Bough*. Fortunately, literary paternity, unlike biological, does not preclude the possibility of more than one father, and Falstaff's family tree has many branches. If to those branches already traced by Stoll and the other literary genealogists, Stewart would add yet another, must we reject it because, for Stoll at least, it means an "instinctive anticipation" of Freud and Frazer?

I would suggest that Sigmund Freud did not endow only twentieth-century man with a subconscious mind. Nor did Sir James Frazer trace the survivals—in England long after Shakespeare's day—of the magical connection between old kings and the lands they ruled, of rites and rituals by which fertility was assured, merely to plague the historical critics of Shakespeare. It is not, however, Freudian psychology (so objectionable to Stoll) but Carl Jung's concept of the collective unconscious of the race which offers a possible further explanation of why, as Stewart claims, the rejection and death of Falstaff are felt to be inevitable and just. Archetypal images of king-fathers and sacrificial rites are our inescapable heritage no less than they were Shakespeare's. We should be neither surprised nor alarmed that Shakespeare, in his greatest moments, penetrates this mysterious, rich, and largely unexplored region of the human psyche.

HAROLD JENKINS

The Structural Problem in Shakespeare's Henry the Fourth

In having the honor to inaugurate a chair of English in this college, I have thought it appropriate to devote my inaugural lecture to the preeminent writer in English. A professor of English who gives to Shakespeare such priority of his attention needs, I hope, no defense. But if defense were necessary, I could of course plead the authority of that distinguished body which has honored me this afternoon by the attendance of so many of its members, the Board of Studies in English, whose collective wisdom has ensured that the syllabus studied in our London school of English gives to Shakespeare a greater prominence than to any other author, not even excepting the author of *Beowulf*. To confine myself to two—or is it indeed only one?—of Shakespeare's masterpieces may be less obviously justifiable. But it cannot be the task of an hour to survey Shakespeare whole, much less Shakespearian criticism. By accepting a restricted scope I must, I am aware, forgo what Dr. Johnson called "the grandeur of generality." But whatever may be the poet's business, the scholar and the critic, in their humbler field, before they can come at the grandeur of generality, must be willing to "number the streaks of the tulip." Though they may properly avoid the esoteric, they cannot ignore the particular. The qualm that I am left with is lest the particular two-headed bloom I have picked for this occasion should not seem the most suitable to present to a women's college. For I am told by one of the most remarkable women

Delivered in 1955 as an inaugural address at Westfield College, University of London, Mr. Jenkins' essay was published in book form by Methuen & Co., Ltd., 1956. Reprinted by permission of Methuen & Co., Ltd.

in the history of the British theater that *Henry IV* "is a play which . . . most women dislike." According to Mrs. Inchbald, "many revolting expressions in the comic parts, much boisterous courage in the graver scenes, together with Falstaff's unwieldy person, offend every female auditor; and whilst a facetious Prince of Wales is employed taking purses on the highway, a lady would rather see him stealing hearts at a ball."[1] That, however, was before the emancipation. It would be small compliment to Westfield College if I failed to recognize the great change that has come about since Mrs. Inchbald's day. I take this opportunity of paying my respect to the part that Westfield College has taken in the education of women and in the consequent enlargement of women's freedom, which has been so conspicuous a feature of recent social history. A subsidiary aspect of this social change, though one that Constance Maynard can hardly at first have envisaged, is that battlefields and even taverns are now less closed to women than they were. So it is without apology that I cheerfully commend to my students the "infinite entertainment and instruction" that Mrs. Inchbald herself admitted might "be obtained from this drama even by the most delicate readers."

The first problem that confronts one in approaching *Henry IV,* and the one about which I propose to be particular, has inevitably introduced itself already. Is it one play or two? Some of you will dismiss this as an academic question, the sort of thing that only people like professors bother their heads about. Some of you will look askance at it as a metaphysical question, which in a sense it is. But it is also, surely, a practical question: how satisfactorily can either the first part or the second be shown in the theater without the other? What is gained, or indeed lost, by presenting the two parts, as the Old Vic are doing at the moment, on successive evenings? And thus of course the question becomes a problem of literary criticism. Until it has been answered, how can the dramatic quality of *Henry IV* be fully appreciated, or even defined? Yet the numerous literary critics who have attempted an answer

1 Quoted in *1 Henry IV,* New Variorum, ed. Hemingway, p. 395.

to the question have reached surprisingly opposite con-
clusions.[2]

Answers began more than two hundred years ago in
the *Critical Observations on Shakespeare* by John Upton,
a man who deserves our regard for trying to scotch the
notion so strangely current in the eighteenth century that
"Shakespeare had no learning." Far from accepting that
Shakespeare's plays were the happy, or the not so happy,
products of untutored nature, Upton maintained that they
were constructed according to some principles of art; and
his examination of *Henry IV* suggested to him that each
of its two parts had, what Aristotle of course demanded,
its own beginning, middle, and end. Upton held it to be
an injury to Shakespeare even to speak of a first and
second *part* and thus conceal the fact that there were here
two quite independent plays.[3] To this Dr. Johnson retorted
that these two plays, so far from being independent, are
"two only because they are too long to be one." They
could appear as separate plays, he thought, only to those
who looked at them with the "ambition of critical discoveries." In these tart words Johnson shrewdly defined
what if not one of the deadly sins, is still a vice and one to
which universities are prone. The "ambition of critical
discoveries," a natural human vanity unnaturally nour-
ished in our day by the requirements of the Ph.D. thesis
and the demand for "publications," has been responsible
for many interpretations of Shakespeare whose merit is in
their being new rather than their being true. Yet one must
not always accept the accepted. Dr. Johnson's contemporaries did not all find it as plain as he did that *Henry IV*
was just one continuous composition. It seemed probable
to Malone that Part Two was not even "conceived"[4] until
Part One had been a roaring success. Capell, on the other
hand, thought that both parts were "planned at the same
time, and with great judgment."[5]

2 For particulars of the most important, see the appended Note, which
will usually obviate the necessity of further reference in the footnotes to
the works listed in it.
  3 *Op. cit.*, 1746. See especially pp. 11, 41–2, 70–1.
  4 *Shakespeare*, Johnson-Steevens Variorum, 2nd ed., 1778, vol. i. p. 300.
  5 *Notes and Various Readings to Shakespeare* [1775], p. 164.

Among present-day scholars Professor Dover Wilson is on Johnson's side. He insists that the two parts of *Henry IV* are "a single structure" with the "normal dramatic curve" stretched over ten acts instead of five. Professor R. A. Law, however, declares that *Henry IV* is "not a single ten-act play," but two organic units "written with different purposes in view." On the contrary, says Dr. Tillyard, "The two parts of the play are a single organism." Part One by itself is "patently incomplete." "Each part is a drama complete in itself," says Kittredge flatly.[6] In short, some two centuries after Upton and Johnson, scholars are still about equally divided as to whether *Henry IV* was "planned" as "one long drama" or whether the second part was, as they put it, an "unpremeditated sequel." A new professor, his ambition already dwindling at Johnson's warning, might well lapse into melancholy, or even modesty. Modest or not, he can hardly escape the conclusion, reached by another eighteenth-century dignitary in a somewhat different situation, that "much might be said on both sides." Like Sir Roger de Coverley, he "would not give his judgment rashly," yet like the late R. W. Chambers, whose pupil I am proud to have been, he may think that the modesty which forbears to make a judgment is disastrous.[7]

Words like "planned" and "unpremeditated" figure largely in this controversy; and of course they imply intention or the lack of it, and will therefore be suspect in those circles which denounce what is called "the intentional fallacy."[8] I am far from belonging to that school of criticism which holds that an author's own intention is irrelevant to our reading of his work; yet, as Lascelles Abercrombie says, aesthetic criticism must ultimately judge by results: a man's work is evidence of what he did, but you can never be sure what he intended.[9] This

6 *1 Henry IV*, ed. Kittredge, 1940, p. viii.

7 See *Beowulf, an Introduction to the Study of the Poem*, 2nd ed., 1932, p. 390.

8 This is actually the title of an article by W. K. Wimsatt and M. C. Beardsley in the *Sewanee Review*, LIV (1946), 468 ff., reprinted in Wimsatt's *The Verbal Icon*, 1954.

9 *A Plea for the Liberty of Interpreting*, British Academy Shakespeare Lecture, 1930, p. 6.

position, with the coming of the Freudian psychology, is finally inescapable, but in its extreme form it seems to me unnecessarily defeatist. When I find *Much Ado About Nothing* beginning with talk of a battle in which those killed are "few of any sort, and none of name," I may infer that Shakespeare intended to write a comedy and not a realistic one at that. But if I wish to play for safety, I may use a phrase of Lascelles Abercrombie's own and speak—not of what Shakespeare intended, but of what he "warned his audience to expect."[10] If we leave aside for the present all question of Shakespeare's intention, what does *Henry IV* itself, as it begins and proceeds along its course, warn us to expect?

The short first scene, filled with reports of wars—wars this time in which multitudes are "butchered"—makes an apt beginning for a history play. But its dialogue announces no main action. Yet certain topics, brought in with apparent casualness, naturally engage our interest. There is talk of two young men who do not yet appear, both called "young Harry," yet apparently unlike. The first of them, Hotspur, is introduced as "gallant," an epithet which is very soon repeated when he is said to have won "a gallant prize." The prisoners he has taken are, we are told, "a conquest for a prince to boast of." Already, before Prince Hal is even named, a contrast is being begun between a man who behaves like a prince though he is not one and another who is in fact a prince but does not act the part. The King makes this explicit. Hotspur, who has gained "an honorable spoil," is "a son who is the theme of honor's tongue," while the King's own son is stained with "riot and dishonor." In the second and third scenes the two Harrys in turn appear. First, the Prince, already associated with dishonor, instead of, like Hotspur, taking prisoners in battle, plans to engage in highway robbery. Then, when he has arranged to sup next night in a tavern, he is followed on the stage by Hotspur telling how, when he took his prisoners, he was "dry with rage and extreme toil." This practice of juxtaposing characters who exhibit opposite codes of conduct

10 *Ibid.*, p. 22.

is a common one in Shakespeare's drama. After the "unsavory similes" that Hal swaps with Falstaff, in which a squalling cat and a stinking ditch are prominent, there is Hotspur's hyperbole about plucking "bright honor from the pale-faced moon." It may not be a classical construction, but there is enough suggestion here of arrangement to justify Upton's claim for Shakespeare's art. We expect that central to the play will be the antithesis between these two young men and the lives they lead. And we shall find that this antithesis precipitates a moral contest which is an important aspect of the historical action of the drama.

The historical action presents Hotspur's rebellion. It is an action which develops with a fine structural proportion throughout Part One. The act divisions, although they are not Shakespeare's of course, being first found in the Folio, may serve nevertheless as a convenient register of the way the action is disposed. In the first act the rebel plot is hatched, in the second Hotspur prepares to leave home, in the third he joins forces with the other rebel leaders, in the fourth the rebel army is encamped ready to give battle, in the fifth it is defeated and Hotspur is killed. Meantime, along with the military contest between Hotspur and the King, the moral contest between the Prince and Hotspur proceeds with an equally perfect balance. The opposition of honor and riot established in the first act is intensified in the second, where a scene of Hotspur at home preparing for war is set against one of Hal reveling in the tavern. The revelry even includes a little skit by Hal on Hotspur's conversation with his wife, which serves not only to adjust our view of Hotspur's honor by subjecting it to ridicule, but also to emphasize that the Prince is—with gleeful understatement—"not yet of Percy's mind." That he is not of Percy's mind leads the King in the third act to resume his opening plaint: it is not the Prince but Percy, with his "never-dying honor," who is fit to be a king's son. At this point the Prince vows to outshine his rival. He will meet "this gallant Hotspur"—the words echo the opening scene—this "child of honor," and overcome him. And so, when the rebels see the Prince in Act IV, he is "gallantly arm'd"—Hotspur's word is now applied to him—and he vaults upon his horse "as if an angel dropp'd down from the clouds"—with a glory, that is, already beyond Hotspur. All that then remains is that the Prince shall demonstrate his new chivalry in action, which of course he does in the fifth act, first saving his father's life and finally slaying Hotspur in single combat. Opposed to one another throughout the play, constantly spoken of together, these two are nevertheless kept apart till the fifth act, when their first and last encounter completes in the expected manner the pattern of their rivalry that began in the opening words. The two have exchanged places. Supremacy in honor has passed from Hotspur to the Prince, and the wayward hero of the opening ends by exhibiting his true princely nature.

What then is one to make of the view of Professor Dover Wilson that the Battle of Shrewsbury, in which the Prince kills Hotspur, is not an adequate conclusion but merely the "nodal point we expect in a third act"? If we do expect a "nodal point" in a third act, then *Henry IV Part One* will not disappoint us. For there *is* a nodal point, and—I am tempted to say this categorically—it is in the third act of Part One that it occurs. In this third act, when the King rebukes his son, the Prince replies, "I will redeem all this . . ."; in the fifth act he fulfils this vow at Shrewsbury, as is signalized by the King's admission that the Prince has "redeem'd" his "lost opinion." Again, in the third act, the Prince swears that he will take from Hotspur "every honor sitting on his helm"; in the fifth act Hotspur is brought to confess that the Prince has won "proud titles" from him.[11] More significantly still, the third act ends with the Prince saying,

> Percy stands on high;
> And either we or they must lower lie;

and then the fifth act shows us the spectacle of the hero looking upon his rival's prostrate form. The curve of the plot could hardly be more firmly or more symmetrically drawn. It does not seem easy to agree with

11 The connection here is reinforced by the Prince's use of his earlier image: "all the budding honors on thy crest I'll crop."

Dr. Johnson and Professor Dover Wilson that *Henry IV Part One* is only the first half of a play.

If this were all there were to *Henry IV Part One,* the matter would be simple. But the Prince's conquest of honor is only one aspect of his progress; the other is his break with the companions of his riots. Interwoven with the story of the Prince and Hotspur are the Prince's relations with Falstaff, and these, from Falstaff's first appearance in the second scene of the play, are presented in a way which leads us to expect a similar reversal. The essential thing about Hal is that, scapegrace that he is, he is the future king—the "true prince," the "sweet young prince," the "king's son," the "heir apparent," as Falstaff variously calls him, with whatever degree of mockery, in their first dialogue together. More than that, this dialogue is constantly pointing forward to the moment when he will come to the throne. "When thou art king"—Falstaff uses these words four times in the first seventy lines and yet again before the scene is over. "Shall there be gallows standing in England when thou art king?" "Do not thou, when thou art king, hang a thief." And so on. With these words ringing in our ears, then, we are continually being reminded of what is to come. The words seem, however, to refer to some vague time in the distant future. The Prince's reign will inescapably become reality, but it is at present apprehended as a dream. Falstaff's irrepressible fancy blows up a vast gaily-colored bubble, and as Bradley recognized,[12] it is because this bubble encloses the dreams of all of us that we feel for Falstaff so much affection. In our dreams we all do exactly as we like, and the date of their realization is to be when Hal is king. Then, everything will be changed—except of course ourselves. *We* shall go on as before, our friend Falstaff will continue his nocturnal depredations, but highwaymen will not be regarded as thieves and punishments will be abolished. Unfortunately, in the real world outside the bubble, it is not the law but we ourselves that should change, as Falstaff recognizes when he says, "I must give over this life, and

12 "The Rejection of Falstaff," *Oxford Lectures on Poetry,* 1909, pp. 262–63.

I will give it over . . . I'll be damned for never a king's son in Christendom." The joke of this is that we know that Falstaff will never give over, nor means to; but the joke does not quite conceal the seriousness of the alternatives—give over or be damned; and the idea of damnation continues to dance before us, now and later, in further jests about Falstaff's selling his soul to the devil, wishing to repent, and having to "give the devil his due." What Falstaff's eventual doom is to be could be discerned more than dimly by a mind that came to this play unfurnished by literature or folklore. And none of us is quite as innocent as that. We cannot help being aware of an archetypal situation in which a man dallies with a diabolical tempter whom he either renounces or is destroyed by; and to the first audience of *Henry IV* this situation was already familiar in a long line of Christian plays, in some of which man's succumbing to temptation was symbolized in his selling his soul to the devil and being carried off to Hell. It is because it is so familiar that it is readily accepted as matter for jesting, while the jests give a hint of Falstaff's role in the play. I merely pick out one or two threads in the very complex fabric of the dialogue: you will be good enough, I trust, to believe that, in spite of some dubious precedents in the recent criticism of other plays, I am not seeking to interpret *Henry IV* as an allegory of sin and damnation. Falstaff is not a type-figure, though within his vast person several types are contained. And one of them is a sinner and provokes many piquant allusions to the typical fate of sinners, whether on the earthly gallows or in the infernal fire. There is also an ambiguity, to use the modern jargon, which permits Falstaff to be not only the sinner but the tempter as well. The jokes of a later scene will call him indeed a devil who haunts the Prince, a "reverend vice," an "old white-bearded Satan." What I think the play makes clear from the beginning is that neither as sinner nor as tempter will Falstaff come to triumph. Even as we share his dream of what will happen when Hal is king, we confidently await the bursting of his bubble.

To strengthen our expectation even further is what we

know of history, or at least of that traditional world where the territories of history and legend have no clear boundaries. The peculiarity of the history play is that while pursuing its dramatic ends, it must also obey history and steer a course reasonably close to an already known pattern of events. The story of Prince Hal was perfectly familiar to the Elizabethan audience before the play began, and it was the story of a prince who had a madcap youth, including at least one escapade of highway robbery, and then, on succeeding to the throne, banished his riotous companions from court and became the most valorous king England had ever had. Not only was this story vouched for in the chronicles, but it had already found its way on to the stage, as an extant play, *The Famous Victories of Henry the Fifth,* bears witness, in however garbled a text. It is hardly open to *our* play, then, to depart from the accepted pattern, in which the banishment of the tavern friends is an essential feature. Moreover, that they are to be banished the Prince himself assures us at the end of his first scene with Poins and Falstaff in that soliloquy which generations of critics have made notorious.

> I know you all, and will awhile uphold
> The unyoked humor of your idleness.

The word "awhile" plants its threat of a different time to come when a "humor" now "unyoked" will be brought under restraint. The soliloquy tells us as plain as any prologue what the end of the play is to be.

Yet although *Henry IV Part One* thus from its first act directs our interest to the time when Hal will be king, it is not of course until the last act of Part Two that Pistol comes to announce, "Sir John, thy tender lambkin now is king." It is not until the last act of Part Two that the Prince is able to institute the new régime which makes mock of Falstaff's dream-world. And it is not of course till the final scene of all that the newly crowned king makes his ceremonial entrance and pronounces the words that have threatened since he and Falstaff first were shown together. "I banish thee." To all that has been said about the rejection of Falstaff I propose to add very little. The chief of those who objected to it, Bradley himself, recognized the necessity of it while complaining of how it was done. Granted that the new king had to drop his former friend, might he not have spared him the sermon and parted from him in private?[13] Yet Professor Dover Wilson is surely right to maintain that the public utterance is the essential thing.[14] From the first, as I have shown, interest is concentrated on the Prince as the future sovereign and Falstaff builds hopes on the nature of his rule. Their separation, when it comes, is not then a reluctant parting between friends, but a royal decree promulgated with due solemnity. This is also the perfect moment for it, when the crown that has hovered over the hero from the beginning is seen, a striking symbol in the theater, fixed firmly on his head. The first words of the rejection speech elevate him still further—"I know thee not"—for the scriptural overtones here[15] make the speaker more than a king. The situation presents many aspects, but one of them shows the tempter vanquished and another the sinner cast into outer darkness. In either case the devil, we may say, gets his due.

The last act of Part Two thus works out a design which is begun in the first act of Part One. How then can we agree with Kittredge that each part is a complete play? Such a pronouncement fits the text no better than the opposite view of Johnson and Dover Wilson that Part One, though it ends in Hotspur's death and the Prince's glory, is yet only the first half of a play. If it were a question of what Shakespeare intended in the matter, the evidence provided by what he wrote would not suggest either that the two parts were planned as a single drama or that Part Two was an "unpremeditated sequel."

An escape from this dilemma has sometimes been sought in a theory, expounded especially by Professor Dover Wilson and Dr. Tillyard, that what *Henry IV* shows is one action with two phases. While the whole drama

13 *Ibid.*, p. 253.
14 *The Fortunes of Falstaff*, pp. 120–21.
15 *Cf.* Luke xiii. 25–7.

shows the transformation of the madcap youth into the virtuous ruler, the first part, we are told, deals with the chivalric virtues, the second with the civil. In the first part the hero acquires honor, in the second he establishes justice. But I see no solution of the structural problem here. For though it is left to Part Two to embody the idea of justice in the upright judge, the interest in justice and law is present from the start. On Falstaff's first appearance in Part One he jibes at the law as "old father antic." And he goes further. Included within his bubble is a vision of his future self not simply as a man freed from "the rusty curb" of the law but as a man who actually administers the law himself. "By the Lord, I'll be a brave judge," he says, making a mistake about his destined office which provokes Hal's retort, "Thou judgest false already." It is in the last act of Part Two that we have the completion of this motif. Its climax comes when on Hal's accession Falstaff brags, "The laws of England are at my commandment," and its resolution when the true judge sends the false judge off to prison. But it begins, we see, in the first act of Part One. The Prince's achievement in justice cannot, then, be regarded simply as the second phase of his progress. Certainly he has two contests: in one he outstrips Hotspur, in the other he puts down Falstaff. But these contests are not distributed at the rate of one per part. The plain fact is that in *Henry IV* two actions, each with the Prince as hero, begin together in the first act of Part One, though one of them ends with the death of Hotspur at the end of Part One, the other with the banishment of Falstaff at the end of Part Two.

Now, since the Falstaff plot is to take twice as long to complete its course, it might well be expected to develop from the beginning more slowly than the other. Certainly if it is to keep symmetry, it must come later to its turning-point. But is this in fact what we find? Frankly it is not. On the contrary, through the first half of Part One the Hotspur plot and the Falstaff plot show every sign of moving towards their crisis together.

Both plots, for example, are presented, though I think both are not usually observed, in the Prince's soliloquy in

the first act which I have already quoted as foretelling the
banishment of his tavern companions. It is unfortunate
that this speech has usually been studied for its bearing on
Falstaff's rejection; its emphasis is really elsewhere. It is
only the first two lines, with the reference to the "unyoked humor" of the Prince's companions, that allude
specifically to them, and what is primarily in question is
not what is to happen to the companions but what is to
happen to the Prince. In the splendid image which follows
of the sun breaking through the clouds we recognize a
royal emblem and behold the promise of a radiant king
who is to come forth from the "ugly mists" which at
present obscure the Prince's real self. Since Falstaff has
just been rejoicing at the thought that they "go by the
moon . . . and not by Phœbus," it is apparent that his
fortunes will decline when the prince emerges like Phœbus
himself. It is equally apparent, or should be, that the
brilliant Hotspur will be outshone.[16] There is certainly no
clue at this stage that the catastrophes of Hotspur and
Falstaff will not be simultaneous.

Our expectation that they will be is indeed encouraged
as the two actions now move forward. While Hotspur in
pursuit of honor is preparing war, Falstaff displays his
cowardice (I use the word advisedly) at Gadshill. While
Hotspur rides forth from home on the journey that will
take him to his downfall, the exposure of Falstaff's make-
believe in the matter of the men in buckram is the fore-
shadowing of his. The news of Hotspur's rebellion brings
the Falstaffian revels to a climax at the same time as it
summons the Prince to that interview with his father which
will prove, as we have seen, the crisis of his career and the
"nodal point" of the drama. That this interview is to be
dramatically momentous is clear enough in advance: before we come to it, it is twice prefigured by the Prince and
Falstaff in burlesque. But not only do the two mock-
interviews excite our interest in the real one to come; the
mock-interviews are in the story of the Prince and Falstaff

16 *i.e.*, This first-act soliloquy looks forward not only to the rejection
of Falstaff but also to Vernon's vision of the Prince and his company before Shrewsbury, "gorgeous as the sun at midsummer."

what the real interview is in the story of the Prince and
Hotspur. First, Falstaff, whose dream it is that he may one
day govern England, basks in the make-believe that he is
king; and then Hal, who, as we have so often been reminded, is presently to be king, performs in masquerade
his future part. The question they discuss is central to the
play: "Shall the son of England prove a thief and take
purses?" Shall he in fact continue to associate with Falstaff? One should notice that although the two actors ex-
change roles, they do not really change sides in this debate.
Whether he acts the part of king or prince, Falstaff takes
the opportunity of pleading for himself. When he is king
he instructs the Prince to "keep with" Falstaff; as prince
he begs, "Banish not him thy Harry's company, banish not
him thy Harry's company: banish plump Jack, and banish
all the world." Falstaff's relations to the future king, a
theme of speculation since the opening of the play, now
come to a focus in this repeated word "banish." And when
the Prince replies, "I do, I will," he anticipates in jest the
sentence he is later to pronounce in earnest. If it were
never to be pronounced in earnest, that would rob the
masquerade of the dramatic irony from which comes its
bouquet: those who accept Part One as a play complete in
itself wrongly surrender their legitimate expectations. In
this mock-interview the Prince declares his intentions towards Falstaff just as surely as in his real interview with his
father he declares his intentions towards Hotspur. One
declaration is a solemn vow, the other a glorious piece of
fun, but they are equally prophetic and structurally their
function is the same. We now approach the turning point
not of one, but of both dramatic actions. Indeed we miss
the core of the play if we do not perceive that the two
actions are really the same. The moment at the end of the
third act when the Prince goes off to challenge Hotspur is
also the moment when he leaves Falstaff's favorite tavern
for what we well might think would be evermore. It is at
the exit from the tavern that the road to Shrewsbury
begins; and all the signposts I see indicate one-way traffic
only. There should be no return.

The various dooms of Hotspur and Falstaff are now in

sight; and we reasonably expect both dooms to be arrived
at in Act V. What we are not at all prepared for is that one
of the two will be deferred till five acts later than the other.
The symmetry so beautifully preserved in the story of
Hotspur is in Falstaff's case abandoned. Statistics are
known to be misleading, and nowhere more so than in
literary criticism; but it is not without significance that in
Henry IV Part One Falstaff's speeches in the first two acts
number ninety-six and in the last two acts only twenty-five.
As for Falstaff's satellites, with the exception of a single
perfunctory appearance on the part of Bardolph, the whole
galaxy vanishes altogether in the last two acts, only to
reappear with some changes in personnel in Part Two.
Falstaff, admittedly, goes on without a break, if broken
in wind; and his diminished role does show some trace of
the expected pattern of development. His going to war on
foot while Hal is on horseback marks a separation of these
erstwhile companions and a decline in Falstaff's status
which was anticipated in jest when his horse was taken
from him at Gadshill. When he nevertheless appears at
one council of war his sole attempt at a characteristic joke
is cut short by the Prince with "Peace, chewet, peace!" A
fine touch, this, which contributes to the picture of the
Prince's transformation: the boon companion whose jests
he has delighted in is now silenced in a word. There is
even the shadow of a rejection of Falstaff; over his supposed corpse the Prince speaks words that, for all their
affectionate regret, remind us that he has turned his back
on "vanity." But these things, however significant, are
details, no more than shorthand notes for the degradation
of Falstaff that we have so confidently looked for. What
it comes to is that after the middle of Part One *Henry IV*
changes its shape. And that, it seems to me, is the root
and cause of the structural problem.

Now that this change of shape has been, I hope I may
say, demonstrated from within the play itself, it may at
this stage be permissible to venture an opinion about the
author's plan. I do not of course mean to imply that
Henry IV, or indeed any other of Shakespeare's plays,
ever had a plan precisely laid down for it in advance. But

it has to be supposed that when Shakespeare began a play he had some idea of the general direction it would take, however ready he may have been to modify his idea as art or expediency might suggest. Though this is where I shall be told I pass the bounds of literary criticism into the province of biography or worse, I hold it reasonable to infer from the analysis I have given that in the course of writing *Henry IV* Shakespeare changed his mind. I am compelled to believe that the author himself foresaw, I will even say intended, that pattern which evolves through the early acts of Part One and which demands for its completion that the hero's rise to an eminence of valor shall be accompanied, or at least swiftly followed, by the banishment of the riotous friends who hope to profit from his reign. In other words, hard upon the Battle of Shrewsbury there was to come the coronation of the hero as king. This inference from the play is not without support from other evidence. The Prince's penitence in the interview with his father in the middle of Part One corresponds to an episode which, both in Holinshed and in the play of *The Famous Victories of Henry the Fifth,* is placed only shortly before the old king's death. And still more remarkable is the sequence of events in a poem which has been shown to be one of Shakespeare's sources.[17] At the historical Battle of Shrewsbury the Prince was only sixteen years old, whereas Hotspur was thirty-nine. But in Samuel Daniel's poem, *The Civil Wars,* Hotspur is made "young" and "rash" and encounters a prince of equal age who emerges like a "new-appearing glorious star."[18] It is Daniel, that is to say, who sets in opposition these two splendid youths and so provides the germ from which grows the rivalry of the Prince and Hotspur which is structural to Shakespeare's play. And in view of this resemblance between Daniel and Shakespeare, it is significant that Daniel ignores the ten years that in history elapsed between the death of Hotspur and the Prince's accession. Whereas in Holinshed the events of those ten years fill nearly twenty pages,

17 See F. W. Moorman, "Shakespeare's History Plays and Daniel's *Civile Wars,*" *Shakespeare Jahrbuch,* XL (1904), pp. 77–83.
18 Book III, stanzas 97, 109–10.

Daniel goes straight from Shrewsbury to the old king's deathbed. This telescoping of events, which confronts the Prince with his kingly responsibilities directly after the slaying of Hotspur, adumbrates the pattern that Shakespeare, as I see it, must have had it in mind to follow out. The progress of a prince was to be presented not in two phases but in a single play of normal length which would show the hero wayward in its first half, pledging reform in the middle, and then in the second half climbing at Shrewsbury the ladder of honor by which, appropriately, he would ascend to the throne.

The exact point at which a new pattern supervenes I should not care to define. But I think the new pattern can be seen emerging during the fourth act. At a corresponding stage the history play of *Richard II* shows the deposition of its king, *Henry V* the victory at Agincourt, even *Henry IV Part Two* the quelling of its rebellion in Gaultree Forest. By contrast *Henry IV Part One,* postponing any such decisive action, is content with preparation. While the rebels gather, the Prince is arming and Falstaff recruiting to meet them. Until well into the fifth act ambassadors are going back and forth between the rival camps, and we may even hear a message twice over, once when it is despatched and once when it is delivered. True, this is not undramatic: these scenes achieve a fine animation and suspense as well as the lowlier feat of verisimilitude. But the technique is obviously not one of compression. Any thought of crowding into the two-hour traffic of one play the death of the old king and the coronation of the new has by now been relinquished, and instead the Battle of Shrewsbury is being built up into a grand finale in its own right. In our eagerness to come to this battle and our gratification at the exciting climax it provides, we easily lose sight of our previous expectations. Most of us, I suspect, go from the theater well satisfied with the improvised conclusion. It is not, of course, that we cease to care about the fate of individuals. On the contrary, the battle succeeds so well because amid the crowded tumult of the fighting it keeps the key figures in due prominence. Clearly showing who is killed, who is rescued, and who shams dead, who slays a valiant foe and who only pretends to, it brings each man to a destiny that we perceive to be appropriate. We merely fail to notice that the destiny is not in every case exactly what was promised. There is no room now in Part One to banish Falstaff. A superb comic tact permits him instead the fate of reformation, in fact the alternative of giving over instead of being damned. It is a melancholy fate enough, for it means giving over being Falstaff: we leave him saying that if he is rewarded, he will "leave sack, and live cleanly as a nobleman should do." But since this resolution is conditional and need in any case be believed no more than Falstaff has already taught us to believe him, it has the advantage that it leaves the issue open, which, to judge from the outcry there has always been over the ending of Part Two, is how most people would prefer to have it left. Shakespeare's brilliant improvisation thus provides a dénouement to Part One which has proved perfectly acceptable, while it still leaves opportunity for what I hope I may call the original ending, if the dramatist should choose to add a second part. I refrain, however, from assuming that a second part was necessarily planned before Part One was acted.

Part Two itself does not require extended treatment. For whenever it was "planned," it is a consequence of Part One. Its freedom is limited by the need to present what Part One so plainly prepared for and then left out. Falstaff cannot be allowed to escape a second time. His opposition to the law, being now the dominant interest, accordingly shapes the plot; and the law, now bodied forth in the half-legendary figure of the Lord Chief Justice, becomes a formidable person in the drama. The opening encounter between these two, in which Falstaff makes believe not to see or hear his reprover, is symbolic of Falstaff's whole attitude to law—he ignores its existence as long as he can. But the voice which he at first refuses to hear is the voice which will pronounce his final sentence. The theme of the individual versus the law proves so fertile that it readily gives rise to subplots. Justice Shallow, of course, claims his place in the play by virtue of the life that is in him, exuberant in the capers of senility itself. He functions all the same as the Lord Chief Justice's antithesis: he is the foolish justice with whom Falstaff has his way and from whom he wrings the thousand pounds that the wise justice has denied him. Even Shallow's servant Davy has his relation to the law; and his view of law is that though a man may be a knave, if he is my friend and I am the justice's servant, it is hard if the knave cannot win. In this humane sentiment Davy takes on full vitality as a person; but he simultaneously brings us back to confront at a different angle the main moral issue of the play. Is he to control the law or the law him? In fact, shall Falstaff flourish or shall a thief be hanged?

It has sometimes been objected that Falstaff runs away with Part Two. In truth he has to shoulder the burden of it because a dead man and a converted one can give him small assistance. Part Two has less opportunity for the integrated double action of Part One. To be sure, it attempts a double action, and has often been observed to be in some respects a close replica of Part One—"almost a carbon copy," Professor Shaaber says. At exactly the same point in each part, for example, is a little domestic scene where a rebel leader contemplates leaving home, and in each part this is directly followed by the big tavern scene in which revelry rises to a climax. And so on. An article in a recent number of *The Review of English Studies* has even called *Henry IV* a diptych, finding the "parallel presentation of incidents" in the two parts the primary formal feature. I do not wish to deny the aesthetic satisfaction to be got from a recognition of this rhythmic repetition; yet it is only the more superficial pattern that can be thus repeated. With history and Holinshed obliging, rebellion can break out as before; yet the rebellion of Part Two, though it occupies our attention, has no significance, nor can have, for the principal characters of the play. The story of the Prince and Hotspur is over, and the King has only to die.

The one thing about history is that it does not repeat itself. Hotspur, unlike Sherlock Holmes, cannot come back to life. But there are degrees in all things; conversion has not quite the same finality as death. And besides, there is a type of hero whose adventures always can recur. Robin Hood has no sooner plundered one rich man than another comes along. It is the nature of Brer Fox, and indeed of Dr. Watson, to be incapable of learning from experience. In folklore, that is to say, though not in history, you can be at the same point twice. And it seems as if Prince Hal may be sufficient of a folklore hero to be permitted to go again through the cycle of riot and reform. In Part Two as in Part One the King laments his son's unprincely life. Yet this folklore hero is also a historical, and what is more to the point, a dramatic personage, and it is not tolerable that the victor of Shrewsbury should do as critics sometimes say he does, relapse into his former wildness and then reform again. The Prince cannot come into Part Two unreclaimed without destroying the dramatic effect of Part One. Yet if Part Two is not to forgo its own dramatic effect, and especially its splendid last-act peripeteia, it requires a prince who is unreclaimed. This is Part Two's dilemma, and the way that it takes out of it is a bold one. When the King on his deathbed exclaims against the Prince's "headstrong riot," he has not forgotten that at Shrewsbury he congratulated the Prince on his redemption. He has not forgotten it for the simple reason that it has never taken place. The only man at court who believes in the Prince's reformation, the Earl of Warwick, believes that it will happen, not that it has happened already. Even as we watch the hero repeating his folklore cycle, we are positively instructed that he has not been here before:

> The tide of blood in me
> Hath proudly flow'd in vanity till now.

In the two parts of *Henry IV* there are not two princely reformations but two versions of a single reformation. And they are mutually exclusive.[19] Though Part Two

---

[19] All this is very well exhibited by H. E. Cain (see appended Note). But his conclusion that the two parts therefore have no continuity is invalidated because, like many others, he is content to isolate particular elements in the problem and does not examine it whole. Except when the views of others are being quoted or discussed, the word "Falstaff" does not occur in his article.

frequently recalls and sometimes depends on what has happened in Part One, it also denies that Part One exists. Accordingly the ideal spectator of either part must not cry with Shakespeare's Lucio, "I know what I know." He must sometimes remember what he knows and sometimes be content to forget it. This, however, is a requirement made in some degree by any work of fiction, or as they used to call it, feigning. And the feat is not a difficult one for those accustomed to grant the poet's demand for "that willing suspension of disbelief . . . which constitutes poetic faith."

Henry IV, then, is both one play and two. Part One begins an action which it finds it has not scope for but which Part Two rounds off. But with one half of the action already concluded in Part One, there is danger of a gap in Part Two. To stop the gap Part Two expands the unfinished story of Falstaff and reduplicates what is already finished in the story of the Prince. The two parts are complementary, they are also independent and even incompatible. What they are, with their various formal anomalies, I suppose them to have become through what Johnson termed "the necessity of exhibition." Though it would be dangerous to dispute Coleridge's view that a work of art must "contain in itself the reason why it is so," that its form must proceed from within,[20] yet even works of art, like other of man's productions, must submit to the bondage of the finite. Even the unwieldy novels of the Victorians, as recent criticism has been showing, obey the demands of their allotted three volumes of space; and the dramatic masterpieces of any age, no less than inaugural lectures, must acknowledge the dimensions of time. The inaugural lecture has, however, this unique advantage: as its occasion is single, the one thing that can never be required of it is to make good its own deficiencies in a second part.

[20] This is a synthesis of several passages in Coleridge. The words in quotation marks are said of whatever can give permanent pleasure; but the context shows Coleridge to be thinking of literary composition. See *Biographia Literaria*, ed. Shawcross, vol. ii. p. 9. Also relevant are "On Poesy or Art," *ibid.*, vol. ii. p. 262; and *Coleridge's Shakespearean Criticism*, ed. T. M. Raysor, vol. i. pp. 223–24.

NOTE

Of the numerous critical writings on *Henry IV*, I have read most and learnt from many. So although my main thesis about its structure has not, as far as I am aware, been previously put forward, it necessarily incorporates some arguments which have. To my predecessors I gladly acknowledge my indebtedness. It is not least to some of those with whom I disagree—Professor Dover Wilson and Dr. Tillyard; from their work on *Henry IV* I have derived much insight and stimulus. The most important discussions of the particular problem are, I think, the following:

Johnson, *Shakespeare,* 1765, vol. iv. pp. 235, 355; C. H. Herford, *Shakespeare,* Eversley edition, 1899, vol. vi. pp. 253–54; C. F. Tucker Brooke, *The Tudor Drama,* 1912, pp. 333–35; R. A. Law, "Structural Unity in the Two Parts of *Henry the Fourth,*" *Studies in Philology,* XXIV (1927), pp. 223ff.; J. Dover Wilson, *The Fortunes of Falstaff,* 1943, p. 4 and *passim;* E. M. W. Tillyard, *Shakespeare's History Plays,* 1944, pp. 264ff.; Dover Wilson, *1 Henry IV,* New Cambridge Shakespeare, 1946, pp. vii–xiii; M. A. Shaaber, "The Unity of *Henry IV,*" *Joseph Quincy Adams Memorial Studies,* 1948, pp. 217ff.; H. E. Cain, "Further Light on the Relation of *1* and *2 Henry IV,*" *Shakespeare Quarterly,* III (1952), pp. 21ff.; Law, "Links between Shakespeare's History Plays," *Studies in Philology,* L (1953), pp. 175–82; Tillyard, "Shakespeare's Historical Cycle: Organism or Compilation?" and Law, "Shakespeare's Historical Cycle: Rejoinder," *ibid.,* LI(1954), pp. 37–41; G. K. Hunter, *"Henry IV* and the Elizabethan Two-Part Play," *Review of English Studies,* n.s., V(1954), pp. 236ff.

For further references, see *2 Henry IV,* New Variorum, edited Shaaber, pp. 558–63.

Suggested References

The number of possible references is vast and grows alarmingly. (The *Shakespeare Quarterly* devotes a substantial part of one issue each year to a list of the previous year's work, and *Shakespeare Survey*—an annual publication—includes a substantial review of recent scholarship, as well as an occasional essay surveying a few decades of scholarship on a chosen topic.) Though no works are indispensable, those listed below have been found helpful.

1. Shakespeare's Times

Byrne, M. St. Clare. *Elizabethan Life in Town and Country.* Rev. ed. New York: Barnes & Noble, Inc., 1961. Chapters on manners, beliefs, education, etc., with illustrations.

Craig, Hardin. *The Enchanted Glass: the Elizabethan Mind in Literature.* New York and London: Oxford University Press, 1936. The Elizabethan intellectual climate.

Nicoll, Allardyce (ed.). *The Elizabethans.* London: Cambridge University Press, 1957. An anthology of Elizabethan writings, especially valuable for its illustrations from paintings, title pages, etc.

Shakespeare's England. 2 vols. Oxford: The Clarendon Press, 1916. A large collection of scholarly essays on a wide variety of topics (e.g., astrology, costume, gardening, horsemanship), with special attention to Shakespeare's references to these topics.

Tillyard, E. M. W. *The Elizabethan World Picture.* London: Chatto & Windus, 1943; New York: The Macmillan Company, 1944. A brief account of some Elizabethan ideas of the universe.

Wilson, John Dover (ed.). *Life in Shakespeare's England.* 2nd ed. New York: The Macmillan Company, 1913. An anthology of Elizabethan writings on the countryside, superstition, education, the court, etc.

2. Shakespeare

Bentley, Gerald E. *Shakespeare: A Biographical Handbook.* New Haven, Conn.: Yale University Press, 1961. The facts about Shakespeare, with virtually no conjecture intermingled.

Bradby, Anne (ed.). *Shakespeare Criticism, 1919–1935.* London: Oxford University Press, 1936. A small anthology of excellent essays on the plays.

Bush, Geoffrey Douglas. *Shakespeare and the Natural Condition.* Cambridge, Mass.: Harvard University Press; London: Oxford University Press, 1956. A short, sensitive account of Shakespeare's view of "Nature," touching most of the works.

Chambers, E. K. *William Shakespeare: A Study of Facts and Problems.* 2 vols. London: Oxford University Press, 1930. An invaluable, detailed reference work; not for the casual reader.

Chute, Marchette. *Shakespeare of London.* New York: E. P. Dutton & Co., Inc., 1949. A readable biography fused with portraits of Stratford and London life.

Clemen, Wolfgang H. *The Development of Shakepeare's Imagery.* Cambridge, Mass.: Harvard University Press, 1951. (Originally published in German, 1936.) A temperate account of a subject often abused.

Craig, Hardin. *An Interpretation of Shakespeare.* Columbia, Missouri: Lucas Brothers, 1948. A scholar's book designed for the layman. Comments on all the works.

Dean, Leonard F. (ed.). *Shakespeare: Modern Essays in Criticism.* New York: Oxford University Press, 1957. Mostly mid-twentieth-century critical studies, covering Shakespeare's artistry.

Granville-Barker, Harley. *Prefaces to Shakespeare.* 2 vols. Princeton, N.J.: Princeton University Press, 1946–47. Essays on ten plays by a scholarly man of the theater.

Harbage, Alfred. *As They Liked It*. New York: The Macmillan Company, 1947. A sensitive, long essay on Shakespeare, morality, and the audience's expectations.

Holland, Norman N. *The Shakespearean Imagination*. New York: The Macmillan Company, 1964. Lively introductions to Shakespeare's theatrical style and thirteen major plays.

Ridler, Anne Bradby (ed.). *Shakespeare Criticism, 1935–1960*. New York and London: Oxford University Press, 1963. An excellent continuation of the anthology edited earlier by Miss Bradby (see above).

Smith, D. Nichol (ed.). *Shakespeare Criticism*. New York: Oxford University Press, 1916. A selection of criticism from 1623 to 1840, ranging from Ben Jonson to Thomas Carlyle.

Spencer, Theodore. *Shakespeare and the Nature of Man*. New York: The Macmillan Company, 1942. Shakespeare's plays in relation to Elizabethan thought.

Stoll, Elmer Edgar. *Shakespeare and Other Masters*. Cambridge, Mass.: Harvard University Press; London: Oxford University Press, 1940. Essays on tragedy, comedy, and aspects of dramaturgy, with special reference to some of Shakespeare's plays.

Traversi, D. A. *An Approach to Shakespeare*. Rev. ed. New York: Doubleday & Co., Inc., 1956. An analysis of the plays, beginning with words, images, and themes, rather than with characters.

Van Doren, Mark. *Shakespeare*. New York: Henry Holt & Company, Inc., 1939. Brief, perceptive readings of all of the plays.

Whitaker, Virgil K. *Shakespeare's Use of Learning*. San Marino, Calif.: Huntington Library, 1953. A study of the relation of Shakespeare's reading to his development as a dramatist.

3. Shakespeare's Theater

Adams, John Cranford. *The Globe Playhouse*. Rev. ed. New York: Barnes & Noble, Inc., 1961. A detailed conjecture about the physical characteristics of the theater Shakespeare often wrote for.

Beckerman, Bernard. *Shakespeare at the Globe, 1599–1609*. New York: The Macmillan Company, 1962. On the playhouse and on Elizabethan dramaturgy, acting, and staging.

Chambers, E. K. *The Elizabethan Stage*. 4 vols. New York: Oxford University Press, 1923. Reprinted with corrections, 1945. An indispensable reference work on theaters, theatrical companies, and staging at court.

Harbage, Alfred. *Shakespeare's Audience*. New York: Columbia University Press; London: Oxford University Press, 1941. A study of the size and nature of the theatrical public.

Hodges, C. Walter. *The Globe Restored*. London: Ernest Benn, Ltd., 1953; New York: Coward-McCann, Inc., 1954. A well-illustrated and readable attempt to reconstruct the Globe Theatre.

Kernodle, George R. *From Art to Theatre: Form and Convention in the Renaissance*. Chicago: University of Chicago Press, 1944. Pioneering and stimulating work on the symbolic and cultural meanings of theater construction.

Nagler, A. M. *Shakespeare's Stage*. Tr. by Ralph Manheim. New Haven, Conn.: Yale University Press, 1958. An excellent brief introduction to the physical aspect of the playhouse.

Smith, Irwin. *Shakespeare's Globe Playhouse*. New York: Charles Scribner's Sons, 1957. Chiefly indebted to J. C. Adams' controversial book, with additional material and scale drawings for model-builders.

Venezky, Alice S. *Pageantry on the Shakespearean Stage*. New York: Twayne Publishers, Inc., 1951. An examination of spectacle in Elizabethan drama.

4. Miscellaneous Reference Works

Abbott, E. A. *A Shakespearean Grammar*. New edition. New York: The Macmillan Company, 1877. An examination of differences between Elizabethan and modern grammar.

Bartlett, John. *A New and Complete Concordance . . . to . . . Shakespeare*. New York: The Macmillan Company, 1894. An index to most of Shakespeare's words.

Bullough, Geoffrey. *Narrative and Dramatic Sources of Shakespeare*. 5 vols. Vols. 6 and 7 in preparation. New York: Columbia University Press; London: Routledge & Kegan Paul, Ltd., 1957–. A collection of many of the books Shakespeare drew upon.

Greg, W. W. *The Shakespeare First Folio*. New York and London: Oxford University Press, 1955. A detailed yet readable history of the first collection (1623) of Shakespeare's plays.

Kökeritz, Helge. *Shakespeare's Names*. New Haven, Conn.: Yale University Press, 1959; London: Oxford University Press, 1960. A guide to the pronunciation of some 1,800 names appearing in Shakespeare.

———. *Shakespeare's Pronunciation*. New Haven, Conn.: Yale University Press; London: Oxford University Press, 1953. Contains much information about puns and rhymes.

Linthicum, Marie C. *Costume in the Drama of Shakespeare and His Contemporaries*. New York and London: Oxford University Press, 1936. On the fabrics and dress of the age, and references to them in the plays.

Muir, Kenneth. *Shakespeare's Sources*. London: Methuen & Co., Ltd., 1957. Vol. 2 in preparation. The first volume, on the comedies and tragedies, attempts to ascertain what books were Shakespeare's sources, and what use he made of them.

Onions, C. T. *A Shakespeare Glossary*. London: Oxford University Press, 1911; 2nd ed., rev., with enlarged addenda, 1953. Definitions of words (or senses of words) now obsolete.

Partridge, Eric. *Shakespeare's Bawdy*. Rev. ed. New York: E. P. Dutton & Co., Inc.; London: Routledge & Kegan Paul, Ltd., 1955. A glossary of bawdy words and phrases.

Shakespeare Quarterly. See headnote to Suggested References.

Shakespeare Survey. See headnote to Suggested References.

Smith, Gordon Ross. *A Classified Shakespeare Bibliography 1936–1958*. University Park, Pa.: Pennsylvania State University Press, 1963. A list of some 20,000 items on Shakespeare.

5. Henry IV, Part Two

Barber, C. L. "Rule and Misrule in Henry IV" in *Shakespeare's Festive Comedy*. Princeton, N.J.: Princeton University Press; London: Oxford University Press, 1959.

Bradley, Andrew Cecil. "The Rejection of Falstaff" in *Oxford Lectures on Poetry*. New York: The Macmillan Company, 1909.

Jenkins, Harold. "Shakespeare's History Plays: 1900–1951," *Shakespeare Survey 6,* ed. Allardyce Nicoll. New York and London: Cambridge University Press, 1953, pp. 1–15.

Jorgensen, Paul A. "The 'Dastardly Treachery' of Prince John of Lancaster," *Publications of the Modern Language Association,* LXXVI (1961), 488–92.

Kaiser, Walter. "Shakespeare's Falstaff" in *Praisers of Folly*. Cambridge, Mass.: Harvard University Press, 1963; London: Victor Gollancz, Ltd., 1964.

Knights, L. C. "Time's Subjects: The Sonnets and *King Henry IV, Part II*" in *Some Shakespearean Themes*. London: Chatto & Windus, 1959; Stanford, Calif.: Stanford University Press, 1960.

Kris, Ernst. "Prince Hal's Conflict," *Psychoanalytic Quarterly,* XVII (1948), 487–505; reprinted in *Psychoanalytic Explorations in Art*. New York: International Universities Press, 1952.

Leech, Clifford. "The Unity of *2 Henry IV*," *Shakespeare Survey 6,* ed. Allardyce Nicoll. New York and London: Cambridge University Press, 1953, pp. 16–24.

Shaaber, M. A. "The Unity of *Henry IV*" in *Joseph*

Quincy Adams Memorial Studies, ed. James G. Mc-Manaway. Washington: The Folger Shakespeare Library, 1948.

——, ed. *A New Variorum Edition of The Second Part of Henry the Fourth.* Philadelphia: J. B. Lippincott, Co., 1941.

Spivack, Bernard. "Falstaff and the Psychomachia," *Shakespeare Quarterly,* VIII (1957), 449–59.

Spurgeon, Caroline. "Note on images as a revelation of character in the drama" in *Shakespeare's Imagery and What it Tells Us.* London: Cambridge University Press, 1935; Boston: Beacon Press, 1958.

Tillyard, E. M. W. *"Henry IV"* in *Shakespeare's History Plays.* London: Chatto & Windus, 1944; New York: The Macmillan Company, 1946.

Traversi, Derek. *"Henry the Fourth, Part II"* in *Shakespeare from "Richard II" to "Henry V."* Stanford, Calif.: Stanford University Press, 1957; London: Hollis & Carter, Ltd., 1958.

Wilson, John Dover. *The Fortunes of Falstaff.* London: Cambridge University Press, 1943; New York: The Macmillan Company, 1944. A selection from this book is reprinted in the Signet Classic edition of *Henry IV* [*Part One*].